BARRY's BOOK

NIGHTMARE ON WALL STREET

Salomon Brothers and the Corruption of the Marketplace

MARTIN MAYER

SIMON & SCHUSTER

New York   London   Toronto   Sydney   Tokyo   Singapore

SIMON & SCHUSTER
Simon & Schuster Building
Rockefeller Center
1230 Avenue of the Americas
New York, New York 10020

SIMON & SCHUSTER and colophon are registered trademarks
of Simon & Schuster Inc.
Designed by Irving Perkins Associates, Inc.
Manufactured in the United States of America

10   9   8   7   6   5   4   3   2   1

Library of Congress Cataloging-in-Publication Data

Mayer, Martin, date.
    Nightmare on Wall Street : Salomon Brothers and the corruption of
the marketplace / Martin Mayer.
      p.   cm.
    Includes bibliographical references.
    1. Salomon Brothers.   2. Government securities—United States—
Marketing—Corrupt practices.   I. Title.
HG4936.M39   1993
332.6'2'0973—dc20   93-14703
                                                            CIP
ISBN: 0-671-78187-1

Photo Credits

1: Courtesy of William R. Salomon
2, 3: Magnum Photos/Cornell Capa
4: Salomon Brothers 1974 Annual report
5, 7, 9, 10: AP/Wide World Photos
6: Tony Palmieri/WWD
8: Courtesy of William R. Salomon
11: Onyx/Joyce Ravid
12: Reuters/Bettmann

for Mary and Charlie Ramond

CONTENTS

PROLOGUE

THE CAT COMES OUT OF THE BAG

LATE WEDNESDAY MORNING, August 7, 1991, a dozen lawyers gathered with top executives of Salomon Brothers, the world's most powerful securities firm, for an extraordinary conference. The meeting was held in a conference room of the Park Avenue offices of Wachtell Lipton Rosen & Katz; the subject was a report on a month's work that the law firm had done to investigate alleged misbehavior by the government bond department of Salomon Brothers. The report had both bad news and good news. The bad news was that the misbehavior had been extensive, repeated, and blatant, involving the misuse of some of the most important names in the financial markets. The good news was that the lawyers could make a case that Treasury Department regulations were so loose, maybe what had been done wasn't really illegal.

The leader of the Salomon delegation, which arrived in limousines (every member of Salomon's "Office of the Chairman" had exclusive use of a limousine and driver), was chairman, president, and CEO John Gutfreund (which he pronounces "Goodfriend"), sixty-one years old, a pudgy, awkward man with a weak chin, thinning hair, and large, thick glasses. He was in a hurry; he had an appointment early the next morning in London and wanted to catch the 1:45 P.M. Concorde from Kennedy Airport. Because he was in a hurry, he seemed brusque and uninvolved in the discussion: He would do whatever others thought best.

Gutfreund's public image was one of arrogance to the point of brutality, reinforced by the big black cigar forever in his mouth or between thumb and forefinger, and by an occasional eruption at social gatherings into the foul language that was commonplace on the trading floor ("You must understand," said someone who was close to him at the firm, "that the word *fuck* at Salomon Brothers was a way to take breath"). But he was a graduate of Lawrenceville, one of the nation's more elegant prep schools, and Oberlin College. His first wife, Joyce Low, had been the daughter of Teddy Low of Bear Stearns & Co., one of the great men of Wall Street. He didn't read much (he told an interviewer in early 1991 that he owned fewer than a hundred books), but he had been an English literature major at college. More than half the partners at Salomon in 1962, when he first became a partner, had never gone to college, and as a residue from that experience Gutfreund considered himself rather more cultured than most of his peers. People who knew him fairly well—he was not a man with many or close friends—thought he was in truth rather shy and more than a little insecure. His father had been a wholesale butcher, and he didn't want people to know it. In the 1980s he had by diligent effort lost his New York accent and acquired a mid-Atlantic way of speaking the English language.

It is almost impossible to exaggerate the importance Gutfreund and Salomon Brothers had achieved in the 1980s. Through most of the decade the firm had been by far the largest dealer in U.S. government bonds, the largest underwriter of corporate securities, the largest entirely nongovernmental packager of home mortgages for sale as securities (which had become Wall Street's biggest business), the largest trader of blocks of stock in American companies, and the largest foreign investment house in Britain and Japan. A cover story in *Business Week* in December 1985 had labeled Gutfreund "the King of Wall Street" and had quoted a competitor's comment about Salomon that "they're in a position now to make of the securities business what they want."[1]

Gutfreund had been with the firm thirty-six years, starting as a salesman and trader of the tax-exempt bonds that states and localities issue to finance their public works. Moving to investment banking–related activities, he rose to a general supervisory role as number-two man to the firm's managing partner, William R. Salomon. In 1978, on Salomon's retirement, he became managing partner himself, until he and his inner circle made themselves multiple millionaires by turning the partnership into a stockholder-owned enterprise. After 1984 he was chairman and chief executive officer of what had become Salomon, Inc. Before the spring 1987 bond market crash (much more devastating to Salomon than the Black Monday stock market crash that made history the following October), he and real estate developer Morton Zuckerman had planned to build the most spectacular corporate monument in New York—a sixty-seven-story skyscraper that would include a trading floor for Salomon alone that was larger than that of the New York Stock Exchange. Far from Wall Street, the new Salomon headquarters would occupy the best site in the whole city: across Columbus Circle from the southwest tip of Central Park, replacing the city's outdated convention center. "The occupancy costs on that building were going to be the highest in the history of Western civilization," said David Stockman, who had come to Salomon shortly before, after a career as a congressman and director of the Office of Management and Budget in the Reagan administration.

Surrounding Gutfreund in the Wachtell Lipton conference room was the handful of New York–based high-ranking Salomon executives who had survived the extensive purges he had carried through in the previous five years. Thomas Strauss, president of the holding company Salomon, Inc., was ten years younger than Gutfreund, bald, very personable, a veteran of the government bonds desk, a graduate of the University of Pennsylvania, and rather condescending to people who had not enjoyed his educational advantages. Vice-chairman John Meriwether, in his early forties with a soft-cheeked face but a military bearing, supervised all of Salomon's bond trading for its own account. Executive vice-president Gedale ("Dale") Horowitz was of Gutfreund's generation; formerly a municipal bond trader but now without direct responsibility for any of the firm's activities, he was one of the founders of the Public Securities Association and in 1991 chairman of the Securities Industries Association. Donald Feuerstein, first in his class at Harvard Law School, was Gutfreund's indefatigable defender and Salomon's general counsel since 1972. ("I don't know what Don's IQ is," said one of his former partners who worked closely with him in the late 1970s, "but it's about half again as high as it ought to be.") Also present was the firm's rather recently acquired public relations director, Bob Baker, a lethargic, elegant Southerner with limited experience in both securities matters and public relations.

The origins of the Wachtell Lipton investigation were very peculiar. The triggering event had been a telephone call to Martin Lipton on July 1 from a friend and client at Goldman Sachs who reported that the FBI was all over that house, seeking expert explanations of exactly what it was that Salomon had done wrong in the May 22, 1991, auction of U.S. Treasury two-year notes. At first Goldman was very unhappy to see FBI men on the property, because the last time they had come their purpose had been to make a public arrest of a Goldman partner. But once Goldman discovered what the mission was, the firm was pleased to cooperate. Goldman had been among the many losers in the aftermath of the May auction and didn't much like Salomon anyway.

Wachtell Lipton, while never Salomon's corporate counsel, had done a great deal of work for the house, and Martin Lipton, the well-publicized leader of the firm, had been one of Gutfreund's best friends for twenty years. Although he was a good deal taller than Gutfreund, they were physically similar types—overweight, round-faced, no animal magnetism, dependent partly on brains, partly on force of personality to achieve leadership. Wachtell Lipton had the highest average income per lawyer in the United States, and Lipton was the most highly paid in his firm. In 1983–84, when Gutfreund was at war with David Tendler, co-chairman and chief executive officer of the company then called Phibro-Salomon, Lipton attended the board meetings where the battles were fought, without an invitation anyone acknowledged issuing, although he was neither on the board nor the company's counsel. When Gutfreund fired Lewis Ranieri, one of the then six members of his executive council, a man who called Gutfreund "Pops" and whom Gutfreund called "Sonny," creator of Salomon's dominating mortgage securities department and arguably the greatest contributor to Salomon's profits in the early 1980s, he did the deed in Lipton's office. It was Lipton, too, who in 1987 first brought Gutfreund the unwelcome word that corporate raider Ron Perelman was planning a run at Salomon, and escorted him (though he didn't stay) to the dinner at the Regency Hotel where Perelman would tell Gutfreund his job was at risk.

Lipton and his wife were also friends of Gutfreund's fabulously self-indulgent second wife, although he had not, as generally believed, introduced them. Susan Gutfreund was well known to the city's fashion and "style" press. She had made headlines by spending an asserted $2 million on a staircase for the Gutfreunds' duplex at 834 Fifth Avenue, a million to put a garage under their town house in Paris, and Lord knows how many tens of thousands on a Lucullan feast for Henry Kissinger's sixtieth birthday. There were stories that she never wore the same gown twice, about trunks and trunks and *trunks* of clothes in the storage room at River House, where the Gutfreunds had departed after using someone else's terrace without permission to hoist to their apartment a Christmas tree too big to fit into any elevator in the building. And that was the tip of the iceberg of stories told truthfully or otherwise in the city's best circles. There had been no publicity, for example, when Susan purchased two seats on the Concorde so a New York confectioner could fly a cake to Paris for John's sixtieth birthday party at the Musée de Carnavalet.

Lipton called Gutfreund's office to report the phone call from Goldman and found that Gutfreund was in Paris; his wife liked to attend the private July 4 receptions at the U.S. embassy. Fortunately, Lipton was also going to Europe. The two friends had dinner there, and Lipton gave Gutfreund the news of the phone call from Goldman. Gutfreund acknowledged that he knew the government thought Salomon might have done something wrong in the May auction; indeed, he had gone to Washington on June 10 to meet with Undersecretary of the Treasury Robert Glauber to try to convince him that the Treasury's concerns were misplaced. Nevertheless, the SEC at the end of June had issued requests for Salomon's records of trading and financing the May notes. The subpoena was being handled by Don Feuerstein and Solly's in-house legal department.

But Wachtell Lipton had developed something of a specialty of internal investigation of securities houses; perhaps the firm should take a look at the Salomon government bonds department. Lipton sent a team to ask questions. By July 12 the answers to those questions had become very disconcerting, and a considerably larger team was committed to the investigation. Three partners were in charge: Lawrence Pedowitz, who had been chief of the criminal division of the U.S. Attorney's office in New York; Michael Byowitz, who had been a staff attorney with the Antitrust Division of the Department of Justice; and Allan A. Martin, who had been part of the SEC's Division of Enforcement. The August 7 conference was to discuss their alarming discoveries and what should be done about them.

SEVERAL SMOKING GUNS

There were two different sets of problems, neither trivial. The problem with the May 22 auction was its results: Salomon had wound up on settlement day, May 31, controlling $10.6 billion of the $11.3 billion in May 1993 notes that were delivered by the Treasury to the winning bidders at the auction. Meanwhile, others had been buying and selling these same two-year notes, still awaiting delivery from the Treasury's capacious womb, in a "when-issued" market that runs from the day a new Treasury issue is announced to the day, about three weeks later, when the Treasury actually gives birth. As a result of these transactions, purchasers of contracts for two-year notes were entitled to receive when they were issued somewhere between $8 billion and $12 billion worth of May 1993 U.S. Treasury notes. The other parties to these contracts, who would have to deliver $8 billion to $12 billion of May 1993 notes when issued, were banks, insurance companies, and speculators who had sold "short" in this informal futures market. Salomon and its allies, having won the auction, controlled virtually all the real notes. The only way the short sellers could make their deliveries and close out their contracts was to buy or borrow the notes from Salomon. In the language of the market, they were "squeezed."

As time passed, the squeeze gripped ever tighter; the most desperate days for the short sellers were July 1 and July 2. Lots and lots of money was involved. On $10 billion worth of notes, a "one-quarter-point move" (twenty-five cents per $100), which occurred in the last week of May, is worth $25 million. Edward Kwalwasser, executive vice-president of the New York Stock Exchange in charge of keeping the membership honest, would later tell the Senate Banking Committee that "our members lost millions and millions of dollars when they had to repurchase those notes after the May auction. People got fired—I mean, traders got fired for what they did because it looked like they were stupid as opposed to being taken advantage of."[2] Putting the worst reading on these facts, however, Wachtell Lipton's lawyers did not believe anybody could tie top management to a preplanned, manipulative squeeze.

The second set of Salomon problems the lawyers had investigated involved a whole bunch of Treasury auctions, going back almost a year and a half and including that of May 22. Treasury rules forbade any one purchaser from bidding for more than 35 percent of the securities to be awarded at an auction. Salomon participated in the Treasury auctions both as a buyer for its own account and as a broker for customers, and there was no limit on how much it could buy in the two capacities together—the rule was only that no *one* purchaser could bid for more than 35 percent of the amount on offer. The purpose of the rule was not entirely clear. During the week or ten days between the auction and the day of settlement, Salomon legally could (and in effect did) buy from its customers all the notes it had bought presumably on their behalf at the auction. Still, the 35 percent maximum bid for any one participant was a rule, and securities houses were supposed to obey the rules written by the Treasury and the Federal Reserve Bank of New York, which ran the auctions.

Paul Mozer was Salomon's chief government bonds trader, with responsibilities that included bidding at the auctions both for Salomon and Salomon's large institutional customers. He was a short, intensely argumentative and humorless thirty-six-year-old with black hair, a broad forehead, and a narrow chin. Gutfreund liked him for his almost violently competitive temperament. Mozer had denounced the 35 percent rule in interviews with the press and had on several occasions ignored it, bidding for more than 35 percent for Salomon's own account. When the Treasury had imposed its limit on him by automatically reducing his bids to whatever would be 35 percent of the amount offered, he had

secretly evaded the rule by putting in bids in the name of customers who had not in fact asked Salomon to bid for them.

In the May 22 auction, for example, Salomon bid for 35 percent
of the issue for itself, and for nearly 60 percent more as agent for
a number of customers. Those customers included Tiger Management, a large private investment partnership mostly for social and
theatrical personalities (among them the singer Paul Simon),
which had authorized Salomon to bid as its agent for $1.5 billion
worth of notes. Mozer, however, bid for $2 billion in the name of
Tiger. When Solly's bid won the auction, that extra $500 million
was ticketed to the Salomon computer as "sold" by Tiger to Salomon. Tiger did not know it had bid for, bought, or sold these
$500 million of two-year Treasury notes. While there was no
evidence that top management had known about this jiggery-
pokery with the Tiger name, Wachtell Lipton's gumshoes learned
that there had been at least one previous occasion when the abuse
of a client name to enter a fake bid for Salomon's benefit *had* been
brought to the attention of Gutfreund, Strauss, Meriwether, and
Feuerstein—and they had done nothing about it.

Someone near the top at Salomon for the first half of the 1980s
said that the Gutfreund he knew would have reacted to such
chicanery with an instantaneous "Fire the fucker." But someone
who was near the top at Salomon in the second half of the 1980s
saw it differently: "John Gutfreund was sitting in his Fifth Avenue
apartment admiring his million-dollar Adams rug when a golden
goose walked in and shat on it. He had a choice: He could kill the
golden goose, or he could try to get somebody to clean the rug.
He made the wrong choice."

A BAND-AID FOR ARTERIAL BLEEDING

Of the two offenses, the Wachtell Lipton lawyers considered the
fake bids by far the more serious. But it was decided not to make
too much of Mozer's folly. After all, as Feuerstein had argued in
the internal councils of the firm, the Treasury had no specific rule
against bidding for invented customers and no penalty specified
for violation of the 35 percent rule, other than rejection of the bid
itself. Lying to the government was itself "a criminal act," Feuer-

stein had told Gutfreund and Strauss back in April, but there was
not necessarily a legal obligation for the firm to report it to the
authorities. At Feuerstein's urging in late July, after Pedowitz and
his colleagues had independently learned about the fake bids, the
Lipton firm undertook its own search of the law and emerged with
an opinion that did not contradict Feuerstein's.

When the Wachtell Lipton lawyers and the Salomon lawyers
met on August 6 to prepare a joint presentation to senior management for the following morning, they were in general agreement. Now that more faked bids had been discovered, all present
agreed that the two young managing directors responsible for
them would have to go—both Mozer and his assistant Thomas
Murphy. The firm could purge itself of sin by disciplining the two
individuals and the clerks who had done their bidding. (Mozer,
sensing what was about to happen to him, exercised options he
had previously earned for forty-six thousand shares of Salomon
stock and immediately sold them for about $1.64 million.) An
announcement to the effect that two managing directors were
being punished should be made to the press as a preemptive strike
against any announcements from a government agency. The argument the firm would use to defend itself in the coming months
was fully developed at the August 7 meeting: The problem was
one of character, not of culture; it had happened that there was a
rotten apple in the barrel. This was not the most felicitous meta-
phor (the problem with the rotten apple, after all, is that the rot
consumes the whole barrel), but it came naturally.

The participants in the Wednesday morning meeting also
agreed that the squeeze which had started the government's investigation could be brazened out. Gutfreund insisted it was the
sort of thing that happened in the bond markets often enough to
be almost a normal event. There had also been a squeeze in the
April notes when Salomon's Mozer had wound up on the wrong
side of the ledger and had lost money—briefly, until he found a
way to join the squeezers. As Gutfreund may have known, short
sellers who complained to the Federal Reserve Bank of New York
that they were being beaten up by the startling premium the May
notes commanded in the market were told that such things were
natural phenomena. After his trip to Washington in June, Gutfreund thought Treasury Deputy Secretary Robert Glauber had

probably accepted his argument, which he had buttressed with charts he left on Glauber's desk, that the difficulties some traders were having with the May notes were a plausible result of a normal auction. Salomon's position was that the complainers about the May notes were crybabies who had misjudged the market and were looking for somebody to blame. And because the call to Lipton had come from Goldman Sachs, public relations director Baker developed a demonology that Goldman, as sore losers, had sicced the Feds onto poor Solly.

What the Wachtell Lipton people thought of Gutfreund's defense is not known. Their internal investigation turned up considerable evidence that Salomon in collusion with several third parties had managed a squeeze of the market for the Treasury's two-year notes due in May 1993. Still, Gutfreund was their client. If they were willing not to contradict Feuerstein's assertion that fake bids did not absolutely *have* to be reported to the government, they would be willing to accept Gutfreund's argument that Salomon in the May notes had been merely the lucky beneficiary of a buyer's market.

Still, when Gutfreund left to board the Concorde for Paris, the men in the law firm's conference room were not happy campers. They were clearly embarking on a journey without a known end. The emphasis in the discussion that followed was on keeping control to assure a public perception that Salomon was on top of the situation and would do whatever was necessary to repair any damage that might have been done to the firm's reputation. Clients would be upset; competitors, notably Goldman, would be out to snare them. There would have to be a press release to announce that Salomon had uncovered some irregularities; it should be issued on Friday so that it would be in the Saturday newspapers, which nobody read in August anyway. It would be important to keep the relevant government agencies informed. Shortly before the press release was distributed, the New York Fed, the Treasury, and the Securities and Exchange Commission should be told that it was going out, and should be faxed their own personal copies. All that agreed, there was an extended discussion of just what should be in the press release.

Work on the press release continued that afternoon, and a draft was finished in time for a Thursday morning meeting at Salomon to which the executives invited someone from the office of Gershon Kekst, Salomon's outside, we-call-you-when-we-need-you public relations counsel. And the mountain delivered a mouse. "Salomon Brothers, Inc.," the statement read, "has reported to the Treasury Department and other government agencies that it has uncovered irregularities and rule violations in connection with its submission of bids in certain auctions of Treasury securities." In the third paragraph it was acknowledged that "the Securities and Exchange Commission and the Antitrust Division of the Justice Department are investigating the May auction and subsequent market activities in the notes." Salomon, the press release continued, "has suspended the two managing directors who were in charge of its Treasury securities trading desk . . . and is implementing procedures designed to prevent any recurrence of these problems." The only name mentioned in the press release was that of John Meriwether, who, the public was assured, "will be assuming direct responsibility for the work of the government bonds department."

In the weeks after the disastrous work-product of this meeting became public, the fashion at Salomon would be to blame Wachtell Lipton. "The press release," Baker said censoriously, "was written by Lipton and Feuerstein and simply presented to us; it was typed on Wachtell machines, wasn't even typed here." But the truth seemed to be that Salomon management had not come clean with its lawyers. At best, moreover, Wachtell Lipton's investigation was limited to what could be found within Salomon itself, and Solly didn't keep much in the line of records of what it did in the government bond business. The bidding slips at the May auction, for example, were numbers scribbled on Treasury Department printed forms, written on the spot and stuffed into a box on a counter at the Federal Reserve Bank of New York. In theory someone somewhere had made copies of those slips for Salomon's own records, but when the lawyers asked to see them, they couldn't be found.

The Wachtell Lipton lawyers were not told about continuing interrelationships between Salomon personnel and the investment funds that had purchased these Treasury notes in the when-issued market—relationships that included investments by Salomon executives in the funds that the Justice Department would later call

Salomon's "co-conspirators." Nor were they told of the presence at these funds of traders who were recent Salomon alumni and kept all their old contacts. And because the lawyers were operating strictly within Salomon, they did not learn that the Treasury, angry about the extraordinary rise in price in the when-issued market for the May notes, had called for help from the Securities and Exchange Commission as early as May 29, two days *before* the actual issuance of the notes.

On the evidence available in June 1991, the SEC staff and the Antitrust Division of the Department of Justice formed a strong initial view that Salomon and several of the other large purchasers had worked collusively to manipulate the market for the May two-year notes. Indeed, the first SEC requests for information on the May auction went out to Wall Street only after the June auction had been completed, because the Treasury and the SEC originally thought that by keeping quiet they might be able to set a trap and catch Salomon and its friends *in flagrante delicto* in June. At a meeting of government agencies investigating the matter, the SEC's director of enforcement was asked where he would place Salomon's offenses on a scale running from individual insider trading to the monstrous deceptions of Drexel Burnham. He said that at first blush he thought the Salomon case was *much* worse than Drexel. And there is a case to be made for that position. As someone involved in the ongoing antitrust investigation of the note auctions put it, "Milken was just fucking around with some corporations; Salomon was fucking around with the United States government."

Everything considered, some in the government were certain to take offense at a press release claiming that Salomon had uncovered "irregularities and rule violations" and was cooperating with the investigation. Because of their limited knowledge of what had happened and was happening, the Wachtell Lipton lawyers did not see many of the major weaknesses in the defense the Salomon lawyers wanted the law firm to offer. Still, as the lawyers worked out what had to be done, they became increasingly nervous, and a call was put through to Gutfreund in Europe to summon him home for a meeting late Thursday night. He would personally have to call the regulators to tell them "what our investigation has uncovered." He would need "talking points" for those telephone calls, and he would want a briefing on how to answer the questions the regulators were likely to ask. Gutfreund's plane back from London did not arrive at Kennedy until nine o'clock, and he did not appear at the meeting until ten. Lawyers, outside public relations counsel Kekst and inside public relations man Baker, and members of the Office of the Chairman hung around, waiting, chitchatting, until a deeply annoyed Gutfreund appeared to sign off on the press release and on the decision that the regulators would be informed of management's long-standing knowledge of one fake bid in another firm's name. But the public would *not* be told, for Salomon could maintain, the lawyers agreed, the argument that what had been done by the firm was not actually *illegal*.

What was wrong with the press release, however, went deeper than any weaknesses of Salomon's case. Legality even if true was not going to protect the firm. What should have but did not strike terror in all the hearts around the conference table was that the three regulators involved in the case would be revealed as having been drowsy if not actually asleep at the switch. President E. Gerald Corrigan of the Federal Reserve Bank of New York, Chairman Richard Breeden of the Securities and Exchange Commission, and Treasury Deputy Secretary Robert Glauber were not only tough and able, but also vain.

Corrigan would inevitably be the most offended, because the New York Fed was on the firing line: It ran the Treasury auctions, and it had been essentially out of the loop. The New York Fed had not had the faintest notion that Salomon had put in fake bids; it had not known about the enormous position Salomon's friends had taken in the when-issued market; it had not tracked the financing arrangements Salomon and its friends had made in the "repurchase" market where the bulk of the profits of manipulation were made. Corrigan, who had been abroad, was being blindsided. A large, rambunctious New Yorker in his early fifties with a Ph.D. in economics from Fordham, he was a man of great intellectual distinction. He was about to become chairman of the committee that writes the world's rules for bank supervision at the Bank for International Settlements in Basel, and he was a brilliant polemicist. By knowing precisely what he was doing and using the full power of his office, he had saved the world on October 20,

1987, when his terrified member banks were refusing to supply funds to the exhausted stock market, and he *made* them lend.

But he would certainly cut a bad figure if Congress began investigating Salomon's wrongdoings.

On Friday, August 9, minutes before Salomon put out the press release, Gutfreund and Strauss called Corrigan to tell him, among other things, that there had been a fake bid, using a customer's name for Salomon's benefit, in the May auction; and, by the way, they had known about another fake Mozer bid since April. The more he thought about it, the angrier Corrigan became. Tom Strauss was a friend; he and Corrigan had had dinner together on several occasions since Strauss had learned of Mozer's fake bid, and Corrigan had been told nothing. And what was this nonsense about vice-chairman John Meriwether assuming direct supervision of the department? Meriwether had been the first member of Salomon's top management to know about the fake bid, and he had done nothing except pass the problem on.

Institutionally, the SEC would be if anything angrier than the New York Fed. On July 29, Salomon had filed a registration statement with the SEC to permit the sale of $5 billion of new unsecured Salomon debt securities. The registration statement made no mention of any possible trouble with the government. On August 8, as Gutfreund was being summoned back from Europe and all the key people at the firm were being called to evening meetings, Salomon asked the SEC to accelerate the effective date of the registration and allow immediate sale of the notes. At no time in the discussions of the Wachtell Lipton investigations and what to do about them did anyone mention the sin dyed deepest cardinal red in the Securities Act: selling securities with a registration statement that knowingly omitted "a material fact."

Glauber would have the best reason of all to be angry. What little Salomon was doing in connection with this mess had, in fact, been triggered by information that the Treasury's cops were on the trail. Gutfreund's visit on June 10 would now look like an obvious effort to put the bloodhounds off the scent. The formulation "Salomon has reported . . . that it has uncovered irregularities" was not only misleading to the public but by inference critical of Treasury authorities who had long before called in the cops.

Thursday night, even while the lawyers and the Salomon executives, like characters in a Beckett play, were waiting for Gutfreund, the first steps toward executing the containment strategy had to be taken. Members of the Salomon board of directors were called—mostly at their summer homes, for this was August 8—and read the text of the press release. Strauss and general counsel Feuerstein made the phone calls and added to the press release the fact that the federal regulators would be briefed on the matter before the press was given the news the next day. Among those who received the calls were Warren Buffett, the famous folksy "value investor" who had put $700 million of his holding company's money into a special issue of Salomon preferred stock in 1987 and had served on the board since then, and Buffett's sidekick Charles Munger, also on the board, a Los Angeles lawyer who ran the S&L owned by Buffett's Berkshire Hathaway. Only Munger, always the bad cop to Buffett's good cop, asked the lawyer's question of what did top management know and when did they know it—and what had they done about it. It seems unlikely that he got an answer.

Don Howard, Salomon's recently arrived chief financial officer (he had come from Citicorp in 1988), definitely was not told the truth. Feuerstein called him midday (he had taken the day off to play with a visiting grandchild) and asked him to come in for a meeting that evening. At the meeting he found "most of the senior people from the firm. . . . The topic at that point was that we had discovered illegal activity in the government bond department. Very confined. There was no indication that night to me at all that top management had known about it for several months and had done nothing. I was brought in because they wanted to know what I thought the impact on the funding would be if they announced this. I said, 'If it's illegal activity and you get rid of the people, I don't think it will be all that severe.' In fact, I still don't think it would have been all that devastating if that had been all there was to it."[3]

The press release itself seemed to go reasonably well with the press. Because the matter was still under investigation, questions that might have revealed the juicier details could be brushed aside. Reporters did notice the contrast between the opening statement that Salomon "had uncovered irregularities" and the admission later in the release that the government was already investigating the May auction. But the *Times* business staff, also somewhat depleted by vacation, pretty much accepted the spin Baker put on the story. There had been only "two, perhaps three" phony bids, nobody except the two managing directors noted in the press release was involved, and Salomon was confident that no further wrongdoing in connection with the May auction would be uncovered. Public relations director Baker was quoted as saying, "These were individuals acting on their own without the knowledge of management." William Brachfeld of Daiwa Securities, who had sat in the head government trader's chair for Salomon in the 1970s, was quoted as saying that "what some people call a squeeze is just the way the market works." John LaWare, one of the governors of the Federal Reserve, told the *Times,* "I don't think that anyone involved in it was significantly damaged by it."[4] Still, it was a Friday in August, when not much happens, and a tale of Salomon's "irregularities" in some Treasury auctions ran at the top of the front page of the paper on Saturday morning.

Gutfreund's calls to the Treasury, the New York Fed, and the SEC had been coldly received. Glauber specifically asked whether management's knowledge of the previous faked-bid episode would be covered in the release and was incorrectly assured that it would be. But nobody seemed to make any threats. Not until Monday morning when the back half of a *Wall Street Journal* front-page story picked apart Salomon's party line[5] did Lipton and the other lawyers realize how thin the ice was—and how unconvincing people more knowledgeable than *The New York Times* business reporters would find the story Baker had given out at the press conference. The SEC, the *Journal* reported, "is expected to bring charges of market manipulation, violations of antifraud provisions of securities laws, and criminal charges of mail and wire fraud." The Treasury said that "discussions with market participants and our observation of market prices lead us to the conclusion that a squeeze . . . did in fact occur." From that *Wall Street Journal* story, too, John Gutfreund learned for the first time how easily regulators who make themselves accessible to the press on a background basis can work their will without leaving a fingerprint at the scene.

Salomon lay doggo for the first two days of the next week while regulatory pressure rose around it like the tide, and then on Wednesday had to give away the game in another press release, one that deserves to be a classic. (Unfortunately, Salomon, which will give inquirers all the other documents it has made public in connection with this event, no longer distributes copies of this one.) Yes, the firm now admitted, Gutfreund, Strauss, and Meriwether *had* known since April about a fake bid the head of its government securities desk had entered in a customer's name. "Management immediately determined that the matter must be communicated to the government; however, due to a lack of sufficient attention to the matter, the determination was not implemented promptly."

That disaster still lay ahead as Gutfreund left his office after his phone calls to the regulators on Friday, August 9. He flew to his summer home on Nantucket, where his wife and five-year-old son were already in residence, for a weekend's rest. He had no hint that it was all about to go—job, limo, income, status—or that Salomon Brothers itself, his life's work, the palace in which he had become the King of Wall Street, was teetering beside the abyss that had swallowed Drexel Burnham just a few months before.

The next day, reading the story that ran in the *Times,* Gutfreund felt a little uncomfortable and asked people whether they had seen it. As his advisers had hoped, many had not. Newspapers are not delivered to people's homes on Nantucket, and many vacationers feel they can skip the papers in August because they will find the same stories on the same pages in September that they remembered from July. So several of the people to whom Gutfreund spoke didn't know what he was talking about. He told them, "There's something on the front page of today's *Times* about Salomon Brothers, and it's a problem, but we have it under control." To some he added, "I've been trying to get hold of Nick Brady [George Bush's Treasury secretary, who had been head of Dillon Read and knew Gutfreund from the New York securities business]. But I haven't been able to reach him."

His wife told her friends, "John says it's like getting a traffic ticket."

Chapter 1

BILLY TAKES COMMAND

ORIGINALLY, there were three Salomon brothers: Arthur, Percy, and Herbert. They were the sons and, until the day in 1910 when they founded their new firm, the employees of an established small-scale money broker who had walked out on their mother, an English-born professional pianist, and then married another woman. The unusual uxoriousness of the Salomon partners while the brothers lived—until the 1970s the incidence of divorce in the firm was unusually low—may be traced in part to the founding partners' reaction to their mother's abandonment.

In its beginnings Salomon Brothers was strictly a brokerage house; that is, it found buyers for sellers and sellers for buyers, taking a commission on bilateral transactions. The instruments brokered were the highest quality short-term paper, "bankers' acceptances" and the like, that banks sold and purchased every day to maintain liquidity or put idle money to work. A picture of the firm in 1910 hangs on a wall in the secretary's room of what is now Billy Salomon's one-man office in one of the new buildings on Sixth Avenue. It shows one desk and a telephone on the wall beside the door, all three brothers wearing their hats indoors to save time in case a client called and solicited their attendance. One of the few amenities the brothers installed when they moved to 60 Wall Street in 1922 was a barber's chair, allowing them to remain in business while getting shaved, a matter especially important to Arthur, the undisputed leader of the firm, who liked to have his mustache professionally tended.

Within a few years of its founding, Salomon had evolved into what the London market called a "discount house," an intermediary that employed its own resources (plus bank loans) to buy high-quality corporate and government paper from banks and bank trust departments that wanted cash, and sell the paper (with luck and skill, at a higher price) to other banks and insurance companies that wanted investments. The firm's achievement of this status was greatly helped by the arrival of Morton Hutzler, scion of a Baltimore department store family. The name of the firm, retained until 1970, forty years after Hutzler retired, became "The Discount House of Salomon Brothers & Hutzler," and the house became a dealer—not just a broker—in most high-grade bonds. By the 1950s the Salomon trading desks were a preferred alternative to the stock exchange for many bonds; indeed, the firm liked to say that the definition of a liquid bond was one on which you could get a bid from Salomon.

Throughout its tenure at 60 Wall, the center of the firm as a social entity was the partners' dining room, a narrow, dark, wood-paneled room with a door to the common hallway at one end and a pair of curtained windows at the other. Its ambiance exhaled conservatism, with English countryside art on the walls, large Georgian chairs marching the length of the long table, hand-knotted Spanish rugs on the dark polished wood floor, and lighting from fluted fixtures. Linens, silver, and crystal were set at each partner's place at the single long table. At no time in the 1950s did Salomon have more than twenty partners, and about half of them came for breakfast every working day. Breakfast, prepared and served by an aging, loyal staff without much turnover, was ready from seven-thirty. Some partners were there by seven-fifteen, although the trading day in that less pressured age did not begin until ten o'clock, and interest in what was happening on the European markets was largely restricted to those who had married into the English aristocracy—a category that did not include anyone at Salomon.

At breakfast the partners might talk sports or tell stories, sometimes rough stories. But mostly they talked shop, for Salomon like any trading house was essentially in the information business.

They discussed yesterday's markets, what the insurance companies seemed to be interested in, and any news picked up at the big
New York banks on which they called daily or more often. Lunch
drew another handful of the partners, those who were not tied to
the trading desk. Sometimes customers were entertained in an
adjoining room, because even in the 1950s the firm had a notable
kitchen, arguably the best on Wall Street after J. P. Morgan's—and
there wasn't any other place at 60 Wall suitable for receiving
customers. Liquor was available and consumed.

Salomon in the 1950s, then, was already a firm of some wealth
but not status. Outside the Wall Street community, nobody had
ever heard of it. The name appears neither in *Our Crowd,* Stephen
Birmingham's popular study of the significant Jewish families of
New York, nor in Vincent Carosso's monumental history, *Investment Banking in the United States,* published in 1970. With only
a handful of exceptions in the 1950s, the Salomon partners were
men who had come to Solly for their first job, most often as
teenage runners and office boys with no more than a high school
education. The Salomon partners' dining room might be elegant,
but 60 Wall Street wasn't: The windows leaked, the elevator lob-
bies were shabby, and there was no air-conditioning. Everywhere
on Wall Street in the 1950s private offices were scarce—indeed,
rather suspect. In firms such as Morgan Stanley and Brown Brothers Harriman, partners sat in large uncrowded rooms at neat dignified rows of rolltop desks, speaking softly. But Salomon's
partners sat in a zoo of a trading room, cheek by jowl with their
clerks and each other, shouting.

Nobody outside Wall Street had heard of Salomon because the
firm did business exclusively with a wholesale trade—banks, insurance companies, the emerging pension and mutual funds—and
its function essentially was to make a private market in which
these large pools of money could trade pieces of paper with one
another. Salomon was a dealer or a trader, not a banker; except on
rare occasions it did not advise clients or raise money for them; it
was the intermediary for its customers' transactions. The process
was one in which Salomon bought from one such institution and
then sold to others, or sold to one and then bought from others,
for any market must equilibrate the needs of buyers and sellers.
The prices at which Salomon bought or sold and the quantities

traded in this market were not a matter of public record, but the participants knew what Salomon's competitors were paying or asking for these securities. At bottom Salomon prospered because it "bought business," trading on lower margins than its more established competitors, who had gone to school with their customers.

Both salesmen and traders worked in the single long, narrow trading room, peering around pillars to see the numbers slotted, white on black, on a board that ran about half the length of the long wall and listed the actively traded government and corporate bonds. As trades occurred, attendants shoved new numbers into the slots on the board, but the news traveled initially by men calling out to each other: "Hoot and holler" was (and is) the fastest way to spread information on a trading floor to all who may need it. Everyone breaking into the firm, after his period of messenger duty and work in "the cage" (where the bonds and the money were taken in and paid out, safeguarded and accounted for), served time on the trading desks, keeping records of his trader's buys and sells, learning how the firm made its money. But often the dominant figures in the room were the salesmen, the people with the client contacts who brought the business to the trading desks.

On a table by the oak door to the partners' dining room was an elongated black-bound ledger book called "the boards" in which was recorded, in handwriting, the firm's positions as of the close of business the day before: its inventory of municipal and government bonds and notes, commercial paper, corporate bonds, bankers' acceptances, and the like. At the back of the ledger—called "the back of the book"—was a list of the firm's own investments, held for long-term price appreciation and income rather than trading profit. The ledger noted the price at which each position had been acquired, both in the trading accounts and in the investment accounts, and the price for which it had sold in the previous day's final transaction—the "market price." Every so often someone entering the partners' dining room would pause at the doorway, open "the boards," and take a look at how the firm was doing. How the firm was doing was synonymous with how the partner was doing, because the rule was that the firm's investments were the partners' wealth. It was understood that apart from their homes, bank accounts, and insurance policies, partners in a trading house like Salomon did not have private interests separate from those of their firm.

In the early 1950s, Salomon's capital had touched $11.5 million, but in the mid-1950s, it went into decline. All earnings were divided among the partners at the end of each year, and they mostly spent what they made or put it into real estate rather than add to their investment in their firm. Partnership compensation was a mix of salary, bonus, and return on investment in the partnership itself. This was a privately held firm: no stockholders, no public reports of activity, profits or losses. In the early 1950s the average partner in the average year took home between $70,000 and $100,000 a year, which was an extremely good income. The youngsters, by contrast, were poorly paid. Gedale Horowitz, who would become executive vice-president of Salomon and chairman of the Securities Industries Association, came to work for the firm in 1955 out of Columbia Law School, for $55 a week, "less than my wife made as a schoolteacher, which is probably the way the world ought to be."

The leader of the firm in the 1950s was not, however, a pure example of the Salomon man. He spent a fair amount of time in his private office, beside the trading room, and he also maintained some private interests independent of the partnership. He was Rudolf Smutny, a tall man with a long face, a bald dome, a go-getter attitude, and a sarcastic manner. Smutny had come to Salomon Brothers out of the Marine Corps right after World War I; he also served a second time as a volunteer in World War II. He was an indefatigable salesman, often calling on the same bank two or three times a day, with a salesman's unquenchable optimism and high opinion of himself, including his capacities to analyze financial statements and to handle booze. When he made a sale in the trading room, he would bellow out, "I dood it, fellas." He developed a cadre of large institutional customers, led by Equitable Life Insurance, for which he structured a $19 million bond swap, a lot of money in those days, to give the mutual insurance company more income and Salomon a capital gain.

Contacts with Equitable led Smutny to relations with land developer William Zeckendorf, whose corporate umbrella, Webb & Knapp, had an insatiable need for both construction and mortgage money and was looking for ways to get it through the market rather than through banks and insurance companies. Smutny and Zeckendorf became friends and drinking and golfing companions, and Smutny put more than $2 million of Solly's capital into Webb & Knapp stock. He made other unusual investments, too. At a time when railroad bonds were still central to the bond market and the railroads were pretending that other modes of transportation were unimportant, Smutny made the ultimately correct call that the future of railroads would be in symbiosis with trucks and ships, and that containers which could be transferred whole from rail-cars to other shipping systems would be the best investments in that industry. One company in particular, Trailer Train, based in Chicago, commanded his attention.

Flouting the unwritten Salomon rule, Smutny accepted election to the boards of Trailer Train, of Zeckendorf's Webb & Knapp, and of Associated Oil & Gas. Taking himself very seriously, he boosted his own share of the partnership income to $12\frac{1}{2}$ percent, double that of partners much his senior, and began to abuse his expense account, charging his children's travel and entertainment (and in one instance, clothing) to the firm. His wife, who was also a formidable drinker—straight gin from eight-ounce glasses—sometimes abused other partners' wives on social occasions.

Smutny installed one of the first car phones in the limousine he insisted Salomon buy for him. He would arrange to have customers call on him toward the end of the day and then would take them uptown in his limousine, making phone calls to impress them. The trading desk acquired a police phone monitor to pick up the calls between Smutny and Zeckendorf, and it turned out that what they talked about was restaurants and golf games (and how nice it was to have a telephone in the car), never business. Some partners were more amused than others.

The companies into which Smutny put the firm's capital did not pay dividends, and he made the earnings on the capital look better by purchasing short-term paper in Europe, where interest rates were higher but currency devaluations could devastate the dollar value of the paper. His domestic investments turned out to be mostly losers (Webb & Knapp wound up bankrupt, and although Trailer Train remained a Salomon client for more than two decades, it never provided much return on its stock). Under

Smutny's leadership Salomon's capital slid to only a little more than $7 million, a fact that was not generally known on the Street or to the firm's employees, many of whom would have sought other jobs if they had been aware of it. And many of the assets in the investment account were highly illiquid and hard to value. Among them, however, there was also one gigantic winner: Smutny's gamble in a little company called Haloid, which became Xerox after his successors sold Salomon's stake. If they had closed the business instead, distributed the Haloid shares among themselves and simply held on to them, the Salomon partners would have been richer than they ever became through their work.

PERCY USES BAD LANGUAGE

Among those who watched these developments in silence was the sole survivor of the original Salomon brothers, Percy, born in 1882 and long retired. He was a slim old man with thin shoulders but erect posture, who wore a high collar and spoke rarely. The gentleman of the three brothers, with a specialty in handling foreign banks and the stuffier trust companies, Percy had been less interested in trading or the theories of the business than his brother Arthur, who wrote and published articles on aspects of finance and designed exotic futures contracts for bankers' acceptances, ways for clients to make sure they could borrow (or lend) at some future time. And he had been less interested in wine, women, song, and oceangoing yachts than his brother Herbert.

When he came in for lunch in the 1950s, which he did every so often, Percy rarely talked about business. But he did once, on a day in the fall of 1956, shortly after the firm closed the books on its October 1 to September 30 fiscal year. He stopped on his way out from lunch and cast his eyes at the ledger book on the table by the door. He took a minute reading the back of the book, then turned to the partners at the table, perhaps eight or nine of them, and said, "You fellows ought to be ashamed of yourselves, dealing in *shit* like this."

Among the partners present was Percy's son William, often "Bill" and more frequently "Billy," a salesman of no great attainments who had come to Salomon from prep school in 1933, having chosen to get married young rather than go to college. Someone who knew him at Horace Mann remembered him as charming, strikingly well dressed, with clothes from DePinna, and more or less vacant. His clients at Salomon tended to be those his father had serviced, and it was thought he had become a partner by reason of consanguinity rather than as a reward for accomplishment. He made the best paper airplanes in the trading room and was deadly with spitballs. Like his father, he was a gentleman, courteous to all. Small, rather delicate, with hair neatly parted on the left, he had not been heard to assert himself in the partnership. Percy, departing, let his eyes rest briefly on each of the other men in the room, including Billy, who had never heard his father use such language before.

The oldest of the partners at the table was Ben Levy, a very tall, angular figure with a heavy head of white hair; he had worked for the Salomon brothers' father and had thrown in his lot with the new generation when they started their own firm. As the only employee in 1910, he had been the one who answered the telephone ("When asked who I was," he told an interviewer many years later, "I'd say, 'The boy in the office' "), kept the books, and carried the documents around Wall Street. Made a partner in 1918, partly as a reward for hard work selling the government's Liberty bonds, he had been the firm's government bond trader (not in those days a very significant market) since the middle 1920s. He called on the Federal Reserve Bank of New York every day to do business. As such he was among that small happy cohort of Wall Streeters who made money when the crash came and government bonds rose smartly in price. Since the 1930s he had been the leader of the partners who wanted to see Salomon go slow on the innovations, cultivate its own garden, take small positions, limit risks.

A grandfatherly figure and a kindly man generous in his judgments of others—people who came to work for Salomon in the 1950s have the fondest memories of him—Levy professionally was a classic short-term trader. All he knew or wanted to know was the feel of the market, for which explanations can always be found (prices are down because the midwestern banks are having trouble with their grain loans and selling governments to get cash, and so forth, which doesn't have to be true for people to believe it). His favorite quote was J. P. Morgan's explanation of why bond prices went up: "There were more buyers than sellers." Like many other leaders of this firm in its earlier years, Levy was greatly influenced by a wife who knew everything he was up to; their marriage endured more than sixty years. In theory he was part of an executive committee that advised Smutny, but Smutny had long gone beyond asking his advice.

The third member of the supposed executive committee was Edward L. (Ned) Holsten, Salomon's first Harvard graduate, who liked to tell people he had written his thesis on Machiavelli's *The Prince* and used what he had learned every day in the markets. He was a large, handsome man with a lordly manner, one of the firm's few Protestants (although the belief among the old-timers is that he was really part Jewish and denied it), recruited originally with the thought that he could help Salomon break into the WASP world of securities underwriting. He was in fact responsible for the firm's first management of a securities issue, $43 million of bonds for the meat packer Swift, and he also brought the house the selling "mandate" for an issue of Socony-Vacuum (later Mobil) bonds. Then Salomon was forced to retire from underwriting by the violent opposition of the established firms. "He was very bright," Billy Salomon said of Holsten, "but very weak."

Holsten had become a sort of supervising salesman of industrial bonds. He had a photographic memory and could recite the prospectuses for corporate issues he had sold, years after the sale and after downing four or five martinis at lunch. Even more conservative than Levy, he used to warn the young salesmen about touting customers on railroad bonds, which the Depression had shown to be very vulnerable to dramatic loss. He, too, was highly uxorious; he was married to a cousin who drove him to work every day and said she had a gun in her handbag that she would use to kill anyone who tried to steal her Ned.

Perhaps the most important of the group to whom Percy addressed his contempt was Jonas Ottens, a short man with a pompadour of white hair; he was lord of the utilities bond desk, which was the most active at the firm. Born Ottenstein, he was a rabbi's son who had married a Catholic woman and had become the kind of convert who talked a lot about religion. His was a teaching talent, anyway. He would stay late to teach the juniors at informal classes that ran from five to seven or eight o'clock, several nights a week in the trading room. Wise students then came back to the office at six-thirty or seven the next morning to bone up on the tables of the bonds sales from the previous day. Ottens would come in and say, "AT&T $2\frac{3}{4}$s sold yesterday at the New York Stock Exchange. What was the price?" After that answer was right he would ask, "Did we buy any? What was the yield at eighty-four?"

Each junior kept his own "basis book" to explain the relationship between the "coupon" (the interest rate paid on the bond) and the true yield (which factored in the difference between the market price and what the bond would pay on the date of redemption). Ottens expected the juniors to memorize the various bond tables, to understand why different bonds had different ratings, why they had different "coupons," and why their prices varied. He was a man with an all but uncontrollable temper, and when the answers to his questions were wrong or when one of his clerks made a mistake at the desk, Ottens blew his stack. "He was a great teacher, but he was extremely difficult to work for," said Stanley Cohen, who came out of the Marine Corps to Salomon in 1955. Cohen considered himself a tough specimen and remembered that the only person in the world he was afraid of was Jonas Ottens. "But out of the office he'd give you the shirt off his back."

Where the firm's name was involved, Ottens could be forceful outside the office, too. As part of his dedication to the youngsters, he coached the Salomon baseball team, which played at the Parade Grounds in Brooklyn. (The team had been an enthusiasm of Arthur Salomon from the first year his firm got big enough to have a ball club; Arthur would go to the games and bet on his boys.) After each game the whole group would go to Burry's on Coney Island Avenue, a bar where you could get a meal in the back room. Most of the first team in the 1950s became partners.

"Joe was the daddy, but you couldn't argue with him," Cohen said. He remembered one game when Ottens was the umpire and called a member of the opposing team safe at first on a close play. The Salomon trader who was playing first base was incensed and yelled at Ottens for missing the call. Ottens told him to shut up and get back to his position, but he continued to yell. After a few minutes of obscenity, Ottens said to his first baseman, "*He's* safe, and *you're* out." The next morning when the clerk came to work, he found a cardboard box on the floor beside his desk with instructions to clear out his belongings and be gone. Ottens was almost always among the breakfasters in the partners' dining room, where he educated the partners, too. Smutny had tried to order him around, and he didn't like it at all.

Others had been offended, too. Harry Brown, who had first come to the door of Salomon as the delivery boy for his father's tailor shop, bringing Arthur a new suit, was made a partner in the 1930s and was sent to Chicago to manage the Salomon office there. As the firm's most organized manager, Brown was pressed into service to spend a day or two every week in New York. He was, said Salomon's star investment banker Ira Harris, who knew him some years later, "the creative brain of the firm, both for numbers and for money." Because Smutny's piggyback railcar company was headquartered in Chicago, he spent a lot of time there and bossed Brown around. At one point, in fact, he tried to fire Brown but pulled back when he found he lacked partnership support. Mrs. Smutny, moreover, had offended Mrs. Brown, whose control over her husband was legendary in the firm. (He went straight home from work, ate an early dinner at home every night, and was in bed by 9:15. "She wouldn't," one of his partners said some years later, "let him take his cock out of his pants in the washroom.") Brown would be happy to join any group opposing Smutny. So would Miles (Mike) Perrin, the senior industrial bond trader, an amusing man (his brother was senior joke-writer for Jack Benny) who had a short fuse and was pushed around on several occasions by Smutny.

Another willing to join a cabal was Charles Simon, who was the firm's contact man with the enormous New York State pension funds, the upstate banks, and some of the city trust departments. He had come to Salomon as an office boy in the spring of 1931 when his father, who was in the cotton business, had to admit that he could no longer afford to keep his son at William and Mary. Simon spent his first year with the firm as the trusted messenger, carrying Jonas Ottens's bootleg booze to a lab to be analyzed, working with marine salvage people who were repairing Ned Holsten's speedboat after an accident in the Hudson, and passing along a monthly payment to a pretty young woman in an apartment in Queens for Herb Losee, Salomon's classically handsome banker type who kept fighting dogs at his Long Island home and was in charge of trading municipal bonds. After a further year watching Mike Perrin trade Canadian bonds, Simon went to up-state New York to see if he could generate business, and he proved astonishingly good at it. Robert Dall, who later handled Salomon's "money desk" and created its mortgage-trading business, said Simon taught him that "salesman is really a sacred word."

In 1992, more than sixty years after his first day, Charles Simon was still at Salomon, looking out a window in a corner office on a high floor of its new building, speaking in military imagery with considerable obscenity, and admiring paintings that showed scenes of the battles he never fought. Simon had liked Smutny: "If there was somebody to restrain him, he was useful, he worked his ass off, he was exactly the kind of man to lead a squad—'Come on, fellows, let's go. Get your ass off those seats, let's go!' He wanted the firm to be big and powerful, but he was just a little slow in the head, and he was always being told by Zeckendorf that he was a genius."

Although a lot of people wanted Smutny out, discussions around the dining table revealed that the senior partners were not willing to take the lead in removing him. He was the firm's contact with several of its largest customers, and he had a habit of leadership nobody in the junta could claim. Truth to tell, they were all afraid of him—all except Billy Salomon, who talked things over in confidence with Leo Gottlieb of Cleary Gottlieb Steen & Hamilton, the firm's lawyers, and then patiently worked the partnership for almost six months, urging a meeting one morning before trading began, on a day when Smutny would be out of town. The stars came into the proper conjunction in April. At the meeting, after he and Ottens had described the financial condition of the firm and the losses on Smutny's pet projects, Billy demanded a vote to buy out Smutny's $12\frac{1}{2}$ percent and dismiss him from the partnership. Levy and Holsten were not prepared to cast Smutny out, but Billy insisted. When Smutny returned from his trip, he found to his horror—for the firm was his whole life—that he had been expelled from Salomon. Charles Simon, who was there, gave the simple explanation: "Billy found he had bigger balls than he'd thought he had."

There was a squib in *The New York Times* on April 20, 1957, announcing that Rudolf Smutny was retiring from the firm of Salomon Brothers & Hutzler. Having moved on to the brokerage house of du Pont, Glore Forgan, Smutny reentered history thirteen years later as the partner in that firm who suggested it might find salvation from its troubles under the wing of the new computer services magnate H. Ross Perot.

YOUR MONEY AND YOUR LIFE

Billy Salomon was forty-four years old in 1957, and he took office as part of a triumvirate with Levy and Ottens, most people in the firm believing that Ottens was the leading figure. But it was Billy who had to resolve the problem of the firm's capital position after Smutny was bought off with a frighteningly high fraction of the firm's liquid assets. He turned again to Gottlieb, a shy man of rigid probity and rarely revealed brilliance (first in his class at the Sheffield School at Yale and then at Harvard Law School), who would continue to practice law well into his nineties.[1] Gottlieb became a limited partner, investing half a million dollars of his own money, and wrote a new partnership agreement for Billy—"a *swingeing* agreement," said Edgar Aronson, who signed it in the late 1960s, using the British slang he picked up as head of Solly's London office. Under the terms of Billy's new agreement, Salomon partners in effect committed to leave most of their share of the future profits of the firm in their capital accounts, not only while they were working for Salomon but for five years after their departure.

Billy ran the firm for the next twenty years. In 1964 he took the title managing partner at the suggestion of public relations adviser Mel Adams, who thought Wall Street was confused because the firm lacked a recognized spokesman (although until the disasters of August 1991, Salomon Brothers was the only major financial house that let its people make their own comments on markets without clearance from their bosses or public relations). And, of course, it was Billy's family name that was on the firm. Retaining his unassuming, rather gentle manner, he became more of a dictator than Smutny had ever been: "When Billy told you to do something," said Michael Bloomberg, who came to Salomon in the mid-1960s fresh out of business school, "you did it. It's like my eighty-three-year-old mother. When she tells me to do something, I do it." And though he was an unusually courteous man outside the office; nobody can remember that he ever said thanks for a service done for him or the firm.

But among the hundreds of partners and "managing directors" who passed through Salomon Brothers in the years of his leadership, there are amazingly few who feel anything but loyalty to the point of love for the Salomon Brothers of the Billy days. (Even the failure to say thanks has its defenders: "You were *supposed* to be good," said one of them.) Morris Offit, who was Salomon's sales director in the 1970s and now has his own private bank, said that "Bill Salomon is the most underrated Wall Street leader. Gus [Levy of Goldman Sachs] and Sy [Lewis of Bear Stearns] and Andre Meyer [of Lazard] and Bobby Lehman [of Lehman Brothers] got the press, but Bill was an architect. He had little compassion, and he did little stroking. He had what I used to call the Pit Theory of personnel management—put all these guys into a pit, and whoever walks out is the survivor. But he kept all the inmates walking in lockstep. He could play the traders and the salesmen and the bankers against each other—that was his genius. He was very comfortable making people decisions, and that's the greatest strength a manager can have."

It was the people Billy Salomon hired and socialized into his firm who made John Gutfreund the King of Wall Street. In the twenty-one years from 1957 to 1978, Salomon Brothers became one of the most important investment banks in the world, hugely profitable and heavily capitalized with almost $200 million (only Merrill Lynch had more). Although some of these activities were still embryonic and would mushroom only in the dark world of the 1980s, Salomon in 1978 was already a pioneer in hedging as well as taking risks, in the creation of mortgage-backed securities, and in finding profitable swap financing for multinational corporations, governments, and international organizations. Its monetary and fixed-income (bond) research operations were the best in the world, certainly in the private sector. Eventually Billy even got some respect: He served on the board of governors of the New York Stock Exchange and as president of the Bond Club, an organization, as one of his partners said rather sourly, "formerly headed by people who had come over on the Mayflower."

For most of those years Billy was in physical pain, limping about the trading room to favor an arthritic hip joint that was replaced in a pioneering and successful operation in the early 1970s. Then another physical disability led him to resign as managing partner in 1978, a year before his sixty-fifth birthday. He had been diagnosed with a brain tumor, and while it proved operable and benign, he was concerned—or so one of his closest friends reported—that after he returned from the hospital he would not have the judgment to know that his judgment was impaired. Billy himself said his reason for taking early retirement was that he and his wife Virginia were entitled to take vacations of the kind they hadn't known since he had taken over the firm in 1957: "We wanted three weeks in Europe, and I could never do that while I was running the firm. The brain tumor told me it was time."

Before going into the hospital, Billy without announcement anointed John Gutfreund his successor. There was in fact no significant rival for the job. Treasury Secretary William Simon had left the firm to go to the second Nixon administration in late 1972 with an understanding that he might return, but the offer made to him when he became free to consider one was for a partnership share less than Gutfreund's. Later, accompanied by Dale Horowitz, who was Simon's best friend at Solly, Gutfreund upped the ante to equivalence and became effusive in his enthusiasm that Simon return so "we can run the firm together." But Simon felt that Gutfreund's real feelings had not changed from their first meeting. In any event Simon wanted to serve on corporate boards and spread some wings, and after the departure of Smutny, Billy had formally forbidden such commitments. Gutfreund had been a successful trader of municipal bonds and the leader of Salomon's move into investment banking before he shed such specific responsibilities to become Billy's alter ego and general adviser. He expected the job, and everyone at the firm expected he would get it.

Billy later said that his wife warned him he would be unhappy with his choice. Gutfreund's great ability as a trader, an underwriter, and an assistant had been his superb instinct for pricing securities and deals, and that instinct had nothing to do with managing people or making policy decisions. Besides, she didn't like him. Billy told very few people at the firm that he was going in for a brain tumor operation, but Gutfreund spread the word to a wider cadre. One morning in 1992, looking at the framed full-length photo portrait of John Gutfreund that sat on the table beside the couch in his office, where he saw it whenever he looked up to speak with his visitor, Billy Salomon said that when his operation was over and the biopsy report was conclusively negative for cancer, his wife called Gutfreund to give him the good news. To which, Billy reported, Gutfreund said, "Are you sure?"

Chapter 2

THE MAGIC OF THE MARKET

MORRIS OFFIT came to Salomon in 1969 from the Mercantile Safe Deposit & Trust Co. in his native Baltimore, to start the firm's first stock research department. He was a quiet, slim, dark-haired, reflective man, destined for banking rather than trading. (Later he would design and operate Salomon's first systematic training programs for employees; when he left, he started his own private bank, which flourished.) During his first afternoon on the job, he was called into Billy Salomon's office and confronted with the management committee: Billy, John Gutfreund, Charles Simon, Robert Quinn, Vincent Murphy. "What do you know," they asked, "about Norwich Pharmaceuticals?"

What had happened, Offit later learned, was that Benjamin Buttenweiser, one of the great figures of Jewish Wall Street, had come over from his own shop at Kuhn Loeb to lunch with Billy, a first-time event of major significance. In the course of conversation Buttenweiser mentioned that Kuhn Loeb's client Revlon had bought 744,000 shares of Norwich in hopes of taking over the company but found that it couldn't do so. This was not an actively traded stock, and Revlon was stuck with the shares. Did Billy have any ideas? On the floor of the New York Stock Exchange brokers were bidding 40½ for Norwich, and brokers were offering to sell for 41. Salomon and Buttenweiser got that information by calling the exchange, which was the only way you could get such information in those days. And at lunch Billy said Salomon would take the whole 744,000 at the 40½ bid, a commitment of more than $30 million, less a stock exchange minimum commission of about $185,000.

Salomon was not, of course, investing in Norwich; Billy wanted that stock sold fast. Offit gathered all the material he could about Norwich and took it back to his room at the Princeton Club, where he was staying until he could find an apartment. He worked all night and by eight the next morning had a document on Billy's desk, near the door on the trading floor (sometimes messengers wandering into Salomon would ask Billy to sign for things, because he was the closest person). The document gave the financials, some analysis of the products and their markets, and what could be learned about investors who already owned a lot of Norwich, because selling stock to an investor who already knows the company is much easier than selling it to someone who is starting from scratch. Billy picked up Offit's document and walked it over to the Dreyfus Corporation, where he had a talk with his friend Dick Johnson, the one-eyed portfolio manager of the Dreyfus Fund, who already had a large position in the stock. At the end of the talk Dreyfus bought the entire 744,000 shares at the price Billy had paid for it the day before, and Salomon pocketed two commissions. Offit didn't remember whether Billy said thank you (he never did), but his own career at the firm was off to a good start. From 1973 to 1980 he would be head of domestic sales and manager of the firm's first training program.

No other firm traded that way. The year before, during the week of the Russian invasion of Czechoslovakia and the frightening anarchy around the Democratic National Convention in Chicago, Salomon had traded ten blocks of stock totaling 902,500 shares, including one trade of 374,000 shares of Control Data (more than $52 million), which for two years (until another Salomon trade supplanted it) held the record as the largest in the history of the New York Stock Exchange. Over the course of a year's work Salomon expected to make money on such activity, but any given trade could easily bomb. Such transactions were Salomon's advertising for its market-making capabilities—and for its habits of mind. Business like this came Salomon's way in part because other firms weren't willing to commit such large chunks of capital to trading. But, Billy said at the time, "really, it isn't capital. It's desire, pride, aggressiveness, the appetite for it."[1] The year Billy launched his stock research department was the year the music stopped—the great '60s bull market faded away as the federal government ran its only budget surplus in the last forty-five years. He made money anyway.

Salomon's qualities and successes as a trader were more than just a source of profits for the firm and its partners. They became a gearing system whereby what was done today in trading influenced what was done tomorrow in corporate finance, and the day after in investment banking, international banking, and currency. For better or worse—and there are arguments on both sides—the world financial structure of the 1990s was created by Billy Salomon and his traders and salesmen in the 1960s and 1970s, then magnified and gold-plated by John Gutfreund and his pinwheel of talents in the 1980s. They entered and then dominated the various kingdoms of finance because they could employ the strengths Salomon drew from its daily contact with the earth of trading.

Because the dominating Salomon knew the buyers but not the issuers of investments, underwriting became increasingly a game of selling stocks and bonds rather than a venture in financing economic activity. Because the value of these pieces of paper was increasingly a function of the price of other pieces of paper, not of real production and consumption, a new financial culture grew that fed on itself. Because what Salomon could offer was a price for a piece of paper, the emphasis in finance shifted perceptibly from the long-standing relationship to the individual transaction— and then to the "product" being bought and sold.

In the 1980s, while Billy Salomon watched from the sidelines with mounting distaste, an apprenticeship and judgment business became a business of quick mathematical insights by people who might or might not understand the significance of what they were doing. Salomon was not, like Drexel Burnham Lambert, a house of fraud, where strengths in traditional banking skills were perverted to "create value" in a flimflam of private manipulated markets; Salomon was never implicated in any of the "insider trading" scandals associated with names like Ivan Boesky, Dennis Levine, and Michael Milken. But the "Salomon culture," the drive to get more and more business, to tie the customer to Salomon with steel fasteners, to trade anything and everything ("They would make a bid on your furniture if you asked," somebody said), would inevitably hit a ceiling—and nobody would know what came next.

External events, especially the growth of giant institutions as the primary lenders to and investors in the modern capitalist economy, provided the force that propelled finance through Salomon's channels. Academic theorizing separated the financial and the real economy, building the walls of abstraction within which only logic mattered, frightening the merely practical men who might otherwise have asked whether so large a piece of the gross national product should really be spent for financial engineering. Salomon's people were not the inventors of markets—Leo Melamed at the Chicago Mercantile Exchange and Richard Sandor at the Chicago Board of Trade created the futures contracts that would expand all the playing fields—but they were the designers of the instruments by which these markets could be tilted. Brilliant kids who knew only what they had been taught were recruited for such purposes, first by Salomon and then by its competitors. When those competitors mastered the trick of these designs and poured their own cleverness into the complicated systems that Salomon had built to funnel profits out of the new markets, it turned out that the youngsters who succeeded to the Salomon name had never learned why there were rules against cheating.

FEELING IS BELIEVING

Salomon got to its line of work by what seems in retrospect a quite natural progression. A discount house is a trading operation, buying paper from one bank to sell to another. Discount houses are necessarily in the market every day on both sides, gathering information from all the banks with which they do business. All financial intermediaries make their living from the information they have that their clients and customers don't have. Most frequently and legitimately, their information derives from being at the vortex of the market, where they can see and feel more than outsiders can.

Robert Dall, a redhead who worked in a red-striped shirt, came to Salomon in the 1960s from eight years as a commercial banker. He learned the difference between borrowing and using the market from William Simon, who was then running Salomon's government bond department. Dall's job was to find the loans for tomorrow morning that would enable Simon to pay for what he was purchasing for delivery tomorrow morning. One day in 1969 when money was tightening, Dall found that he could not, as Simon had assumed, "buy" (that is, borrow) overnight money at 5¼ percent. He went to Simon with some concern, and Simon said, "All right. Then sell it [lend] at 5¼. Keep selling. As the rates go down, sell more."

Dall did as he was told, lending money he didn't have. Rates dropped quickly as others in the market assumed that some new major lender had arrived on the scene, and Dall then turned around, bought back what he had sold, and ultimately got the loans Simon needed from the money market at rates as low as 4½ percent. By the time he was done he had funded Simon's position at something less than the 5¼ percent Simon had wanted to pay, and had made money for the firm while doing so.

The instruments the discount houses bought and sold could almost always be financed with loans from the banks, at the lowest available rates, because they were the highest quality instruments and were pledged to the loan. It was essentially through the discount houses that the central banks executed monetary policy. The Bank of England conducted its open market operations, buying paper from the market to put money in the system and selling paper to take money out, through the group of discount houses in the surrounding streets. Jonas Ottens was in the offices of the Federal Reserve Bank of New York several times a day in the 1920s for the same reason. Part of the creditworthiness of the discount houses was the belief at the banks that the government's central bank would make sure no banking customer of a discount house would lose money if a discount house failed. If money was intolerably tight in the market, the central bank would "rediscount" the paper bought by the discount house to keep it out of serious trouble. After World War II, in the United States the term "primary dealer" replaced "discount house," and only Discount Corporation of America kept the name, but the principles didn't change much.

It was Arthur Salomon who saw that the information gained in a discount house business could be used to improve a firm's chances when trading bonds. The risks to the trading house were greater in the bond market, because changes in interest rates do not greatly affect the price of instruments with only a few days or weeks to run but will really jolt the price of paper that will pay the old rate for years to come. The principles of dealing, however, are the same: To "make a market" profitably, the trader has to know the current attitudes of players on both the buying and the selling sides, not the intrinsic value of the bonds. On any given day the prices in a financial market are determined not by the "fundamentals" but by the participants' belief in where prices will be tomorrow. The intermediary who was both buying from and selling to the insurance companies and the bank trust departments would have much better information to guide his own decision-making than a market participant who for the day was either a buyer or a seller.

The bond trader, then, "priced" the bond, bid to buy at one price, and offered to sell at another, slightly higher price. He had to have in his head the prices currently being paid for bonds at this interest rate for similar companies, the quantities that some customers seemed to be putting on offer as against the quantities other customers seemed to be demanding. He had to know the firm's own inventory: Did he feel Salomon could profit by holding more of this paper, or was the position already too heavy? What other chunks of this stuff might be for sale? In whose hands? Were the firm's other customers likely to want it or sell it? What did the market know about Salomon's inventory?

Like Dall's lending money to reduce the cost of borrowing it, a trader with a heavy inventory nobody knew about might buy more to push up the price and create the public interest that automatically follows rising prices. But if others did know Salomon had an inventory to sell, they would gleefully short the security to meet Salomon's demand for more, and then wait for Solly to get tired of holding it and dump it at Solly's loss, the others' gain. If there was no inventory and the customer wanted to buy, how easy would it be for Solly to serve his wishes by acquiring the bonds he wanted, either buying them or borrowing them? If Salomon sold short to serve a customer who wanted to buy, would its subsequent bids to buy and clear its position send the price up, making the deal unprofitable?

Sometimes the trader felt he was in a competitive situation, that the customer was soliciting bids or offers from other traders as well as from Salomon; sometimes he felt he was alone, and the prices varied accordingly. The firm made its profit, after all, on the "spread" between the price the trader paid to buy the security and the price he was able to charge when he sold it. The less he paid one customer, the more he charged the other customer, the higher the profits of Salomon Brothers. But the Salomon trader's price on both sides was strongly influenced by the Salomon contact man whose customer's wish to buy or sell had begun the transactions. In *Liar's Poker,* young salesman Michael Lewis is asked sarcastically by a trader, "Look, who do you work for, this guy or Salomon Brothers?"[2] In the 1960s, for all the go-go reputation of the decade, the answer to that question would have been easy and different from the answer the trader expected from Lewis in the 1980s. The Salomon salesmen of the 1960s were trained to know that it's the customer who writes everybody's paycheck, and if the customer wasn't satisfied, Salomon wouldn't make money anyway.

Billy Salomon liked to say that if a customer wasn't happy he might try to do his business down the street and might find he liked it there; Salomon couldn't afford that. Harry Nelson, who came from Merrill Lynch to be Salomon's sales manager in 1966, inherited a trade in which the customer felt cheated. It was a big trade with a lot of money involved. He took the problem to Billy, who said, "If he doesn't like the price, tell him to write his own ticket." Reflecting on that statement, Nelson said, "Billy was a great believer in creating a sense of obligation on the client's side." That was different but not a great deal different from what Salomon's competitors in the market liked to say, which was that Salomon "bought business." It was also not incompatible with a senior trader's comment that Billy sometimes failed to recognize "who was a customer and who was screwing the firm to the wall."

The salesmen were always a force for holding down the spreads. They were not credited or debited according to the profit or loss on the sales they made; they were measured solely by the volume of business they did, the revenues they generated. The success of the trading desk, by contrast, *was* measured—and measured daily—by the profitability of the trades. Although the traders were sometimes salesmen themselves, working the telephone consoles to rustle up bids for their merchandise (and conscious that the people on the other end of the phone calls listened differently depending on how they had done on their most recent trades with Salomon), there was a palpable tension between them and the sales force. The two groups needed each other but they had different agendas.

Often enough the prices the trader quoted were a function of the salesman's clout. Continental Bank in Chicago was Harry Brown's account. Brown was the number-two partner, second only to Billy himself. He saw to it that Continental got the best prices. "You know, we referred to accounts by numbers," William Simon remembered from the days when he was head of two Salomon trading desks. "Continental Bank was two-eleven. Whenever I heard it was a two-eleven, I winced. They were *embarrassed,* all the money they made on us. They'd call and say, 'We'll make it up to you.' "

Bill Simon remembered an occasion when Charles Simon (no relation) came to his municipal bond desk with the unwelcome news that the State of New York was about to come out with a $250 million issue of 4¼ percent bonds to finance some worthy purpose, and Charlie had told New York State comptroller Arthur Levitt that Salomon would take $70 million of it. "What do you mean, we'll take seventy million?" Bill screamed, terrifying his side of the trading room. "That shit should be 4½. How am I going to sell it? What are you doing to me?" And Charlie explained what Bill knew, that Arthur Levitt was his biggest and best account, and the New York State retirement funds that Levitt controlled gave Salomon more business than any other institution in the world. "We'll make it back in a week in trading," Charlie said; and Bill, not wishing to be in a fight with his best salesman, bought the bonds. "But Levitt would never call to say he'd make it up to you," Bill Simon remembered. "And three months later I'd have the administrative committee on my neck, asking me why that shit was in my portfolio, telling me to sell it at a loss."

Asked whether his recollection of this incident departed drastically from Bill's, Charles Simon thought awhile, then shook his massive jowly head and growled, "Spread's too wide." At $4\frac{1}{4}$ when the bonds should have been paying $4\frac{3}{8}$, was the story plausible? Charles Simon nodded. Yes, that might have happened.

Billy Salomon, said a man who joined the firm as a bright boy in the 1970s and stayed until 1990, really understood the Las Vegas principle of trading: If you do ten deals, you have to be right on six of them to make money; if you do a thousand deals, you have to be right on only 501. The trader's odds are better: The more business he does and the wider the range of customers with whom he does it, the smaller the chance that he will be fucked (to use professional terminology) by someone who knows more than he does. Billy Salomon told newcomers to the firm that "we want to do as much business as we can as often as we can with as many customers as we can."

The essence of the bond business as Salomon practiced it was that there were always customers who had to do something. The bank trust department had to pay the estate tax, the insurance company needed cash for the owner of the insured property that had burned down, the pension fund had to pay the pensions: They had to sell from their portfolios. Or the widow sold the department store, the insurance company was booking the semi-annual premiums, the pension fund received its payment from the corporation, and they all had to buy for their portfolios. Sometimes the portfolio managers were changing their investment strategy; they wanted safer or short-maturity bonds although they yielded less, or were willing to increase the proportion of riskier and longer-maturity bonds to increase their income. Or they had heard about something they really thought they should own and now wanted to sell something less interesting to pay for it.

Part of the function of the Salomon contact man was to make the bonds Salomon had in inventory look interesting. The perfect call on a customer was one where the customer was persuaded to buy something Salomon's trader had in inventory, and to pay for it by selling Salomon something that allowed the firm to cover a short. Salomon salesmen, knowing their traders' inventory, could sometimes put ideas in their customers' heads. The fact that Salomon's trading activity in bonds often revolved around swaps for customers gave both salesmen and traders habits of mind that would have great resonance in the firm's development in the 1980s.

Billy Salomon always insisted that trading in bonds, even government bonds, was riskier than what the firm did in stocks. Life insurance companies, the largest market for government bonds, tended to buy them to hold. Their actuaries told them the amount of money they would need each year, and they covered a percentage of those needs with government bonds that would be redeemed that year. But the government issued bonds according to the size of the deficit in the year of issuance, and the quantity coming due each year bore no relation to the insurance companies' needs. If Salomon in the course of trading purchased an issue that would expire in a year for which the insurance companies were already fully covered, there might be a vacuum under the bond, no bids at all in the market—at *any* price. This problem would disappear in the later 1970s when the Chicago Board of Trade began trading a Treasury bond futures contract that could be satisfied by the seller's delivery of any bond that had more than fifteen years still to run. But at the time when Salomon became the nation's premier government bond trading house, the firm needed a lot of guts to permit traders to take large positions in Treasury bonds.

So Billy Salomon found somebody who never got scared: a lean young man named William Simon who wore big horn-rimmed glasses and an intense expression. Simon had gone from Lafayette College to Union Securities in the early 1950s and became head of that posh firm's trading operation after only two years on the job. Union had merged with Eastman Dillon, where, Simon recalled, "I was being told to cut positions, do this, do that. One day they're bullish, one day they're bearish. They live for up markets, and whenever the market turns, they're in trouble." He wanted out, and Weeden & Co., an ambitious trading house that wasn't a member of the New York Stock Exchange, hired him away in 1963 for what was then the enormous salary of $125,000 a year. A year later Billy bought him away from Weeden for less—$50,000 a year plus the promise of "consideration for a partnership" in Salomon in September—to become the chief trader in the municipals department. Simon also fit fine into Salomon's social structure: "We'd always had Catholics," said Dale Horowitz; "just no Protestants."

Simon proved to be one of the greatest traders ever. "I was competing against Joe Cross at C. J. Devine," he later said modestly. "You learned or you were dead. Of course," he added, relieving himself of the burden of maintaining modesty, "people could say the same thing about me." Standing at the corner of his desk, telephone in at least one ear, drinking glass after glass of ice water while others drank coffee and got nervous, he kept exchanging shouted information with his traders, working the phones, sensing whether this was the time to go with or against the market. When the market closed, he would retreat to the partners' dining room with his assistant Dale Horowitz, and they would have a drink or two together while playing endless games of gin rummy. Sometimes the games lopped over onto a table at Oscar's, where bond traders from other houses, especially Morgan Guaranty, might join them. And Simon would be back in the partners' dining room early the next morning. Like John Gutfreund, who had graduated from the municipals desk to "the syndicate department" that tried to get Salomon included in corporate underwriting deals, he was a regular at breakfast. "We'd just sit and listen and learn," said one of the men who was a young partner in the early 1970s. "What Bill taught me most," said another, "was that on a trading floor you have to listen separately with both ears."

In 1966, which was a bear market year for bonds, Salomon had sizable losses buried in its governments trading portfolio. The head of the governments desk was Girard Spencer, colorless and not very smart, but handsome. One of the firm's few divorces in the 1950s happened when another partner's wife divorced him to marry Spencer; and both men remained partners. Spencer had played it cool and cautious under Ben Levy's watchful eye. Now he and his chief salesman were both asked to retire early, and Billy asked Simon to take over the governments desk. He agreed only if he could keep the municipals portfolio; he could handle both, he told Billy breezily, because they were both at the same end of the trading room. As summer wore on, Simon sensed that the Fed was about to relax; he plunged the firm's capital into long-term governments, buying every time the market softened.

Ben Levy was displeased. Now into his seventies, he still came to the office every day and sat at his desk, available to juniors for advice and counsel. Ira Harris, then new to the firm and carrying its torch in Chicago as one of the nation's first experts in mergers and acquisitions, would stop by Levy's desk whenever he came to New York. "He was a wonderful, wonderful man," Harris said. "He was terrific with the younger partners. I loved to talk with him whenever I was in New York." Simon was less enthusiastic. "Levy wandered around," Simon said recently, "and ate lunch." Billy listened to him, but Simon's department was Simon's show. Harry Brown was still coming in every week from Chicago, the second most important partner in the firm, and he, too, took to hanging over the governments desk. Finally one day Simon shouted, "I'm not going to be second-guessed. If you don't like my position, you can take it and stuff it up your ass"—and Brown and Levy both decided to stay away. Simon made a ton of money for the firm and was appointed chairman of the compensation committee, because he was ideally placed to tell grousers that they shouldn't expect to be paid more than other partners just because their desk showed high profits.

Simon's freedom to commit the firm's capital by building a trading inventory of government bonds was enhanced, of course, by the fact that the banks were happy to lend against the security of such inventory. Moreover, the firm could take a degree of comfort from the fact that the Federal Reserve Bank of New York knew everything that was going on. Every Thursday morning a senior person from the Treasuries desk—Spencer, then Simon, then Bill Brachfeld, then Dall, then Tom Strauss, not infrequently Billy Salomon himself—would go to the Fed's fortress on Liberty Street and talk things over with first Alan Holmes and then Peter Sternlight, operators of the Fed's "open market" desk. On an informal basis the Salomon trader would lay bare for the Fed his firm's position and his view of what others in the market were doing. In early 1970, when Solly decided to bid for a large amount of the new six-month bills at the usual Monday Treasury auction, Billy called to make sure the Fed had no objections. Dall remembered a gentleman's understanding that unless the Fed gave prior approval the firm wouldn't take more than 25 percent of an issue.

Governments were not the only area where Billy gave traders

authority to build inventories. At four o'clock on the afternoon before the Federal Deposit Insurance Corporation seized the Franklin National Bank in the summer of 1974, an officer of the bank called utilities bond desk chief Stanley Cohen and asked him to value the bank's bond portfolio by the opening of business the next morning. Cohen said, "What if I want to buy it tonight?" The officer said, "Fine—just call before nine o'clock tomorrow morning." The FDIC had no special desire to hold a heavy bond portfolio and greatly preferred having cash to pay off what were a remarkable collection of claims (including a giant claim by the Federal Reserve Bank of New York, which had been carrying Franklin's underwater foreign exchange position). Cohen bid the price he thought Franklin would take. "If the market's 81-3," he said reminiscently, "you're not going to bid 81, because, after all, you're buying so much." There was a cushion here, too, because the Fed was surely going to prop the markets up in the aftermath of what was at that time the largest bank failure in the nation's history. Franklin accepted Cohen's bids on $100 million worth of bonds, and Salomon made millions on the resale. Billy had no notion at the time that any such transaction had happened. Cohen didn't know whether Billy ever found out about it. He didn't say thank you.

BLOCKS OF STOCKS

Salomon as a dealing house had little involvement with stocks traded on the New York Stock Exchange, although it did at all times make markets in over-the-counter stocks, especially bank stocks, most of which for technical reasons were not traded on exchanges until the 1960s. Its clients were institutions, and institutions were bound by the "prudent man" rule, which most courts interpreted as severely limiting if not forbidding investments in common stock. But as the 1950s ground on, judicial views of "prudence" changed. Bank trust departments for their managed accounts, insurance companies, growing pension funds—and, of course, mutual funds, most of which were common-stock funds—were acquiring ever-larger positions in stocks. Eventually they would want to buy or sell in large quantities if they could.

But the stock exchange was a system organized to process large volumes of small orders. If an institutional investor placed a large order to buy or sell, he found his order pushed market prices way up or way down. The "specialists" at the exchange, who were pledged to maintain orderly markets in the stocks assigned to them, simply did not have enough capital to handle "blocks." Skilled brokers might be able to "work" a large order on the floor over a period of weeks or months to get it filled without major price disruption, but there was always a danger that knowledge of the order would leak to other market participants. In any event, an investor who had made a decision to get in or get out often wanted to implement that decision now, not over a period of weeks or months. What the institutions wanted before they would commit to buying quantities of stock was a market that could move large blocks without major impact on the price.

There were barriers and benefits for the brokers in "block trading" of common stocks. New York Stock Exchange rules until 1975 fixed the commissions that customers had to pay their brokers on shares traded at the exchange. The commission was calculated by the one-hundred-share "round lot," which meant that a ten-thousand-share trade paid the broker a hundred times as much as the minimum commission on a round lot. Brokerage houses that were not members of the exchange could offer to handle block trades much cheaper than member firms, and a few of them (including Weeden & Co., which had paid Bill Simon $125,000 a year) had indeed opened a beachhead for block trading in a so-called third market. Salomon could not trade in that third market, because New York Stock Exchange rules required member firms to expose all customer orders to the market and execute them on the floor. The only public interest in the enforcement of such rules is to ensure a public record of transactions, and as time passed the Securities and Exchange Commission insisted that companies be permitted to "list" their securities for trading on exchanges other than the New York Stock Exchange. These regional exchanges (in Chicago, Philadelphia, San Francisco, and so forth) did not necessarily enforce minimum commission rules, which gave the NYSE members that joined them somewhat greater flexibility in large transactions. Salomon joined all of them in 1965. And there was always, of course, some play in the joints: The price of the stock itself could be adjusted, or a side deal finagled, to effectively let the institution off the hook for some of the commission.

If block trading was to work, there had to be an intermediary willing to buy and hold (to "position") those pieces of the block that the market was not willing to take at that price, gambling that he could get out without a loss in the near future if not now. Block trading in stocks, then, was like the kind of bond trading Salomon did every day—and both Joe Ottens and Billy Salomon saw the opportunity as early as the 1950s. But Salomon was not, in fact, the first kid on the block to play with this toy. The pioneer was Salim L. (Sy) Lewis of Bear Stearns, an aggressive human being (big and bulky, he had been a semi-pro football player) and an aggressive trader who had worked for Salomon Brothers in the 1920s without leaving any mark at all. But in 1933, as an employee of Bear Stearns & Co., he had the instinct to buy corporate bonds, as Nathan Rothschild put it, "when there's blood in the streets."

On the basis of those winnings Lewis had become the Street's premier arbitrageur, making small but sure profits by simultaneously buying and selling securities that were trading at slightly different prices in two different markets. He extended that business to trades in convertible bonds versus the stocks into which they were convertible, and then merger-and-acquisition situations where for some months the stocks of the two companies that were to merge continued trading at prices that fluctuated around those implied by their merger agreement. This game was particularly interesting in the 1960s when "conglomerators" bought companies not with cash but with "Chinese money," shares of their own stock, so that the deal was worth the market price of the stock that would be created for the purpose. Gus Levy of the larger firm of Goldman Sachs had the reputation in that business (and as a public-spirited fellow who served on many charitable boards, a much greater status in the public eye), but Lewis was the man the Wall Street community feared and followed. And it was Lewis who began offering the institutions the services of Bear Stearns as a block trader. "I watched him putting on those five-hundred-thousand-share blocks," Salomon recalled, "and I said, 'They don't know any more than we do.'"

There was nobody at Salomon with experience in equities. In the early 1960s, Billy tried a succession of traders in stocks, most of them more or less crazy, most of them, in the end, money losers. In 1964, Billy hired Harry Nelson from Merrill Lynch to be Salomon's sales manager—"an interesting but impossible job," Nelson said, "because the salesmen were partners and I wasn't. My first day at Salomon," he added, "was especially difficult. At Merrill Lynch I had been assistant to the manager for national institutional sales and then manager of the New York institutional office. I'd thought I knew something about pricing bonds. It was a shock to go to Salomon and find out how much there was to learn."

John Gutfreund as manager of the "syndicate department," handling Salomon's relations with the big underwriting houses, was closer to equities than anybody else, because the big houses let crumbs of equity underwritings fall from their table for him. He supervised the minuscule stock trading desk with help from Billy himself. Soon after Nelson arrived, three young men were hired to be trader-salesmen to the equities market: Hans Kertess, an exceedingly well dressed and polished man who chain-smoked at the desk and would later be Salomon's floor member on the New York Stock Exchange (still later the boss of the large Tokyo office of Salomon's rival, First Boston, and later still at Salomon, once more as an equities manager); Michael Bloomberg, the firm's first Harvard MBA, later to build, own, and operate the fastest growing information service of the 1990s; and Salim B. (Sandy) Lewis, Sy's son.

Young Lewis was the oldest of Sy's four children and had borne the brunt of his father's unpredictable mix of bullying and affection. At the age of ten he had withdrawn so deeply into himself that his parents took him to Bruno Bettelheim's Sonia Sankman Orthogenic School in Chicago, where over a course of half a dozen years he became one of the German refugee psychologist's outstanding success stories. (Years later, when Bettelheim was retired and writing his books about his concentration camp experiences, children's education, and other subjects, Sandy, a wildly successful manager of a risk arbitrage partnership, would send him a new Mercedes-Benz every other year.) To Bettelheim's delight Sandy was accepted at the University of Chicago, but he didn't like college much and dropped out. After working briefly at

Bettelheim's school—and over Bettelheim's worried objections—he decided to challenge his father on his Wall Street turf. Billy Salomon gave him a job in Chicago but opposed his going to New York on the grounds that he wouldn't be able to stay away from Sy. Gutfreund thought it would work out, and up to a point it did.

Lewis, Kertess, and a more experienced trader named Robert Spiegel began to put Salomon on the equities map. Sandy and Kertess would go on the road together and visit Sy on their return, dissecting their results sometimes until three in the morning. Like his father, Sandy coupled trading ability with insight into what the customers were looking for, and he wanted total control. He had a war with Salomon's Boston office, where the salesmen wanted to maintain their status as exclusive contact with the large mutual funds headquartered there.

Functionally, less than two years after his arrival, at age twenty-seven, Lewis was head of Salomon's equity desk, with Gutfreund and Salomon hovering over him some part of every day. Slim and strong (Bettelheim was big on calisthenics), he was exceedingly brilliant and a startlingly quick study, but he couldn't accept authority. "I came out of the orthogenic school," he said later, "and I set up standards for other people." He found salesmen arranging contributions to customers' favorite charities and demanded they be disciplined as "dishonest." He refused trades the salesmen wanted to make, and cursed the firm when he couldn't do the trades he wanted to do. Billy Salomon heard him on the telephone saying to his father, "These goddamn dopes who run this firm don't know what they're doing." Salomon remembered, "He abused everybody: 'You're disruptive. You're destructive.'" Finally Sandy called Billy an asshole in the middle of the trading floor, and Billy called him at home that evening to tell him he was history at Salomon. Sandy said, "Have you consulted with your partners?" and Billy hung up.[3]

None of the new people had quite the specific gravity to make the big-bucks decisions on block trading and positioning, which were on the rise in the later 1960s, and Salomon and Gutfreund handled these still infrequent opportunities themselves. By and large, until 1968, they took other people's deals, especially Sy Lewis's. One of the men who was then a youngster on the desk remembered going over to Billy's desk with grim news. The desk was working a twenty-five-thousand-share position acquired when Bear Stearns had called to say that Sy was taking on fifty thousand shares and would give Billy the privilege of buying half of it, at a slightly concessionary price. The young trader came to tell Billy, "We've been fucked. I have a man in the crowd on the floor, and he tells me Bear Stearns just sold their twenty-five thousand and then some. Now there are no bids, and we'll take a bath." Billy waved him away with a seraphic smile. "We're learning," he said. "We're still learning."

Among those with whom Sandy Lewis had trouble in 1966 was Richard Rosenthal, a New York high school dropout who had been working on Wall Street since he was fifteen, only ten years before. A tall man with black hair and a toothy grin, he had dark eyes that roved behind thick glasses. His was by general agreement the most brilliant and most devious mind ever employed at Salomon. One of those who watched Rosenthal at the peak of his powers said that "you could take the most complicated corporate structure in the world, give Dickie the papers and put him in a closet with a glass of water, and he'd be out in an hour or two with a complete analysis of the situation." Rosenthal invented new ways to play arbitrage games in the merger-and-acquisition world; indeed, he was the father of the sort of "risk arbitrage" trading Ivan Boesky later made famous. And he was among the first to spot Boesky for what he was. Michael Zimmerman, who worked under Rosenthal and later became head of Solly's merchant banking division, remembered Rosenthal telling him to fire anybody in his department who had dealings with Boesky. "He's got to be getting inside information," Rosenthal said, "because nobody is that much smarter than I am."

Rosenthal was a partner in the firm at the age of twenty-seven. Gerald Rosenfeld, who became Salomon's chief financial officer in the later 1980s and looked into the history of the firm's finances, said that Rosenthal's four- or five-man stock and convertibles trading department consistently made heavy money, supporting the scores of people who worked elsewhere in the equities departments, who mostly didn't make money. And there was more to Rosenthal than that. Before anybody used the term "corporate finance" to describe the bells and whistles and Christmas ornaments that could be hung on what had once been straightforward corporate debt or equity offerings, Rosenthal was figuring out new kinds of paper. Although Gutfreund got the credit for the preferred stock issue that rescued GEICO insurance in 1976 (an action that earned him the loyalty of Warren Buffett, the largest investor in GEICO), it was Rosenthal who had been the designer.

In 1981, Rosenthal was the driving force behind the sale of the firm to Phibro, making Salomon a publicly held corporation rather than a partnership, unquestionably the watershed in Solly's history. By 1982, Rosenthal was gone, to the accompaniment of contemptuous statements about how the firm was losing its edge, and two years after that he was dead in the wreckage of his private plane, having plugged an empty tank into his fuel system as his engines sputtered. He had been kind and helpful to some of the younger people, even providing financial backing for one who went out on his own. He had led an exemplary private life: married to a high school sweetheart, three kids, absorbed in expanding and rebuilding his house with some of the money he had made when the firm was sold. And in the Salomon mold he had been charitable, making significant contributions to schools and hospitals; the funeral services were packed with people. But few of his Salomon partners were among the mourners.

Duplicitous to an extreme (if he noticed that somebody was watching while he had a talk with Billy, he would look for an opportunity to say to that person—as a friend, of course—that it was too bad but Billy didn't like him), Rosenthal was indicted by virtually all his former partners as a pathological liar who took special pleasure in disturbing people's relations with one another. When he went on the board of a Westchester private school, a Salomon partner warned the chairman of that board, who had invited Rosenthal to join, that he was going to have a horrible year—and in less than six months the chairman quit over a quarrel with Rosenthal. But in the work he did for Salomon, popularity did not matter: Arbitrage is a zero-sum game in which the winner makes money because he is smarter than other people and sees necessary price relationships before they do—and this is not a business where a trader needs or even wants friends.

Still, for all his politicking, it took Rosenthal the better part of a decade to establish domination over the equities trading desk, because starting in 1968 he had to put up with the nearby presence of Jay Perry, almost as young, equally black-haired, thin-shouldered, and myopic, equally frenetic and untrustworthy (but not vicious). Perry came from Hot Springs, Arkansas, where he practiced the art of selling by recording his sales pitches into a tape recorder and playing them back to himself over and over again. He started in the securities business as a salesman for Merrill Lynch in Des Moines. In 1964 he joined Salomon as a salesman in its St. Louis office, where he married money and did well enough to become one of the rare out-of-town employees to be awarded a partnership. Billy decided he was really a trader and the man Salomon needed to handle block trading. He did not, however, tell Perry about his decision, bringing him to New York instead to be a junior on the utilities desk—where the first thing he revealed, said a man who was on the next desk, was that "he didn't know shit. He sat there, eyes a-ga-ga, trying to figure it out." When Perry asked Billy what he should do, he was told, "Learn." Only after he had spent three months watching the bond traders did Billy tell him he was going to be Salomon's block trader on the equities desk.

Perry quickly became one of the best in that business. "If I had one trade to do in the world," said a man who worked closely with him, "I'd want Jay to do it. But I wouldn't have a friend in the world when he was finished." Perry was also by far the most publicized block trader. He and Salomon welcomed press attention, and there were articles in all the business magazines about his attitudes and behaviors, including the inadvertently predictive comment by *Business Week* in 1969 that he "seems perpetually on the edge of hysteria, even when the market is closed."[4] In *The Last Days of the Club,* Chris Welles wrote a description of the desk as it was in 1974:

> "O.K., let's go!" Jay Perry said sharply, putting down the phone.
> He swung around in his chair, stood up, picked up the phone again, and pressed a button that hooked it into the public address system. "O.K., here's one we need your help on," he said into the receiver. His words reverberated throughout the huge trading room and were relayed to Salomon Brothers' ten regional offices. "Rohm & Haas, last sale 94, up 2 on the day. We're asked to make a bid for 90,000. We're going to do this block."

Within seconds, trader-salesmen were systematically punching buttons that gave them direct wire connections with the trading desks of 120 major institutional investors throughout the country. *Punch*. "Rohm & Haas, do you care?" *Punch*. "Doing a piece of Rohm & Haas. Do you give a shit?"

Meanwhile, Welles wrote, Perry, having looked up reports on what the mutual funds held, was giving instructions to his crew:

"Bobby, the Chemical Fund, they own tons of it. What do they say? . . . Jack, the largest shareholder is ICA, what do they say? . . . Dick, have you been to Dreyfus?". . . Perry stood up and looked around at the team of 15 traders. "Come on, come on," he urged, like a football coach at the half. "We want this block!"[5]

The trader-salesmen on these calls were getting rather than giving information. They were not asking the customers whether they wanted to buy or sell this stock, just whether they had an interest. The question would have been the same whether the original customer wanted to buy or wanted to sell, whether Salomon's position risk at the end of the trade would be that it owned a big piece of the stock or that it was short a big piece of the stock. If there were lots of others who wanted to sell and not many who wanted to buy, Perry would have had to tell his caller that the price had to be some distance below the 94 of the last trade in the market, which probably would have meant giving up the sale. If there were lots of others who wanted to buy, Perry would know he could dispose of the stock, collect the commissions, perhaps even make some money in a day or two on any part of the block he positioned (kept in his inventory), and move on without worrying about committing Salomon's borrowed money to a long-term stake in Rohm & Haas.

During the course of this telephoning there was at least a chance that news of the Rohm & Haas block would leak to other block positioners (especially Robert Mnuchin of Goldman Sachs, with whom Perry played a ceaseless game of Batman and Joker, the two alternating their roles), who would then move to poison the wells. All trading has a substantial games element to it. When the Treasury auctions its notes and bonds, the dealers spend the final

half-hour before the auction in incessant chatter with one another, back and forth, talking about who does and does not have
a position in the when-issued market, which clients are bidding in
which quantities, whether the bonds will wind up in "strong
hands" or with dealers looking to resell them fast, and so forth.
Billy Salomon said he once asked Bill Brachfeld (then, in the
mid-1970s, Salomon's trader and later the head of the Treasuries
desk at Daiwa Securities' branch in New York, a power in that
market wherever he went) why he was making and taking all
those phone calls.

"I'm getting information from the other dealers," Brachfeld said
impatiently.

"But you're giving them a lot of information about our positions," Billy said.

"But I'm not telling them the truth," said Brachfeld.

"And what makes you think," Billy asked, "that *they're* telling
you the truth?"

By then Morris Offit had a stock research group that could have
given Perry and his traders a lot of information about Rohm &
Haas, but they didn't want it. They were pure traders, interested
only in market sentiment, the feelings of prospective buyers and
other sellers. (Billy needed the information on Norwich he demanded from Morris Offit because he was not a trader, he was a
salesman, and he was going to make a pitch to someone who was
going to take the lot.) Laszlo Birinyi, Jr., who developed research
programs for Salomon and taught the trainees about equities in
the 1980s, told the story of the day Salomon positioned a sizable
block of Mesabi Trust in the belief that it was a Japanese bank and
learned only after the position was sold that it was a mining company.

There was a special logic to not knowing much about the company when the question was one of positioning a chunk of its
stock. In the block trading business the customer was likely to
know more about the company than the broker/positioner *could*
know, however much work he did; the only thing the broker/
positioner was likely to know that the customer didn't was the
state of the market. Will K. Weinstein, who headed the block
trading desk at Oppenheimer & Co. when that company was run
by Leon Levy and Jack Nash, intellectually the strongest executive

team on Wall Street, wrote an article about his problems for *Institutional Investor* in June 1970:

> Block position trading, by definition, is a loser's game.... Because security prices are determined strictly by supply/demand considerations, the block trader, in almost every instance, starts out wrong. He substitutes himself only in the absence of a natural, real buyer or seller and only after a worldwide search for the missing side has been conducted by his firm. He does not pick the stocks in which he wants to play. The choice is made for him by his clients.[6]

The Securities and Exchange Commission, studying this business at the behest of Congress in 1970, found that block positioning "was essentially a loss leader." Blocks *did* move prices, and the prices did not bounce back. If the stock was selling for 30 before the block and the block crossed at 29, the brokerage house that got stuck with a position usually had to sell it for less than 29. On average in 1970, the SEC found, the block trader wound up holding 23 percent of the trade, and on that 23 percent he lost one-half of 1 percent.[7] But the original customer's commission on the full block would more than pay off that loss, and commissions from both sides of the trade (which the block trader would earn on the two-fifths of the average block that was sold to institutional investors) would provide profits. When the move to negotiated commissions took away that cushion, block trading became unprofitable, even for Salomon Brothers—until the rise of futures and options markets in the 1980s allowed houses like Salomon to make money by playing these "derivative" markets with knowledge of their large customers' large orders in the central market.

Once block trading was unprofitable, Rosenthal could get rid of Perry, who had in fact deteriorated considerably under the strain of his job, having lost his wife to divorce and having acquired a drug habit. It may have been of some significance to the development of both Salomon Brothers and the block trading systems that now account for more than half the volume on the New York Stock Exchange that Jay Perry was, as Charles Simon put it, "a mentally disturbed young man." In 1976, Billy sent him off to Dallas to open a Salomon office there; nobody in Dallas could stand him, inside or outside the office. Presently he was working for another firm, and then he was dead.

THE GRANDEUR OF "THE ROOM"

In 1970, Salomon moved from 60 Wall Street to spectacular new space designed for its needs on the forty-first through forty-fifth floors of One New York Plaza, the southernmost office building in Manhattan. The two-story-high trading room ran the length of the building, with a floor space of seven thousand five hundred square feet and desks with built-in telephone consoles for 187 traders and salesmen, including Gutfreund and Billy. Public relations counsel Mel Adams persuaded Billy to run ads acclaiming The Room as one of the world's great securities markets, the place where institutional owners of stocks or bonds could always get a bid. The dining rooms (now there were seven of them, plus a cafeteria for the lesser breeds) overlooked the East River and Queens; visitors to The Room could stand on a balcony and look out over the traders to New York harbor. Under the visitors ran a telex board more than ninety-six feet long, where the numbers whirred to show the moving prices on the most heavily traded debt instruments; at both ends of the room ticker tapes of light bulbs presented the trades on the New York and American stock exchanges. There wasn't a computer screen in sight.

The Room was noisy, very noisy when there was business to be done, and its designers had not done anything much to mitigate the noise. Pairs of desks were surrounded on three sides by waist-high hardwood partitions; the carpeting was thin squares on concrete; the pillars were covered with a painted plaster; the ceiling, too far away to make much difference, was inset with tiny metal floodlights and was only lightly covered with a rough acoustical spatter. Visitors to the balcony over The Room were often astonished by the zoolike roar that rose from the floor when, for example, the Federal Reserve came into the market at 11:30 in the morning to do its business with the primary dealers.

Since the late 1960s, Salomon Brothers & Hutzler had published an annual report with a certified statement, although as a partnership it had no obligation to do so. The 1974 report contained a map of The Room, showing the breakdown into departments: International, U.S. Government and Federal Agencies, Tax-Exempt Securities, Corporate Bonds, Preferred Stock, Public Utility Bond Trading, Transportation Bond Trading, Listed and

Unlisted Common Stock Trading and Sales, Arbitrage and Convertible Securities Trading, Syndicate Department, Dealer Contact, several areas simply labeled Generalist Sales Units, and Managing Partner—a solitary desk dead center at the end of The Room closest to the elevator. Salomon and later Gutfreund were there almost every day, although both also had private offices off the floor. Of the thirty-three New York–based partners in 1974, twenty-seven worked on the trading floor. The research and the investment banking people had desks in The Room, because everything at Salomon was based in trading, but there was also a floor of private offices for them to make phone calls where they could hear themselves think.

The image of a trading room as a constant maelstrom of hyperactivity has more to do with movies than with markets. Except in a handful of the pits in the commodities and options exchanges, traders live lives like those of airline pilots or firemen: hours of boredom, moments of panic. There is an orderliness about the organization, because different individuals trade different instruments, even within the departments, and often when one sector of the market is busy, others are dull. People call their wives or girlfriends, ticket agents, bookies, 900 numbers for jokes or sexy talk, or traders in other houses to see if anything's doing there. Practical jokes, often childish and sometimes quite cruel, are hatched in these moments when men (and now women) are simply swiveling their chairs and looking around.

Today, of course, there are the omnipresent computer screens to look at—two, three, four per desk, programmed individually for each trader or salesman to cover what can easily be a dozen markets. In the dullest moments everybody can keep an eye on the dancing numbers and the lines on the charts, or push a button to see what other dances these numbers may be learning, what art can be appreciated on the charts. Like television itself, the data screen tends to isolate people in their own solipsist world, knowing what they think they want to know, nothing more and nothing less. There is less shouting than there used to be and infinitely less sense of a common enterprise.

The Room has become history, abandoned the same month in 1991 that Paul Mozer put in his crazy Mercury Asset Management bid. After twenty-one years at One New York Plaza, Solly moved to the huge unoccupied monolith at Seven World Trade Center, built by the developer Larry Silverstein in theory as a speculation but, in fact, in the soon useless knowledge that Drexel Burnham would want it. Here there were two two-story Rooms, one for equities trading and one for fixed-instrument and foreign exchange trading, with private offices for the big wheels at the river end to give them the view. There was thick carpet on the floor, the most absorbent materials on the ceiling, cloth on the walls— which turned out to be psychologically wrong. The Salomon trading rooms didn't *feel* exciting anymore. Visitors who knew the old Room found them disturbingly decorous and quiet, apparent evidence of the firm's decay.

Traders remain people of vast and insatiable ego, however; their reward comes far more from the instant gratification of the successful trade than from the money they make. Unfortunately, those ego needs clash with the first requirement of successful trading, which is that the trader recognize and get rid of his losing bets as quickly as possible. The system by which these needs are recognized is called "mark to market." At the close of every trading day, every piece of paper an investment bank owns is at least in theory revalued to show what it was worth as the sun fell. Thus traders are compelled to face what is happening to their own position and its components, and managers can find out whether the traders are getting the firm in trouble.

"The great strength of Salomon," said Dr. Henry Kaufman, for many years the firm's director of research and vice-chairman, "was that if the market went down the next day, there was a great markdown to *liquidation* value [that is, the trader had to estimate how much throwing his whole block on the market might depress the price; he could not just value the block at the price of that day's last trade, which might have involved only a couple of bonds or a couple of hundred shares]. You were held accountable if your holdings were marked down only to a market price and that market price didn't stick." The results of that exercise had been written every night in the elongated ledger on the table at the entrance to the partners' dining room in 60 Wall Street. Vincent Murphy, the firm's chief of operations and Billy's sidekick, stayed late every night in the 1960s and 1970s to write the numbers in the book.

There is no way for management to get its reports from the

maelstrom of tickets and money that descends every night on the cage where the trades are cleared. Traders have to tell their bosses what they have done. If they have a loser, they are always tempted to bury the slips in the desk and wait to report the trade when the market has come back. Even the most sophisticated traders overstay their markets once in a while. Murphy remembered being warned by Harry Brown to go through the traders' desks every night before making up the ledger. That was one of the things Brown had always done on his weekly trips from Chicago. Hans Kertess and Robert Spiegel, when they sat side by side on the Salomon industrials trading desk, found their own system to keep ego down: One day a month each traded the other's position, getting rid of the dogs. Every so often Billy would take dramatic action, arriving in the morning with the message that he thought the bond market was about to crack and he wanted all the traders to sell out their positions now. Then he and Murphy would examine the carnage that night.

In the 1980s keeping track of the firm's positions became infinitely more difficult; indeed, individual traders themselves often did not know whether they were effectively "long" or "short." Instead of selling his mistake, a trader whose best-laid plan had gone agley might buy an option to sell or sell a futures contract on a related index or even enter into some complex swap involving a foreign currency and a bet on interest rate movements as well as the security that showed a loss if you just looked at the individual trade. By the later 1980s a trader could make misleading reports to management with a good chance that nobody would catch him. The result, said a banker who was on the Salomon executive committee, was that "everybody told lies."

As the 1980s wore on, Salomon's trading activities were driven less by customer orders and more by the mathematical analysis of what Deryck Maughan, a Welshman and alumnus of the British Treasury who had risen to prominence at Salomon in Tokyo and became the company's chief executive officer after the 1991 debacle, liked to call "anomalies." The best publicized of these was "index arbitrage" between the futures contract for the S&P 500 stocks and the cash market for these stocks on the New York Stock Exchange. When the price of the futures contract fell below the total price of all the stocks in the index, the quick trader could buy the index and sell the stocks, guaranteeing himself a profit; and ditto, of course, in reverse when the index was higher and the profit came from selling the contract and buying the stocks.

This activity tends to misallocate resources and reduce the nation's productive potential, because the economic purpose of a stock market is to *discriminate* among differing investments—rewarding stockholders in more successful companies with share prices higher than the prices of shares in less successful companies—not to jiggle the value of entire portfolios up and down according to market movements of an artificial "commodity" called a stock index. But an even greater problem lay below the surface, for it was easy for trading houses with considerable market power—Salomon being primus inter pares—to *create* the anomalies by which they profited. Proliferating marketplaces—options exchanges, unpublicized markets in London, Reuters computers—opened wide the opportunities to move prices in one market by manipulating another. As the 1980s wore on, proprietary trading by the big houses came to look more and more like the "pools" activity that dishonored the stock exchange in the 1920s.

The *morality* of trading rested on the fact that the trader got his scars on the front of his face, and it was a true morality. In a society where lawyers proliferated and contracts grew like Jack's beanstalk, John Gutfreund virtually never signed a piece of paper. Where the rubber meets the road, where real money had to be paid for real securities, Gutfreund and Salomon worked almost entirely on a basis of trust: People lived up to what they said on the trading floor or on the telephone or at lunch.

Like all moralities, this one was unpopular with some of those bound by its strictures. Its forcefulness rested, as is usual with moralities, on the likelihood of getting caught. But it's hard to expose incorrect valuation of an interest-rate swap when there are four different ways to "mark" such swaps to market, and they give four different results.[8] And then there arises the problem posed by E. Gerald Corrigan of the New York Fed in his 1992 speech to the New York State Bankers Association: "Off-balance-sheet activities . . . must be understood by top management as well as by traders and rocket scientists."[9] Salomon at year-end 1991 had about $800 *billion* of off-balance-sheet assets of the kind that let traders conceal what they're doing. Nobody in the Salomon management even pretended to understand them. But the profit position booked on the difference between off-balance-sheet assets and off-balance-sheet liabilities was *half* the firm's claimed equity.

People no longer worked in a nexus of customer/salesman/ trader, where the need to maintain continuing human relations influenced and sometimes governed behavior. Absent that nexus, the discipline of shame and the fear of shame were lost; quite a lot of supervision would be needed to keep markets honest. In John Gutfreund's Salomon, nobody much wanted to supervise departments that were making money; in Ronald Reagan's and George Bush's administrations, nobody much wanted to regulate anything that was making money. Greed was good; more greed was better. Fraud was undesirable but only a frictional inefficiency, and, after all, the best people were doing it.

Chapter 3

THE WITCHERY OF MATHEMATICS

IN THE 1950s the division of responsibility between the Salomon salesmen and the Salomon traders meant that only the salesmen knew or cared what was going on in the great world outside the trading room. From the traders' point of view, bond selling was easy work: You took the customers to the hoops and the pucks and got them laid, and when they returned home, they would happily pay $2 more per bond. The hard work was grasping the state of the market so closely that the prices bid and offered were both acceptable to the customer and profitable to the firm. From the salesmen's point of view, the traders were Irish and Italian drunks and gluttons who knew the price of everything and the value of nothing, and made the salesmen's life more difficult by trying to unload their decaying inventory on customers.

For Charles Simon in the 1950s the isolation and insularity of the trading room also meant that the firm lost profitable business because its competitors were giving better prices. He would be on the phone with a customer, quoting the price his trader gave him on something the customer wished to buy or sell, and—especially when the trade was government bonds—he would be told, Nope, we can do better elsewhere. Simon was always on good enough terms with his customers to find out who was beating him, and most of the time it was the firm of C. J. Devine.

But Devine wasn't making a market inside Salomon's markets—quoting both lower prices to buyers and higher prices to sellers. Most often it was quoting better prices to sellers only on bonds that would go up over the next few days, and better prices to buyers only on bonds that were heading down over the next few days. In other words, Devine's people were smarter than Salomon's people: They improved their profitability by guessing right about where the market was going. Chris Devine was a parking-lot attendant who had been befriended Horatio Alger–fashion by the president of the Bank of New York. Why would he be smarter than Ben Levy, who was then in control of Solly's governments trading, or Gerry Spencer, who was the active trader on the desk? And the answer, Simon soon decided, was that on one day of each week Professor Marcus Nadler of New York University left what passed at NYU for the groves of academe and came to sit on the C. J. Devine trading desk with Devine's government bond traders.

Nadler, who was a German refugee, taught a night course on financial markets, a big lecture course with almost two hundred students. Simon enrolled. He got Rudolf Smutny to go with him, and then Billy Salomon, for a few weeks. "We wanted to know," Simon recalled, "why when Uncle Sam borrowed so much money his credit rating didn't decline. Why did rates go down rather than up? Nadler explained that the more the government borrowed, the more money there was. This was stunning to those of us who had no background. Nadler's great ability to teach inspired those of us who had never gone to college. Smutny had no education and didn't really want an education; he went because he wanted to know why I idolized Nadler. I called him 'Doc.' He lived at 86th Street and Riverside Drive, and I would drive Doc home after class every night. I was very privileged to have that time with the old man."

Simon soon learned that there was a lot more to bond trading than whether there were more sellers or more buyers. There was a long history of established ratios between the yield (the semiannual interest payments) on government bonds as against the yield on AA-rated utility, railroad, and industrial bonds. Trading opportunities were created by discontinuities in the "yield curve"—the line on the graph that showed the different interest rates on U.S. Treasury issues with different lengths of time to go before their expiration. Normally, rates on short-term Treasury bills were substantially lower than rates on long-term Treasury bonds (the yield curve ran from the bottom of the left-hand side of the graph to the top of the right-hand side), but sometimes the curve would flatten or even invert. When the shape of the yield curve or the premium for higher quality changed, knowledgeable traders who saw it coming could make a lot of money. Less knowledgeable traders could get their clock cleaned.

Nadler invited Simon to join a "club" he had formed at NYU, the Money Marketeers, which met monthly to talk about what business taught them. At these meetings Simon, who was part of Billy's youth movement in the Salomon executive committee (Billy was forty-three, Simon, forty-five), came to know the older monetary economists. But the name Sidney Homer first swam into Simon's ken from work rather than from study, at the Buffalo Savings Bank in the mid-1950s. The bank's portfolio manager, Edward Koons, told Simon that he had been advised to sell Central Jersey 5's (that is, 5 percent bonds) at the going price of 103, and switch the money into Atchison, Topeka & Santa Fe 4's at 95. Homer had been the source of the advice. Simon said, "I don't think I know as much as Mr. Homer does, but surely you'll be upgrading."

"When you get back to New York," Koons said, "could you see how Homer's considered and whether we should listen to him?"

Sidney Homer was the son of Louise Homer, one of the earliest great American singers, a mezzo-soprano much loved at the Metropolitan Opera and also a lieder singer on concert stages. Homer, who had gone to Harvard but considered himself a self-trained "bond man," worked for Scudder Stevens & Clark, an investment management firm for financial institutions. "I called Homer," Simon remembered, "and asked whether I could take him to lunch at Massolletti's, which was then the best restaurant downtown, and he said, 'Yes, I'll come lunch with you. Who are you?' I knew he was solid gold when he told me the city of Vienna had had fives outstanding for one hundred years, the loans rolled over from monarchy to monarchy. I just loved it; I was fascinated with him immediately. He would pontificate to anybody about the bond market and Wall Street. He was *the* example of the intellectual

WASP on Wall Street. In those days I ran an annual investment seminar for New York State bankers, and I invited him to give a lecture at it."

Homer, who did some trading for Scudder Stevens & Clark, also became one of Simon's customers. "If ever there was a chiseling son of a bitch on price, it was Homer," Simon recalled. "It was always 'I have to call you back.' What a tough guy he was to do business with, but I admired him all the time. I used to tell him, 'You have to write a book.' It fell into my lap that he lived in Gramercy Park, in an ancient apartment that must have been used by Charles Addams, with the oldest furniture I ever sat on. It was across the street from Ned Holsten, who was sick with cancer, and his wife drove him to the office every day. I arranged for them to give Sidney a lift. That Greek god, that arrogant fellow, came under Sidney's spell on those rides; he was learning about supply and demand. Homer had a rule of thumb: If AAA [top-rated] bonds yielded twenty percent more than Treasury bonds, you buy them; if they yielded less than fifteen percent more than Treasury bonds, you bought the Treasuries. I remember one day in the trading room, Holsten called Bankers Trust and said, 'The spread is unusual,' and I knew he was hooked. Ned became a fucking oracle on the subject of bonds.

"Then I saw in *The New York Times* that Scudder Stevens & Clark had elected five new officers. Homer had never been an officer, and they hadn't elected him. I talked to Billy, told him I thought we could hire Homer, and he gave me the go-ahead. We had lunch at '21,' and I told him. He made one condition: He would have to come in as a partner." In 1960, Homer became the first person to join Salomon as a partner, beneficiary (in part) of a killing the firm had made in the market for AT&T convertible bonds, which had left extra money for such a luxury. Homer was an apparently owlish man with a brush mustache, thick glasses, and a solemn manner that was quite deceptive, for he was in fact an amusing fellow; he wrote a continuing series of in-house articles called *Fun with Bonds,* pieces with titles like "Twenty-one Ways to Say No to a Bond Salesman."

At the beginning Homer's role was mostly to educate the traders, both by his presence at the partners' table (he was rarely on the trading floor) and by his writings, which in his last years with the firm were supplemented by mathematical analysis from his nephew-in-law, Martin Leibowitz, a Ph.D. statistician who became a Salomon partner. (He was hired originally by sales director Harry Peterson, who was intrigued by something he had done in his previous job: training a computer to bid for carpeting contracts for commercial office space.) Their collaboration was entitled *Inside the Yield Book*.[1] Gradually the salesmen recognized that Homer was giving them the raw materials of their trade: reasons why customers should swap from one bond to another, making two transactions through Salomon Brothers. A salesman could get a hearing on a much higher level of his customer's firm if he had Homer in tow.

"He thought up all those hedges," Billy Salomon remembered. "When you should buy the two-year and sell the five-year." In fact, what Homer did was far more significant than that: He revolutionized the valuation and the trading of fixed-income instruments (bonds), multiplying the volume and profitability of Salomon's business and transforming the investment and trading patterns of insurance companies and charitable foundations. Salomon's enormous strength in trading was in large part the result of Homer's work, which rested in the end on a single simple insight. What Homer and nobody else had seen was that all the tables in Joe Ottens's yield book, which every Salomon apprentice had memorized under his lash, were simply wrong. They assumed stable interest rates, and interest rates were not stable.

The subject is worth a moment's exploration for its intrinsic importance as well as its significance in the Salomon story. *(Inside the Yield Book,* published in 1972, had by 1987 gone through no fewer than twenty-two printings.) Take, for example, two $1,000 bonds with twenty years to run, one of them paying $50 interest a year at a time when the prevailing interest rate is 5 percent and thus selling at par (face value, one hundred cents on the dollar), the other paying 4 percent, or $40 interest a year. Ottens's yield book said that the correct price for the 4 percent bond should be roughly $900. The $100 profit on the sale twenty years later ($5 a year) would bring the yield of the 4 percent bond to $45, which was 5 percent of $900. The calculations in Ottens's yield book were, to be fair, a little more complicated than that, but not much.

The problem with this analysis was that it neglected the reinvestment of the twice-yearly coupons, "the interest on the interest." If interest rates were going up, a $900 price for a $1,000, 4 percent bond—a $100 discount—would leave its purchaser well behind the purchaser of the 5 percent bond, because the owner of the 5 percent bond would have more income from the interest payments to invest every year at the higher rates. On the other hand, if rates were going down, the $100 discount on the 4 percent bond would leave its purchaser ahead of the game, because it had been calculated to offset the difference between the 4 percent the bond would pay him and the prevailing market rate of 5 percent at the time he bought. If you carried this to its extreme, Homer and Leibowitz pointed out in an aside—not taking the possibility seriously themselves (as of 1972, no company or government had ever issued or seriously considered issuing such a piece of paper)—people who thought interest rates were going down should want to buy a *zero-coupon* bond. In such a bond the interest instead of being paid out would accumulate every year, compounding at the promised interest rate, until a final payment that returned principal and all the accumulated interest. In effect, such a bond guaranteed the purchaser that he would reinvest his annual earnings at today's interest rate until the day the bond was paid back.

A few years after *Inside the Yield Book* was published, Bill Brachfeld asked the Federal Reserve Bank of New York whether it would object to Salomon's "stripping" a thirty-year Treasury bond, then selling its customers two separate investments. One of these instruments would be a zero-coupon bond, offering the face value of the bond as a lump-sum payment (at 6 percent interest, a $1,000 thirty-year bond would sell for about $175); the other would represent the right to the sixty semi-annual coupons (at $30 each, for a 6 percent bond). The first instrument would be for people who thought interest rates would go down and wanted to lock in their 6 percent; the second instrument would be for people who thought interest rates would go up and wanted the chance to reinvest the coupons at the higher rates. Because it would be tapping the two markets separately, Salomon would be able to sell the two pieces of the stripped bond for a total price higher than the going price on the whole bond. The Fed said it wished Salomon wouldn't do that, and for almost a decade Salomon didn't. When it did, in 1981, four years after Sidney Homer died, the "stripped" coupons (called Certificates of Accrual on Treasury Securities, or "CATS") were listed for trading on the New York Stock Exchange.

Salomon extended such analyses much further, to tailor investment instruments for people who thought interest rates would rise in the short run and then fall in the long run, or vice versa. Variants of Homer's insights transformed trading in stocks as well as bonds and underlie the work of the "asset/liability committees" that sit on the mountaintops of virtually all modern financial institutions. Most of the fancy "derivative" securities, the futures and options contracts designed in the 1980s and 1990s by the hotshots in the investment houses, started from Homer's analyses as put into algorithms by Leibowitz and now programmed into computers. But Homer as a historian knew that while rules of thumb were useful, they served as a foundation rather than as a substitute for judgment, and not all of those who followed him remembered that.

For Salomon the significance of Homer's quick partnership was that research would not be subordinate to either the traders or the salesmen. It was understood that Homer's work was completely independent of their needs or desires: *He* would decide what would be useful for *them.* In fact, he put most of his time into a monumental book, *A History of Interest Rates,* a path-breaking survey that traced rates from Sumeria (how much corn did the farmer have to repay the merchant who lent him the seed corn?) to the modern money markets. In his 1977 preface to the revised edition of this book, Homer noted that "when this book was a mere forty pages of jumbled notes and tables, my friend Mr. Charles Simon, a partner in the bond firm of Salomon Brothers, gave me that enthusiastic encouragement which was essential to convert the idea into a book."[2] Homer's scholarly output was widely disseminated by the firm, especially after Mel Adams was hired as its public relations counsel in 1963.

Homer sat in on the lunch when Billy engaged Adams, an unusually small man, both short and slight, whose previous experience had been entirely in aerospace. "We'll know in six months," Homer said rather coldly, "whether or not you're any good." Adams publicized Homer's work to give Salomon a bipolar image:

They were tough traders who bought business with price, but they were also the house that supported and publicized fundamental research into financial matters, something the established houses, the Morgan Stanleys and First Bostons and Goldman Sachses, had never done. "Mel Adams," said Edgar Aronson, who ran Salomon's foreign department in the 1970s and left in anger in 1980, "took these guys from being a bunch of four o'clock pinochle-playing nose-picking apple-knockers and made them investment bankers." Even Charles Simon, who as a member of the executive committee had counseled against hiring a public relations firm ("If you're good, people will find out about you"), grew close to Adams; at his request Adams spent two months cleaning up some reputation problems at NYU, and then he persuaded Billy on public relations grounds to give the university $3 million to create a Salomon Center at the business school.

DR. DOOM'S *COMMENTS ON CREDIT*

In 1961, Marcus Nadler spoke to Simon about one of his best pupils, Henry Kaufman, who received his Ph.D. from NYU while working during the day at the small People's Industrial Bank, where he had become credit manager at the age of twenty-four. His dissertation subject was loans to small businesses. Fully endoctored, he had gone on to be assistant director of research at the Federal Reserve Bank of New York. He also became one of Nadler's Money Marketeers; a generation later, full of honors, he still listed his membership in the Money Marketeers in his *Who's Who* entry. Homer was a financial historian; Kaufman was a master of the contemporaneous flow-of-funds analysis by which the Fed was beginning to seek new understanding of what was happening in the economy. His skills were well matched to the needs of an investment house.

Simon brought him to 60 Wall Street to lunch with Homer, and Kaufman noted approvingly that all the partners were sitting in the trading room. "I thought to myself," he said later, "that they took good care of their money." Homer was impressed with Kaufman and delighted to have a partner who would look ahead while he looked at history. Adams remembered that one day, a few months after Kaufman had joined the firm, he arranged a meeting at which Kaufman would make a presentation. Homer summoned him and asked whether he was really sure that this meeting would contribute significant business to Salomon, "because Henry's time is extremely valuable."

From Billy Salomon's point of view, Kaufman was the first of a breed it later became fashionable to call Fed watchers. ("A commodity item today," Kaufman says, "but a rarity then.") At about the time Kaufman came on board, the U.S. government was under pressure to defend the dollar against the decreasing willingness of foreign governments to use dollars rather than gold as the reserves for their currency. Presidents Kennedy, Johnson, and (until the summer of 1971) Nixon committed themselves to defend the price of gold at $32 an ounce. It was, in retrospect, idiocy: Milton Gilbert, guru of the Bank for International Settlements in Basel, noted that the U.S. government was unhappy in 1968 because it could no longer buy gold at the price it had fixed for the metal in 1933; but if the U.S. government wanted to buy Chevrolets or tomatoes in 1968 for the price it had paid in 1933, it wouldn't be able to buy them, either.[3] Lyndon Johnson's insistence on a budget that gave him both guns and butter created an overheated economy. Both for the maintenance of the foreign exchange value of the dollar and the avoidance of domestic inflation, the Federal Reserve became a key instrument of government. But when the Fed moved to raise or lower short-term interest rates, which it could do easily enough by selling or buying Treasury bills, the price of all debt instruments changed. The longer the "maturity" of the bond (the longer the time that had to pass before the principal was paid back), the bigger the change in the price.

Billy Salomon himself, as head of the firm that was the largest dealer in government securities, maintained professional and social contact with Federal Reserve Board chairman William McChesney Martin, who had been president of the New York Stock Exchange some years before he went to Washington. When Martin was succeeded by the academic Arthur Burns, Kaufman, as a fellow academic, invited him to lunch at Solly, where he and Billy did not hit it off at all. "The most egotistical man I've ever met," Billy recalled. "He'd light his pipe and say, 'I'm different from the other chairmen of the Fed. They always let the other governors vote first, and they voted last. I always vote first. Why should I let the others go wrong?' " Both Martin and Burns, of course, were careful never to tip their hands about what the Fed might do. Kaufman, a veteran of the economics department at the New York Fed, was equipped to diagnose the future course of interest rates without tips from the center. Not least because Henry Kaufman gave them some confidence that they could predict what the Fed would do in the short run, Salomon's traders were willing to take much larger positions than their rivals. And the growth trend fed on itself, naturally. Competition diminished: Merrill Lynch bought C. J. Devine, didn't understand the business, and pulled back to a clearly secondary position.

A rather solemn man with a slight accent, slicked brown thinning hair over a high and broad forehead, and vests as well as jackets, Kaufman was the son of a German refugee but not one of the intellectual refugees. His father was a butcher, and Henry was the first member of his family ever to go to a university. Both his thought and his speech were characterized by great precision; there was about him even as a young man a *gravitas* that created trust. And he was never a creature of fashion: A pupil of Nadler and Homer, he always stressed the price more than the quantity of money. When monetarism was at the height of its influence, his motto was "Money matters but credit counts." After 1979, when President Jimmy Carter appointed Paul Volcker chairman of the Fed despite Volcker's demand for a guarantee that the White House would never criticize actions his board might take to reduce inflation, Kaufman's analyses of the supply and demand for credit became astonishingly newsworthy. His weekly *Comments on Credit* was distributed to no fewer than thirteen thousand Salomon clients and other interested parties, and he became a public figure under the press sobriquet of "Dr. Doom."

As much as Billy Salomon, much more than John Gutfreund, Henry Kaufman was the public personification of Salomon Brothers through the glory years. Three or four times a week he would lunch or dine with important Salomon customers, usually at one of the firm's airy and elegant dining rooms on the floor above the trading floor high in One New York Plaza. He traveled often to the firm's out-of-town branches, where ballrooms would be rented for his "private briefings," for audiences up to five hundred people.[4]

A partner in 1967, he became a member of the firm's "administrative" committee in 1972. In the 1980s his mid-December predictions for the coming year became an invitation-only big-time event, an annual presentation at a late-afternoon lecture that filled the grand ballroom of the Waldorf-Astoria with people sitting row on row, not at tables. When the presentation was over, the assembled customers and competitors gorged on one of the great spreads of the year, including a two-kilo can of caviar (the press was directed initially to a side room to question Kaufman on his presentation and to assure that the caviar was not wasted). Aficionados of the global power struggle saw the locus of monetary authority in the world move when Solly added a sushi bar to the groaning boards offered following Kaufman's presentation.

Kaufman's first demand was the independence of his department. Unlike Homer, he did keep a desk on the trading floor and liked to be there once in a while, close to the stream of information passing through the traders' telephones, but that did not mean he was tipping the traders to what he would tell the outside world. His people were not to know—and if by chance they did know, were not to care—whether the traders were long or short bonds or interest-sensitive stocks. "The traders would call," he remembered, "and say, 'Why did you say that? You know our positions are long.' Usually research has a subordinate position on Wall Street and must be done in the interests of the firm. Commands are handed down. But I could not be influenced."

If the research department's opinions were to be made public, Salomon's traders and salesmen had to learn about them as the public learned about them—a restriction that became increasingly necessary as the Kaufman name and legend spread through the Wall Street community, and Dr. Doom's diagnosis became a cause of feverish activity in the markets. On the outside many people believed that Salomon profited by advance notice of what Kaufman was going to say, and history did record a couple of days when Salomon traders in the morning seemed to know what Kaufman would say that afternoon, but there was no question that Kaufman labored mightily to preserve the secrecy of his analyses until they were released to the world. His greatest coup came in August 1982 when, after two years of proclaiming the damage that was about to be done by the straitjacket the Fed had fitted to the money supply, he announced that the tide had turned and the Fed would ease, thereby correctly forecasting a bull market that would more than triple the Dow-Jones Industrials and make immeasurable fortunes for the holders of bonds and mortgages.

"It was a Tuesday morning," Kaufman recalled, "and there was an executive committee meeting at the Waldorf. I was in the process of preparing a memo of change of views, which I had finished Monday night. Going to the Waldorf at 8:00 A.M., I gave the driver a memo to give to my secretary to put on the screens, and I told her to call me when it was done. The meeting had started when my secretary called. I was on the phone with her, and John [Gutfreund] called, 'What's so important?' Ira Harris was there, Tom Strauss, Dick Schmeelk. I called out to them what I was doing, and John shouted, *'You said that? It's going out now?'*"

By no means was everyone at the firm happy. Kaufman's department grew from the six or seven people he remembered from 1967 to more than four hundred people in 1988. His people participated in the profits of the firm, of course, over and above their salaries, just as the traders and salesmen did, and there were partners who couldn't see what they did to earn their bonuses. "Henry's department cost us as much as fifty million dollars a year," said a trader who was on the executive committee with him in both the '70s and the '80s, probably echoing what had become Gutfreund's view, "and what did we get for the money? It *is* true he didn't tell us what he was going to say. I always thought he should, but he wouldn't. And then we didn't get commission business from the customers who received *Comments on Credit*, because they felt they had to reward the traditional sort of 'research' on individual stocks they got from the other houses. I used to have lunch with people who would tell me how much they appreciated *Comments on Credit*, and when I asked them whether they ever sent any orders to us to say thanks, they always said, 'No.'"

Kaufman's invariable conservatism also provoked irritation on the executive committee. Another colleague on that body, this one from the banking side, remembered that "Henry would yell, 'Look at the risk you're running for what is only incremental business.'" It was to stop hearing this kind of resistance to his expansionary plans that John Gutfreund in 1986 removed Kaufman from the inner executive committee of Salomon Brothers, trying to keep him, meanwhile, on the publicized but less influential board of the holding company Salomon, Inc. Kaufman, who had accepted losses on a number of policy issues in the 1980s, quit on the question of his personal status. If he wasn't in Gutfreund's executive office, he didn't feel he could protect his researchers from the wrath of traders and salesmen who had lost money or customers when the research department's predictions savaged their positions or recommendations.

From his perch in the Chicago office of Lazard Freres, former Salomon banker Ira Harris pointed to Kaufman's departure from the old firm as the end of an era: "When they removed Henry, they got rid of the last of the old guard." Less than a decade after Billy left the firm, no one remained on its decision-making levels who had played a prominent role before Gutfreund took over.

THE BLOOMBERG AND BIRINYI

Fixed-income (bond) trading had always been the heart of Salomon's profitability, and it was the heart of the firm's research effort. But from 1969 there was always an equities research department. The problem was that the people who did the glamorous part of equities work—the block trading—were not interested in what the stock might be "worth" next year, only what it might be sold for next hour. And Salomon's customers, the money managers for the institutions at whom all the Wall Street houses aimed their equities research, were already doing the bulk of their bond business with Salomon and thought they should spread the wealth when allocating stock brokerage commissions.

The value of training in stock research was that the researchers got to know the companies. Salomon more than any other firm had always permitted its people to find for themselves where they could be useful to the firm, and the equities researchers began to drift over into corporate finance, the construction of packages that mixed bonds, stocks, warrants, futures, and options in ways that arguably both minimized the funding costs of a corporate client and maximized the profits of the investment banker. It should also be noted, however, that in this context, where cleverness was all, even the Salomon salesmen could lose what had once been their lodestone: the interests of the customer who would buy the paper.

Morris Offit left research to become Solly's sales manager and was succeeded by Bobby Bernhard, Gutfreund's old classmate from Lawrenceville, son of Adele Lehman and nephew of Robert Lehman. Bernhard left a partnership at Lehman Brothers to come to Salomon. "A wonderful thing for me," he said later, although he left Salomon with bitterness, "because it got me out from under the yoke of my family. At Salomon I could be my own man." Nominally in research, Bernhard, who had the best connections of anyone at Salomon, became increasingly involved with clients whose paper the firm could underwrite rather than with the analysis of investments for clients. He was especially well liked by the younger bankers, who could count on him to come out to Denver on short notice and be the eminent adult presence they needed when making a pitch to a potentially important client.

What brought talent into computerized research at Salomon was Rosenthal's war against Jay Perry. Perry's number two was Michael Bloomberg, a handsome, startlingly intelligent, and bluntly straightforward young man who had been hired by Harold Nelson or Sandy Lewis in 1966 (both claim credit). He was the first Harvard MBA to come to Salomon and one of relatively few in the firm in those days to have an engineering degree (from Johns Hopkins). While his family background was not that different from Rosenthal's, the high school dropout was intensely resentful of the Harvard MBA. Neither Nelson nor Lewis remained long with the firm, and Bloomberg had no rabbi other than Perry. He thought he had Gutfreund, but he was wrong.

Partnerships were awarded at Salomon in September, just before the close of the fiscal year, and Bloomberg anticipated getting his in 1972. He was indeed called into Billy's office with three other favored candidates, but he emerged, with a forced smile, still a contract employee. Among the things in his life of which he is truly proud was his capacity to swallow that disappointment and tough it out. That December, when Bill Simon was summoned to Washington to be Deputy Secretary of the Treasury, the rules were broken and Bloomberg's elevation was proclaimed just before the end of the calendar year. He had been working on a computer system to communicate market information to the equity trading desks, and in honor of his promotion he activated it a few days early to send as its first message the news that Michael Bloomberg had become a partner in Salomon Brothers. In 1974 at age thirty-two Bloomberg was made chief of the firm's equity trading. Then May Day came and went, commissions were negotiable, Perry was banished to Dallas, and the equity desk became unprofitable. This left Bloomberg very disadvantaged when Rosenthal was elevated to Salomon's executive committee. Rosenthal pushed Bloomberg all the way out to Salomon's back office, to work with operations manager Allan Fine on problems relating to automation.

This could have been an extraordinary piece of luck for Solly. At a time when the computer was acquiring the capacity to manipulate databases and discover (even create) trading opportunities, Salomon in 1978 assigned to this problem perhaps the only man in the whole world who knew about both computers and trading. Bloomberg got on well with Vincent Murphy, who was Billy's right hand, and after Murphy left he was among Gutfreund's familiars at the breakfast table. Unfortunately, Allan Fine, son of a taxi driver, a heavyset man with neat instincts, reserved his deepest admiration for people like the senior clerk in the cage who was the world's fastest counter of bond certificates and had never mislaid a one of them. Fine saw Bloomberg as a threat, discouraged others from working with him, and resisted allocating any substantial sums to the computers, mostly on the argument that Salomon's business was changing so fast, you couldn't stabilize an automated system.

Bloomberg found things he could do with the limited budget and staff he squeezed from this hostile situation. While still on the equity desk, he had steered Salomon to the Quotron system for stock quotes, against the competition of GTE, which was one of the firm's few steady investment banking clients (Gutfreund's personal client, too). Working with the Quotron system, a computer screen supplying the latest bids and askeds for all exchange-traded securities, Bloomberg added a "B screen" that gave Salomon's positions in detail and, as he got funds to expand the database, the record of all Salomon's proprietary trades (trades for its own account) in this security—prices, volumes, sellers, buyers. The salesmen got hooked on it and had to be warned that when visiting customers they could not illustrate Salomon's services by pulling up a B screen, because nobody except Salomon had a B screen.

Slowly, slowly, Bloomberg expanded the subject matter of the databases—government bonds, corporate bonds, the list of the instruments the firm traded. The theory was that as the computers learned the historical relationships of the yields on many thousands of different bonds, swapping and arbitrage possibilities could be uncovered with the push of a key. Moreover, as the new futures and options contracts grew more significant in the marketplace, computers would be an important—perhaps the only—way to track the opportunities they offered. The bond traders reacted like Luddites: Their skills were being turned over to a machine, and they wanted no part of it. "Gutfreund," said a man who was on the executive committee at the end of the 1970s, when Gutfreund took over from Billy as managing partner, "didn't understand any of this and didn't want to understand it." Every aspect of what Bloomberg wanted to do was expensive, and it wasn't just Fine who didn't want to spend the money. In 1981 when the partnership was bought out and a new corporate entity created, Bloomberg was one of the six partners who was not hired by the new company.

"Fully liquefied" in the transaction, and several times a millionaire as a result, Bloomberg started his own independent financial information service, using different computer equipment and different programs. He took two people with him from Salomon under an arrangement whereby they promised to destroy anything they had in their files from the Salomon systems they had helped build. The costs of starting afresh were more than even a fully liquefied Salomon partner could carry, and Bloomberg sold 30 percent of his company to Merrill Lynch under a contract that restricted him for five years from offering the service to any other of the dozen largest primary dealers. (The prohibited group was Bankers Trust, Bear Stearns, Citibank, Daiwa Securities, Drexel, Credit Suisse–First Boston, Goldman Sachs, J. P. Morgan, Kidder Peabody, Morgan Stanley, Shearson Lehman, and Salomon.) By 1986 "the Bloomberg," a screen hooked into his mainframes through his proprietary programs, had become an indispensable tool for every bond trader who worked for someone not on the restricted list, and in 1988 Merrill relented, allowing Bloomberg to sell to anyone, for a consideration not yet a matter of public record but believed to have been much more than Merrill's original investment.

By 1992, Bloomberg Financial Markets, now available to one and all at a price of $1,500 a month for the first screen, $1,000 a month for each additional screen, was perhaps the most successful electronic publishing venture anywhere, with revenues approaching $300 million a year. It consisted of three floors in one of the fanciest office buildings on Park Avenue, large modern offices in Princeton for the people building the database, and a conventional news staff that was sixty strong and growing. *The New York Times* had nobody on duty all day at the Securities and Exchange Commission, *The Wall Street Journal* had one reporter, the AP had half a reporter—and Bloomberg had two, covering both the room where corporations filed their registration statements for new issues and the room where quarterly reports, proxy statements, and other such informational material (including SEC decisions) were made available to the public. These were in addition to more than two hundred programmers and keypunchers continuing to expand the historic database to municipal bonds, mortgage instruments, common stocks, traded bank loans, and currencies. In 1992, Bloomberg took over a New York radio station, more or less for the hell of it, and began offering a twenty-four-hour business news service to the general public.

"Bloomberg Fair Value," a line on a graph on a CRT tube, has become the reference standard for bond trades throughout the market, and more famous financial information services such as Reuters, Telerate, and Knight-Ridder have been in a losing struggle to keep up. The handful of old-timers still at Salomon tend to be bitter at "Michael" (not "Mike"—this was another dignified trader) because he disadvantaged his old friends during the years when his contract with Merrill prohibited him from selling to his former partners. The overwhelming majority of those who had been Michael's partners—more than 90 percent of them no longer with Salomon—of course had somewhat greater freedom to think what idiots they had been when they let Dickie Rosenthal persuade them that Bloomberg could add no value to the firm. And some of his old partners were proud of him. (I first met Bloomberg

when he was still shy about talking with the press, because Salomon veteran Dale Horowitz, being helpful on another project,
permitted me to use his name. When I thanked Bloomberg for
seeing me, he said, "I had to. The man used to be my partner.")

Among those Perry and Bloomberg left behind was Laszlo Birinyi, Jr., a slim young man with a talent for wry observation; he
had been recruited from the firm of Miller, Hutchins because he
seemed interesting. He came July 1, 1976—"Just in time for the
tall ships," he remembered. "Bloomberg said, 'You're not going to
sell, you're not going to trade, you're not going to do stock research. You have to find out what you're going to do.' It was
typical Salomon: If you're as smart as you think you are, you'll find
something. I did the things that fell between the cracks. There was
no real structure to the firm, no training program. So I wrote a
book. I began training the newcomers. I'd tell a kid, Pick up the
phone and call me. Pretend I'm a customer. I built systems to take
information and make it succinct for the trading desk: When are
corporations reporting? What are the expectations? That sort of
thing. In 1979 I got the computer department to automate the
ticker tape so that traders could pick up that day's transactions in
the stock. We had a computer department and a trading department; the trading people didn't understand computers and the
computer people didn't understand trading—except for Michael,
and he was too busy. We established automated reporting on
blocks to make sure we knew that when we saw a hundred-
thousand-share block on the tape we knew who traded it.

"We had lots of quantitative data, thanks to Henry [Kaufman]. I
made arrangements with an outside vendor to feed that data to
him and have him send back nice color graphs, overnight. The first
month was November 1977, and our bill was ten thousand dollars.
Three members of top senior management stopped me in the hall
that day and said, 'Nice idea, Laszlo—but *a hundred thousand
dollars a year?*' "

When Birinyi began working on Salomon's data, computer ter-
minals tended to be typewriters without screens, and the easiest
thing to do with them was the old "point-and-figure" technical
analysis, which showed a stock's trades during a day, X's for sales
at a price higher than the previous different price, O's for sales at
a price lower than the previous different price. While arranging to

have information of that sort presented in a more usable form, Birinyi thought of a simple, useful service that would look at the *volume* of trading done for each stock on upticks or downticks. The proposition was that sales at a rising price (an uptick) meant the buyer hit the offer and there was new money coming into the stock, while sales at a falling price (a downtick) meant that a seller hit the bid and somebody was getting out. The real question for a stock analyst in the late twentieth century is whether the institutions are accumulating or distributing. Institutions buy and sell in quantity. Thus one could be encouraged about the future of a stock that went down in price even for several straight days if the sales that seemed to move it down were a few hundred shares each and the sales that braked the fall were in twenty-thousand-share lots. Similarly, a stock that had been rising in price would not be a good buy if the volume picked up on every brief retreat. The nice thing about Birinyi's service was that it answered questions stock by stock, and one could indeed develop a library that indicated the stocks for which the predictions were more or less likely to be correct on differing time horizons.

Birinyi remained at Salomon until 1989 and developed the Salomon-Russell International Index, designed to let speculators place their bets on all the world's stock markets at once. When he left he took his "money-flow" service with him and got a number of institutions to subscribe. But by 1989 this sort of common-sense data-based system was not complicated enough for Solly. In the 1980s the world of securities research had become one of analyzing embedded options through the use of second order partial differential equations and trying to cash in on the analysis by playing the prices on the Chicago Board Options Exchange against the prices on the Chicago Mercantile Exchange against the prices on the New York Stock Exchange against the prices in hidden markets that didn't report the transactions. Morgan Stanley had pioneered the use of higher mathematics in securities trading, but Salomon followed close behind. It made money for the firm and, oddly (for they were the losers in this game, receiving used information), the customers expected it. "These things," Birinyi noted sourly, "are not done by *market* people. They're done by people eighteen to twenty-six months out of school, and they're based on the notion that the market will be steady, it will just stand there and let you do what you want to do. I complained once about one of the quants [common shorthand for quantitative analyst] who wasn't a market technician at all but a salesman who liked to look at charts, and they said, 'Well, he gives us something to talk about.' What use is that? I left because I'd been there too long."

EXOTIC DANCING, FOR MONEY

In 1975, Leo Melamed of the Chicago Mercantile Exchange came calling on Billy Salomon and John Gutfreund to sell them on a new contract he was about to introduce to trading: futures on Treasury bills. Solly was the biggest dealer in such instruments and in longer-term Treasury bonds. It would be to Salomon's advantage to have a contract that would allow the firm to hedge its exposure, providing a trading floor where at some time in the future Solly could contract to sell today's inventory at today's price even if the market went down, or buy out today's short position at today's price even though the market went up. Billy did not like it at all, but he was courteous as always and told Melamed that if by some chance he made this contract work, Salomon would be big users. In 1978 when it was clear that the T-bill contract was going to be heavily used by both speculators and hedgers, Tom Strauss of Salomon called Melamed apologetically and asked if the firm could still buy a membership in the financial instruments section of the Merc. Later Strauss would be a member of the Merc board of directors and useful to Melamed as a defender of his S&P index contract at a time when others wished to blame it for the violence of the stock market crash of 1987.

Although Salomon was a trading house, the cleverness of the firm was rarely exerted to find new trading instruments. Once they were in use, Solly of necessity became an aggressive customer for the contracts developed in Chicago, but it was never an inventor. Where the best brains went in Salomon from the late 1970s to the late 1980s was neither to trading nor to research but to the creation of new *financing* instruments. Many, although by no means all, of the swaps, segmentations, caps, and straddles that transformed corporate finance in the 1980s were invented at Salomon Brothers by very bright and competent men (and a few women), nearly all of whom had departed the firm by 1989. In 1987, Salomon claimed credit for a typed list eighteen double-spaced pages long of "innovations" from 1980 through 1986. There were zero-coupon insured term deposits for banks to sell consumers, and tax-exempt financing in London for Boeing to lease airplanes to American Airlines; "COLTS" ("Continuously Of-fered Longer-Term Securities") for the World Bank and "CARS" ("Collateralized Automobile Receivables") to package car loans into bonds for sale both in the United States and Europe; and GM's "Class H" common stock as part of that company's acquisition of Hughes Aircraft.

Then there were things like "SPINS," debt securities paying only 2 percent interest, issued in 1986, that would pay back four years later according to the rise or fall of the Standard & Poor's 500-stock index. As the stocks in the index were all but certain to pay more than 2 percent in dividends, this was a slam-dunk for Solly, which could acquire the stocks, take a little markup on the SPINS, and pocket the difference between the dividends the com-panies paid and 2 percent. The question of why anybody would buy such paper can be answered more easily than you might think: This was the heyday of Solly's involvement with the S&Ls, and the guys who sold paper to the S&Ls were masters.

Salomon's move to complicated, hybrid, derivative instruments was in hindsight a natural progression; Salomon salesmen had always arranged swaps of bond positions for their customers, and Sidney Homer had been the first to see the range of options em-bedded in what looked like straightforward bonds. What was needed was to apply traditional skills to new times. The high interest rates of the early 1980s, for example, made it possible for corporations to "swap" their own stock for their own bonds in what Salomon called "debt for equity" trades. With interest rates at 14 percent, the 8 percent bonds of a company might sell for perhaps seventy-five cents on the dollar. A company with excess cash could make a $2.5 million profit by purchasing $10 million of its own bonds on the market for $7.5 million. Unfortunately, that profit would be taxable. The tax could be avoided, however, Sal-omon argued—with help from its law firm, Cleary Gottlieb, where the whole scheme may have originated—if instead of paying cash for the bonds the company issued stock to pay for them.

Then Salomon (not the company) could buy the $10 million of bonds in the market for $7.5 million and swap them with the company for whatever quantity of the company's stock the two parties agreed would be $7.5 million. The company could book the $2.5 million as profit but did not have to pay tax on it. Salomon, the IRS ruled, had to be at risk in selling the stock if the company was to qualify for a tax-exempt gain on the bonds, but the risk didn't have to be more than the risk Solly ran when it acquired any block of stock. The IRS had no objection to Salomon harvesting expressions of interest in such a block before completing the deal with its corporate client. Warren Foss, who had come to Salomon in 1976 to work as part of a four-man client contact team that sat on the trading floor and helped corporations sell commercial paper, did the first of these debt-equity swaps for Quaker Oats in 1980. The numbers were $14 million face value of bonds purchased by Salomon for $9.1 million, 287,819 shares of stock issued to Salomon by Quaker Oats as payment for the bonds, and almost $9.5 million paid by Salomon's customers for the stock, leaving the firm a neat $350,000 profit for its time.

From debt-equity swaps it was an easy step to "defeasance," a way for companies to use cash to redeem bonds cheaply. In 1982, for example, Salomon brokered a deal between Exxon and Morgan Guaranty. Exxon bought $312 million face value of U.S. Treasury 14 percent bonds with the same redemption dates as some $515 million face value of its own older 5.8 percent to 6.5 percent bonds. Morgan then bought the Treasury bonds from Exxon by agreeing to pay the twice-a-year coupon and ultimately the principal of the outstanding Exxon bonds. The difference between the 14 percent paid to Morgan by the Treasury and the 6 percent or so Morgan had to pay to the Exxon bondholders would accumulate and pay off the principal of the Exxon bonds when due. Morgan's profit, by the Homeric analysis, would be a function of the interest rates at which it could reinvest the $42 million a year the Treasury would pay on the bonds, but there would almost certainly be *some* profit. Exxon could book a *tax-free* $203 million profit, which even for Exxon was no small potatoes. And the ghost of Sidney Homer rode again.

Currency swapping grew out of the experience of Neil Benedict, a young Englishman who came to Salomon from Dillon Read in 1976 and had an interesting introduction to the firm. Benedict got his shirts from a London shirtmaker who, it turned out, also made Billy's shirts. When he told the man to send the shirts *he* was ordering to Salomon Brothers in New York, the shirtmaker asked whether Benedict could take back with him some shirts just finished to Billy's order. The morning Benedict came to the office with the shirts, he happened to ride up in the elevator with Billy, whom he recognized although they had never met and who gladly received the shirts and would have tipped the delivery boy if it hadn't been a crowded elevator. Later that morning Benedict was the junior man at a closing that was important enough for Billy to visit and applaud those who had done the work, going around the table and shaking everybody's hand. When he came to Benedict, his eyes filled with wild surmise, which Benedict encouraged by touching his collar suggestively.

For four years Benedict did almost nothing at Salomon but "back-to-back loans" for British and American corporations. In 1976, Britain still had currency controls—stiff ones, indeed, in the aftermath of the near collapse of the pound. British banks were not allowed to lend pounds to American companies that might convert them into dollars, and British companies were allowed to borrow dollars from American banks only in a special market where they had to pay a higher rate. Benedict would make arrangements for American companies borrowing in the U.S. market to swap the resulting dollars for pounds procured by British companies borrowing in London.

In 1981, Benedict had a client that wanted to borrow 100 million pounds in the Eurosterling market (the market for British pounds to be used outside Britain). To see if he could work a deal with the international agency, he went to Eugene Rotberg, chief financial officer of the World Bank, a rotund alumnus of the SEC with a well-warranted self-confidence in his ability to make academic schemes practical. Rotberg, it turned out, did not want to get involved with Eurosterling, but the World Bank did want to borrow $300 million worth of Swiss francs and deutsche marks without disturbing the Zurich or Frankfurt markets, where it already had a number of issues outstanding. Meanwhile, Salomon's Jon Rotenstreich had done a deal of about that size for IBM, which had borrowed Swiss francs and deutsche marks at the bottom of the dollar's 1979 weakness and now wanted to lock in its foreign exchange profit. The World Bank, which had a perfect rating in the United States, wanted Swiss francs and deutsche marks and could borrow dollars in the American market very cheaply. When the dust had cleared, Salomon had underwritten a dollar deal for the World Bank in New York, IBM had the dollars and the obligation to repay them, and the World Bank had the Swiss francs and deutsche marks Salomon had raised for IBM in the Swiss market and the obligation to repay *them*. Both sides had what they wanted at an interest rate lower than either would have had to pay to borrow the money directly—value added by Salomon as broker.

Clearly, this principle could be extended to other top-quality borrowers. The Republic of Austria had a large number of bonds outstanding in the Swiss franc market and could raise new money there only at a punitive interest rate, despite its AAA credit rating, which would qualify it for the lowest rates in the dollar market. The Canadian provinces had a lesser credit rating but had no paper in the Swiss franc market, and could sell bonds there at a lower interest rate. Benedict, with help this time from Richard Schmeelk, Solly's Canada expert, set up a pair of underwritings in 1982 for Austria and Canada, which swapped the proceeds when the customers paid for the bonds.

This work was then interrupted, an omen for the future, by Salomon politics. Benedict's deals were of course essentially banking—otherwise "capital markets"—transactions, and Rotenstreich urged that Benedict be made part of the corporate finance section of the firm. Tom Strauss, whose fief by 1982 extended to foreign exchange as well as fixed-income trading but not to corporate finance, insisted that what Benedict was doing was really foreign exchange and that Benedict should report to him. Rotenstreich, who had other grievances, too, went off to become the treasurer of IBM and then the chairman and chief executive officer of Torchmark Insurance, and Benedict went to Salomon's Tokyo office, en route back to Dillon Read.

Most of what Salomon did in the spirit of Sidney Homer involved the segmentation of once apparently (not really) simple instruments. Options that had always been present in the bond were dug out and put on sale—or options that could be added to the bond were hung on the tree to be admired and purchased. The pioneer of segmentation at Salomon was Robert Scully, who spent the decade of the 1980s, which was also the decade of his thirties, thinking up what he described as "ideas that give value for our customers and advantages to the buyers, and make money for ourselves." Scully was considered to have all the virtues, brains, good looks, and candor, and he was very much a company man— his wife worked at Salomon and later became a managing director. Salomon veterans bemoaned his departure in the fall of 1987 perhaps more than that of anyone else who left. He thought of endless variations on the theme of interest rate swaps where one party borrowed at a fixed rate and the other at a floating rate, and the two then exchanged their obligations.

One of the more exotic of Scully's instruments was the "Heaven and Hell warrant," which required the issuer to pay more in one unlikely set of circumstances or allowed him to pay less in another equally unlikely set of circumstances. On March 18, 1986, for example, Scully sold an issue of yen-denominated bonds for the Kingdom of Denmark. The yen was then at about 170 to the dollar. By the terms of this bond, Denmark would have to pay back more yen in 1991 if the yen were weaker than 263.55 to the dollar, and would be permitted to pay back fewer yen if the yen were stronger than 90.01 to the dollar. In principle Salomon did not want to hold either side of this contract and would find a purchaser for the bond, presumably at a price higher than it paid Denmark. This did not always work, but it worked often enough so that similar bonds were issued for American Express, IBM Credit, the Republic of Austria, the Province of Saskatchewan, and a U.S. Federal Home Loan Bank. In the time frame of the Kingdom of Denmark bond, neither Heaven nor Hell claimed the seller or the buyer.

Salomon did not by any means have a monopoly on such cleverness. "Today," Scully said in 1986, "a company raising money calls in a bunch of bankers from around the world and runs a beauty contest. We compete with ideas. Companies like IBM and GM are besieged with people from all over the world with ideas on how to raise money. The half-life of a new idea in this business is about half a heartbeat. A few years ago Shearson Lehman originated the capped floating rate note [a note with varying rates that cannot go above or below a certain limit]. They did five billion dollars in the first month even though we developed our own variant of it the afternoon we heard about it."

Not all these stories had such happy endings. In the late 1980s, Salomon developed an instrument to solve a big problem at the Japanese insurance companies, which by Japanese law were allowed to pay annuities or other guaranteed income contracts to policyholders only from the interest and dividends and rents on their holdings. They could not sell their stocks or properties and use the profits on the sale for distribution, the way insurance companies could everywhere else in the world. With Bankers Trust (*nobody's* name was on this one by 1992), Solly developed a one- to three-year index-linked bond that paid several points of interest higher than the prevailing rate in the Japanese market. In return for paying the insurance company that purchased the bond a higher rate of interest, which allowed the company to promise a higher return to policyholders, the issuer of the bond received the right to reduce its principal payments when the bond came due by 3 percent for every 1 percent fall in the Nikkei index of the 225 most heavily capitalized stocks on the Tokyo Stock Exchange. Some $23 *billion* of such bonds were sold in 1989 and early 1990 when the Nikkei sold at prices ranging from 30,000 to 39,000. In the spring of 1992, with the Nikkei around 18,000 and the bonds expiring, it looked likely that the debtors on the bonds would pay back to the insurance companies something like $3.5 billion of the $23 billion original face value. The profitability of Salomon's Tokyo office in 1990–92 was in large part the result of this and other bets against the Japanese stock market. This somewhat diminishes the long-term value of the Tokyo franchise: The Japanese have long memories.

In retrospect the trouble with creating all these fancy options, like the trouble with trading off the statistical analyses, was that they had no morality. Even after a generation of MBAs had studied the Black-Scholes option-pricing formula that is taught at the business schools, the ability to find the "right" price for such options was very unevenly distributed through the community of bond buyers and bond traders. Shortly after the 1987 crash, Hans-Joerg Rudloff of Credit Suisse–First Boston made scornful reference to those who "sold hybrid securities to the public at premiums of 12 and 14 percent, hiding their profits behind the sophisticated structure of their instruments."[5] He was talking about Salomon more than about any other firm—except, perhaps, his own. Scully was an honorable man, but this was a business that invited the last measures of greed. If the customer believed he got value, why should the quant disagree?

To the extent that the purpose of the new instruments was to "shift risk," the dangers were especially great. By and large the most risk-averse component of the investing community—the pension funds and the insurance companies—is the sector most capable of bearing the risk. Salomon had once been a risk seeker, but by the later 1980s it had become addicted to the sure things promised by the mathematicians. The surviving risk seekers are houses of cards—traders bouncing in the pits of the Chicago exchanges, many of them backed by no more than the market price of their seat and a $50,000 deposit of Treasury bills at the clearinghouse, highly leveraged banks and investment banks with typically no more than 3 percent of their resources from their own money, the rest borrowed short-term. In the end, it turns out, the promoters of risk shifting, who are free-market enthusiasts to a man, rely on the government to bail out the risk takers through deposit insurance, charitable bank regulation, or immense infusions of cash, as in October 1987.

When the bell rang in August 1991, Salomon was carrying $155 billion of assets and something approaching $600 billion of off-balance-sheet contracts on a capital base of less than $4 billion. Presumably the quants had hedged the exposure, but the credit quality of those who sold the hedge, their capacity to live up to their part of the bargain in hard times, was beyond the competence of quants who knew only what their computers told them. When the giant Canadian real estate house Olympia and York started down the tubes in 1992, Salomon took a write-off on the profits it had booked on its hedges with O&Y. The essence of probability math, which nobody wants to talk about, is that the normal curve of distribution has a long tail in both directions, and the things that as a practical matter "can't" happen in fact probably will happen at some time—such as a 508-point drop in the Dow Industrials in a single day's trading. Comfort thyself, saith the dying King Arthur in Tennyson's poem about the grail; what comfort is in me?

"High-tech banking and finance has its place," E. Gerald Corrigan of the New York Fed told the New York State Bankers Association in early 1992, "but it is not all that it is cracked up to be.

For example, the interest-rate swap market now totals several trillion dollars. Given the sheer size of the market I have to ask myself how it is possible that so many holders of fixed or variable obligations want to shift those obligations from one form to the other. Since I have a great deal of difficulty in answering that question, I then have to ask myself whether some of the specific purposes for which swaps are now being used may be quite at odds with an appropriately conservative view of the purposes of a swap, thereby introducing new elements of risk or distortion into the marketplace—including possible distortion to the balance sheets and income statements of financial and nonfinancial institutions alike."[6]

Some of this Billy Salomon may have seen—not understood, for he was not an intellectual, but seen—from the aerie to which he had semiretired, still looking over the trading room, in the summer of 1978. When he learned the following year that Jon Rotenstreich was hedging Salomon's exposure in an IBM underwriting, he was livid. Billy had welcomed the Sidney Homers and Henry Kaufmans, but in the end he thought that taking the risk was Salomon's function; sloughing off that role to others would eventually diminish Salomon, make it more like the other houses on Wall Street.

And the years ahead, beyond Billy's ken, were not going to be a time when Salomon could risk becoming more like the other houses, for the definitions of what constituted ethical behavior would change for the worse throughout the financial markets. George Gould, who came out of the institutional house of Donaldson Lufkin Jenrette to be James Baker's Deputy Secretary of the Treasury, remembered recently his early days on the Street when he worked for Jeremiah Milbank and one day proudly brought the old man a trade he had been offered that was nothing less than a sure thing. Milbank, he recalled, looked at him seriously for a minute and then said, "Mr. Gould, *we* don't *do* that." Gould wondered aloud about how long it had been since he had heard somebody reject a deal on the grounds that "we don't do that."

Salomon under Billy had been tough but scrupulous. No action by Salomon Brothers before 1987 was ever censured or penalized by the Securities and Exchange Commission. As outsiders the Salomon partners knew they would be held to the highest standards of the Street. As those standards dissolved in the years after the partnership became a corporation, the Salomon employees were given wider and wider range to exercise cleverness. Their cleverness, after all, was the way their employers made money. In the end there was nobody at the top who cared about anything but the money.

"That's unfair," one of the old-timers complained. "It wasn't just Salomon. It was everywhere on the Street." But the Salomon that was better at trading and better at math would also be better at fiddling with the rules, once that fiddling became acceptable.

Chapter 4

THE MASTERY OF MONEY

ONE DAY IN THE SPRING OF 1981, Philipp Brothers president David Tendler and his executive vice-president Hal Beretz came to Salomon to breakfast, for no particular purpose but simply as part of the firm's keeping up with its customers. Philipp Brothers—or Phibro, as it was soon to be called—was the largest trader in almost a hundred commodities, from jute to silver to oil, and had profited hugely from the commodities boom of the 1970s. From 1975 to 1980 its annual revenues had gone from $5.8 billion to $23.7 billion, and its profits from $95 million to $467 million. (Among its assets, which proved somewhat less valuable than originally believed, was the right to explore for oil in the Beaufort Sea, which Philipp had acquired in return for surrendering some $665 million of claims against the Hunt family for silver contracts on which the Hunts had welshed.) The company occupied five floors in the McGraw-Hill Building in Rockefeller Center. It had gone public as part of its separation from Englehard Minerals, and its success had created a complicated set of restructurings that left Minorco, a South African–owned mining company (part of Harry Oppenheimer's Anglo-American empire), as the largest stockholder, with a 27 percent interest.

Depending on the size of its fluctuating inventory, Philipp had both bought and sold commercial paper as a Salomon customer, trading directly with Dickie Rosenthal. Just a few months before, Rosenthal had worked with Philipp on the possible acquisition of a midwest insurance company, which had fallen through in January at the last minute. Beretz lived in the same suburban community as Salomon's Dale Horowitz; the two men went to the same temple and were friends. The term "power breakfast" was still hidden in the mists of time, but the Salomon dining rooms, with their pastel portraits of sailing ships in the New York of a hundred years before, were a pleasant place to start the day and compare notes on the world and its affairs.

The breakfast was convivial but businesslike. Among those in the group from Salomon, in addition to Horowitz and Rosenthal, was Henry Kaufman: Philipp was an important, and potentially an even more important, customer who would be grateful for Henry's guidance. Conversation was dominated by the relentless rise in interest rates that Paul Volcker's Fed was imposing on the economy to combat the potentially inflationary effects of the tax cut Ronald Reagan had proposed to the Congress, and by recent megadeals involving Wall Street firms—Equitable had bought Donaldson Lufkin Jenrette, Prudential had bought Bache, Bechtel had bought Dillon Read, and American Express was buying Shearson Loeb Rhoades in a deal brokered by Salomon's former equity trader Sandy Lewis.

Kaufman felt these deals, which greatly increased the capital resources of the investment houses involved, presaged a new world in the securities business. "Either we've got to get bigger or smaller," he said. "And to get bigger we'd have to have a lot more money." Salomon was a partnership. Unlike a corporation, which could increase its resources either by selling stock or issuing bonds that were obligations of the company, Salomon could grow its capital only through retained earnings or by borrowings that left the partners themselves personally on the hook. Tendler recalled that Kaufman added, "And I'm not going to sign any more notes"; Kaufman didn't remember phrasing it quite that way, but he did make it clear that he didn't think Salomon should borrow any more money than it already owed.

After pondering the significance of such comments and thinking about the compatibility of Philipp and Salomon—the only over-laps in their business were gold trading and government bonds—Tendler called Rosenthal to suggest that instead of acquiring an insurance company, Philipp might acquire Salomon. "We had an enormous amount of cash," Tendler recalled. "We were sitting on top of the commodities boom." Especially if it wished to expand as an underwriter and investment banker, Salomon needed capi-tal: The size of the participation the firm could take in an under-writing was a function of how much money it had to put at risk. Philipp had worldwide offices. Salomon's overseas presence was limited to a few hundred people in London and trivial represen-tation in Hong Kong and Tokyo, and there was still a debilitating fight within the firm about which of these cities it should use as its base for the penetration of Asian markets. As the securities busi-ness grew increasingly international, Salomon would need a much greater presence abroad.

Tendler felt comfortable with Salomon. A short, chunky man in his forties with a mane of black hair, he was a City College product who had joined Philipp as a part-time banana trader during school vacations. Like both John Gutfreund and Dale Horowitz in 1981 he spoke with a New York accent. "They were a trading house, we were a trading house," Tendler said. "We had similar back-grounds." Like the old Salomon, Philipp had recruited most of its people from the ranks of high school graduates and office boys, who learned their trade by apprenticeship. There were synergies (the buzz word of the time). When the deal was finally done, John Gutfreund would discourse solemnly and foolishly about the pos-sibility of currencies backed by baskets of the commodities Phil-ipp traded, and Tendler would speak of Salomon financing Philipp projects for minerals and energy development in the Third World. And, of course, if Salomon was acquired by someone, the partners could get their money out.

The official explanation of the Phibro deal has always been that Salomon needed the capital to grow and that the firm could never have become the largest underwriter on Wall Street without what a member of its executive committee called "mainlining the Phibro money." But for many of the Salomon partners the incen-tive was obviously to cash out on the firm's success. Under Billy Salomon they had become wealthy but not rich. "We made what were for me fantastic amounts of money," said James Wolfensohn, who organized the Chrysler bailout for Salomon and moved on to his own consulting firm, "but we got paid like commercial bankers." Their money was buried in the partnership accounts, and by the terms of the partnership agreement they could not get it out. "They used to come to me," Billy recalled, "and say they wanted to buy a house, could they borrow ten thousand, twenty thousand dollars from their partnership account? And I'd say, 'Why do you need such a fancy house?' They didn't often get it."

Billy had retired in 1978, but the compensation system at the firm was still the same in 1981. People at Salomon worked on three different plans. Most galley slaves simply got a salary, usually no better and sometimes worse than the Wall Street average. (When Don Howard came to Salomon from Citibank in 1988 to be chief financial officer and supervisor of the back offfice, he found that people in Salomon's cage were paid less than he had paid people at Citibank, a condition Salomon could sustain because people wanted to work at Salomon and not at Citibank.) In almost any job, however, an employee could "go on contract," which gave him a tiny but not (from his point of view) insignificant share of the firm's profits for the year. The people who worked their way up from the mail room at Salomon remember the day they went "on contract" as vividly as the day they were made partners. Contract employees were not at risk, because Billy regarded the previous year's contract bonus as inviolable: The firm's post-Smutny history showed one losing year (1973), because Billy paid out bonuses to the employees greater than the profits.

Partners received a monthly drawing account in cash, which was their salary, plus a percentage of the profits, most of which had to be reinvested in the firm to grow the capital. "One year I made a million dollars," said a man who was a partner throughout the 1970s, "and I had to go to my mother to borrow ten thousand dollars to meet expenses." Salaries were not very large—in 1981 there may have been more partners with drawing accounts under $2,000 a week than over it—and the only part of the profits that could be taken in cash was a 5 percent dividend on the partners' share of the capital. They were also permitted to draw from their capital the taxes due on this income; among the perks of partnership was free preparation of tax returns by Oppenheim, Appel & Dixon, Salomon's accountants. In addition, partners were permitted to draw from their accumulated capital (including this year's contribution, of course) the maximum they could give tax free to their families: $3,000 a year per person in the early years, later $6,000 a year. Only one other invasion of the capital was permitted: To encourage partners to contribute to charity, Salomon allowed them to take out another $10,000 a year for that purpose. By 1981 the 5 percent dividend on a partner's pro-rata share of the capital was substantial, averaging $200,000 per partner (more than $1 million for Gutfreund)—but it was still only 5 percent, and in 1981 you could get more than 14 percent on a savings account. And Reagan was reducing the tax rate.

Salomon partners could not immediately cash in their capital by leaving the firm. Partners who departed had to spread their withdrawals over five years. If they retired, remaining limited partners, they would get a better income from their stake in the firm, that year's pro-rata share of the profits rather than a mere 5 percent, but they still could take out the principal only piece by piece. The only exception was the partner who left for government service, which made it *illegal* for him to remain a partner. The general belief around Salomon was that Bill Simon resigned from the governments trading desk and accepted appointment as Deputy Secretary of the Treasury not from love of Richard Nixon but to get paid what he'd earned in Billy Salomon's service.

Not everyone was resentful of being kept on Billy's short leash; reporters visiting the firm were introduced to people who were grateful to Salomon for making them save so much money. But the profits of the volatile 1970s and especially of 1980 (when the firm's $200 million of capital had grown to $300 million) made that pool of money irresistibly tempting—"like a big lake for a herd of thirsty cattle," as a man who was there put it. Even people who were making $300,000 a year were powerfully drawn to the $6.8 million, most of it in cash, that was the average each of the sixty-two Salomon partners would take from the Phibro deal.

Billy believed in partnership as the only way to organize a firm like Salomon Brothers. He was willing to have the partnership borrow money. In 1960, Charles Simon parlayed his contacts with U.S. Trust Co. into a $15 million issue of Salomon subordinated debentures that gave its holders 6 percent guaranteed, 8 percent if Salomon's earnings exceeded a certain figure (and they almost always did)—plus the right to sell the bonds back to Salomon for one hundred cents on the dollar at any time with one year's notice. (When a new pharaoh arose at U.S. Trust that knew not Charlie, a request was made for the bonds' redemption, and Salomon bought them back *immediately*.) Billy was also willing to take limited partners, who would receive a prearranged share of profits every year. These were mostly distinguished people who could bring him information as well as money, such as former Supreme Court Justice Arthur Goldberg, Marietta Tree, Leo Gottlieb, and Newton Minow of Chicago's Sidley & Austin (a friend of Ira Harris and a former chairman of the Federal Communications Commission). "He'd ask for advice every once in a while," Minow recalled. "For me, Salomon was very much like a law firm."

In partnerships, Billy felt, people worked together. When people lost money, it was the group as a whole, not this or that individual, who lost. (Nobody who worked for Billy can remember being criticized by him for a losing trade, although others in the partners' dining room might make jokes with a barb in them.) When they made money, they made it for everybody. "You were working," said one of the smartest men there in the 1970s, "for your reputation, to earn money to create wealth." Until the middle 1980s people at Salomon who left the premises felt deeply that they represented the firm, not themselves, to the outside world. Of course there was competition within the firm, and partners didn't necessarily *like* each other. But except for people of extraordinary malevolence, like Dickie Rosenthal, it was rare indeed for anyone actually to wish another man ill. Indeed, that was the secret of the emotion the alumni felt for their old firm.

Almost without exception the partners from the old Salomon spoke of Billy's talent for keeping people who didn't much like each other working smoothly in the same harness. Ken Lipper remembered that when he came to Salomon's investment banking department from Lehman Brothers in 1976, he found looming over his desk on his first day a six-foot-four figure who identified himself as Ray Golden and said, "I was against your coming here. I don't think we need people from outside, but now that you're here we're going to make money together." Jon Rotenstreich, a terrifyingly smart Alabaman who left in 1982 after winning the firm the cachet of being investment banker to IBM, said sadly, "It was such a beautiful period in my life. Even today when I open the paper, that name jumps off any page it's on. I flinch when I see it. I wish they'd changed the name."

In terms of individual compensation, the decision was always made at the end of the year for *next* year. The judgment was made, in other words, not in terms of the profits your desk showed in the year just past but on the evaluation of your future importance to the profitability of the firm as a whole. Bill Simon served as chairman of the compensation committee in the early 1970s and remembered that contract percentages (which were supposed to be secret and sometimes were) were always a judgment call. "People would complain," he said. "They'd say, 'I made a bundle for the firm, *he* barely broke even. How come he's getting a bigger percentage than I am?' And I'd say, '*He* had a tough market last year, you had an easy one. Anybody could have made money on your desk; most people on his desk would have lost money. He was worth more than you were.' If they didn't like it, they could quit." An appeal could be taken to Billy; Vincent Murphy recalled that the result was always the same: "He'd say, 'Well, let's hope the same percentage will be a bigger piece of pie next year, because we're going to do better.' " Laszlo Birinyi remembered from his days as an observer on the floor that anybody who went up to Billy with a demand for something was soon receiving a brisk handshake and all good wishes for his future somewhere else.

THE BIG DEAL

Although the impetus for the Phibro deal came from Rosenthal (who would later, perversely, argue against it at the partnership meeting), the negotiator for the firm was Ira Harris, a large New Yorker (he had two sets of clothes, one for when he was dieting and weighed only about 235 pounds, the other for when he wasn't dieting and might weigh more than 300 pounds) who had adopted Chicago. He had been recruited from Blair & Co. by Billy in the late 1960s while still in his early thirties, to be the nucleus of an investment banking business based on his friendships with the

likes of the Crown, Pritzker, and Tisch families; the deals he had
designed included the Tisches' acquisition of the insurance company CNA, Esmark's spin-off of its Swift & Co. meat business,
Marvin Davis's puchase of Twentieth Century-Fox, Norton Simon's
acquisition of Avis, and much else. He was a prowler who walked
incessantly around both his office and his home with a fat man's
waddle, whether or not there were others in the room. His life
was punctuated with incessant telephone calls, some business,
some quasi-business, some friends just checking in. When I
needed a hotel room in Chicago on a night when a convention
had filled the town, Harris found one—at a discount price. Charles
Simon thought he was a character out of Damon Runyon, Big Julie
from Chicago (but Big Julie was a muscleman, and Harris used
smarts). He was one of the least likely of the partners to be influenced by the money he himself might make from a deal; unlike
almost everyone else at Salomon, he had come to the firm a rich
man from the proceeds of his years with Blair.

"I was *not* the dealmaker in this transaction," Harris said some
years later. "You could call me the dealmaker on the Esmark and
Playtex things, because those were my idea. Here I simply negotiated the terms of the transaction. And this was not a deal like
other deals. Every investment banker would be a better banker if
at one time in his life he would negotiate a deal where he's the
principal." Looking back, he would be proud of the structure of
the deal, but not of the "due diligence," the investigation of the
business, that had preceded it. "If we had done for a client the job
we did for ourselves," he once said, "they'd have had a case against
us."

Going into the negotiations, Phibro and Salomon shared an attitude each wished to keep secret from the other—that the last
few years had been an aberration, and that their business would
never again be so profitable as it had been. "They did it out of
fear," said someone who would soon be but was not yet on Salomon's executive committee, speaking of his partners. "It was a
public demonstration of their lack of faith." Harris spoke of Salomon's potential weaknesses. "The capital in the firm to do business," he said, "was about one hundred and fifty million dollars.
The rest was in illiquid oil and gas investments the Salomon Brothers partnership had made. From 1979 to 1981 a very large part of

Salomon's profits had come from private partnership investments, not from the trading business. And in 1981, with interest rates where they were, you could make more on your money buying Treasury bills. A number of the older partners had retired, and they were taking their capital out as fast as the partnership agreement allowed them to take it."

Phibro's due diligence was no better than Salomon's, although in the end Phibro's stockholders would come out far ahead. In the months just before the deal closed, the bond market dropped steadily, hammered by Paul Volcker's ratcheting interest rates; and in a falling bond market, the inventory of a bond trading house generates losses rather than gains. In the summer months of 1981, Salomon may have lost as much as $50 million in bond trading. But Tendler assumed in his calculations that Salomon's profits were about $100 million a year, and on that basis the $550 million Phibro was paying (not all of it now) was a bargain. Nearly half the $300 million the Salomon partners would take home in cash was an investment portfolio, and Phibro could replace the working capital by reallocating liquid assets on its own books. The banks would let Salomon borrow to carry its inventory (which was at least thirty times the capital) as a subsidiary of Phibro, without any added capital in Phibro itself. The remainder of the $250 million paid to the partners was in the form of ten-year notes carrying a 9 percent interest rate, convertible over time—one to five years—into stock of the new Phibro-Salomon. For Tendler, this equated to a stock bonus down the pike and, he said, "we had always given our employees bonuses in the form of stock." Tendler estimated the real out-of-pocket cash outlay by Phibro at something like $150 million.

At Salomon both the partners and the younger "managing directors" were well rewarded. The cash from the partnership might be the partners' own money, but they couldn't put their hands on it without a deal of this sort. The notes would be convertible to stock that could be sold only gradually, over five years, but then they were going to be a giant honey pot for the *active* partners, who took them all. The difference between the status of the active partners and the status of the inactive partners created public dispute about how good a deal Salomon got. *Fortune* estimated that Phibro paid a total of $554 million and argued that "by almost any measure that looks like a world-class steal." It was less than twice the book value of the company in a year when Prudential Insurance had paid more than twice book for the much less well run Bache, and American Express had paid more than three times book for Shearson. Harris was furious and spoke by telephone with the author of the article (Carol Loomis) on Thanksgiving Day to chew her out. If you removed from the calculations the $135 million or so in the investment accounts which were simply bought from the partners at their market value, Phibro had paid something more than $400 million for the firm as a going concern, which was more than two and a half times the pro-forma book value of the working capital.

Knowledge that these negotiations were under way was kept from everyone at Salomon except the executive committee, and the partners were not especially curious when they came to a retreat at the Arrowhead Conference Center in Tarrytown, New York, for a weekend in late July 1981. Such weekends-with-your-partners had become relatively common in the late 1970s, most of them in the investment banking department but some for the firm as a whole. Some partners came a great distance, grumbling, from summer homes where they had been on vacation. At least one of these, Bobby Bernhard, made a trip of seven hours from a remote corner of the Bay of Fundy in Canada to learn not only that his firm was being sold but that he was not going to be employed by the new firm Phibro and Salomon were forming together.

The minute the doors were closed on the group after dinner on Friday, Gutfreund announced that the purpose of the meeting was to confirm a deal to sell Salomon to Phibro on a basis whereby a holding company called Phibro-Salomon would own both businesses. Each half would retain a corporate identity; Tendler and Gutfreund would serve as co-chairmen of the joint venture, but Tendler would be listed first and would have the title of chief executive officer. Members of Phibro's board would become part of Salomon's board and Tendler would become part of Salomon's executive committee, but nobody from Salomon would become part of Phibro's board. People would get most of their money now, but except for the seven partners who would not be hired by the new company, they would be expected to remain with Salomon and they would have to sign "noncompete" contracts forbidding them to work for any other securities house for at least

three years. The members of the executive committee were sign-
ing contracts that pledged them to work for Phibro-Salomon for at
least five years. After all, a securities firm was nothing but its
people.

To ensure that key people who were not yet partners would
remain, Harris had set up (over some resistance from Phibro, but
Harris said this was "a deal breaker") a special provision creating
"units" to be given to significant Salomon employees and partners
too junior to be receiving much benefit from the sale. Each unit
would be redeemable by key employees and junior partners who
stayed for five years for whatever the highest price of the stock
had been on any day during the five-year period. If the stock
touched 60 (which it did), the unit would yield $60, even if the
price five years after the merger was lower than $60 (which it
was). The distribution from cashing in the units would be entirely
separate and apart from the bonus pool of that year. Almost 2.5
million of these units were handed out in packets of five thousand
to twenty thousand. In theory, people were eligible to receive
units only if their salary was above a certain level, to avoid charges
of favoritism; in fact, the people were given units to a large extent
because of who their rabbi was. It had been Billy Salomon's special triumph that nobody felt he played favorites. With the allocation of the units among the younger people, a new and corrosive
envy spread in the trading room.

Five years later the unit holders were handed lump sums from
$300,000 to well over $1 million in what was not one of the firm's
most stellar years. The total paid to the holders of units was $145
million. There was some feeling among the beneficiaries that the
money was handed out grudgingly in 1986 (Harris by then had
left the executive committee), because the big shots who had
convertible notes rather than units couldn't get for themselves the
$60 a share paid to the juniors. In any event, many of these juniors
left soon after receiving their reward for remaining.

Retired and other limited partners had not been invited to Tarrytown; Billy was at his home in Southampton at the end of Long
Island. Once Gutfreund made the initial announcement, there was
little question in anyone's mind that the partnership would approve the deal: A rejection would have meant that the entire story
would leak to the outside world, impairing Salomon's credit standing. There were opponents who lamented the loss of the partner-

ship ethos ("He sold my birthright," complained Lewis Ranieri, whose mortgage securities department was finding its feet). Gutfreund went off on a friend's yacht for several days to commune with the numbers and decide whether he liked the deal. On some level it clearly disturbed him: To the end of his time at the firm he referred to those who worked closely with him as his "partners." In the end, which came on Sunday morning, few voted no. By the time the Phibro deal closed, October 1, 1981, there were virtually no doubters: The bond market was in free fall—the first week in October was the absolute bottom of the worst bear market government bonds had ever seen—and the Phibro deal had become a perfect safety net.

Right after the vote was taken, Gutfreund, Henry Kaufman, and Richard Schmeelk took a helicopter to Southampton to tell Billy, who was utterly surprised but managed to keep his emotions under control for the duration of the meeting, although not much longer. They may or may not have sold Ranieri's birthright, but they definitely had sold Billy's name. He had had an earlier opportunity to take the firm public, as early as 1969 when a delegation from First Boston had come calling on him, Bill Simon, Charlie Simon, and Harry Brown: $70 million, $80 million, Bill Simon recalled. "So much money I couldn't fathom it"—until Billy said deliberately, "This is not our firm to give away." Moreover, Billy was furious that Gutfreund had gotten for himself more than three times as much money as he had gotten for Billy, who not unreasonably believed he had made a greater contribution to the value of the firm. "I should have thought," he told *Business Week* icily, "that those of us who had been here forty years deserved to share in the gain."

Harris finds the comment unfair to Gutfreund. "The fact of the matter is," he said, "that everything was done according to the partnership rules, which were Billy's rules. He had created them. When those rules came back and bit him, he didn't like it." Those rules were that the "investment account" belonged to the partners who were still active, and retiring partners got back only their contributions to that account plus the profits already booked on it, not their share of its market value. Edgar Aronson actually sued for the money he felt Salomon owed him because he was paid off only on the purchase price of the oil and gas assets in the investment account, and Bill Brachfeld never forgave Billy for what Brachfeld considered a cheat on the limited partners. The Phibro deal, Harris argued, was in fact more generous to the retired partners than Billy had been when he was running the show. The executive committee of the firm allocated $10 million from their own share of the proceeds to buy twenty annuities yielding $125,000 a year for ten years for the retired partners, as an ex gratia compensation. Billy was particularly wrong to complain, Harris insisted, because shortly before his own retirement to limited status in 1978, he had arranged to grandfather himself, to write up the book value of the oil and gas properties in the investment account for himself but not for old colleagues like Harry Brown, Charles Simon, and Robert Quinn, who had recently retired. By one informed estimate, Billy had taken $25 million out of his Salomon capital before the $10 million that came to him from the Phibro sale.

But the more Billy thought about what his former partners had done, the angrier he became. Cleary Gottlieb were still the lawyer's for the firm. Billy went to Judge Simon Rifkind of Paul Weiss Rifkind Wharton & Garrison and asked Rifkind to sue for him, but Rifkind told him to calm down. Over the course of the next weeks Billy was bought off rather than brought around. He would retain his secretary and his office at the firm, with its window overlooking his beloved trading room; he would be an honorary chairman; he would be paid $450,000 a year to do nothing; and he would keep his car and driver. And he could continue to criticize the deal, which he did.

Now that the people who had been partners were no longer building wealth but were working for the stockholders in a publicly owned corporation, they had to be paid more to keep them happy. The salaries of the men who had been partners rose to an average of well over $300,000 a year. By 1986 there were more than five hundred officers of Salomon Brothers who made more than half a million dollars a year.

IT'S MONEY MAKES THE WORLD GO ROUND

What did the partners do with the money from the sale to Phibro? Billy liked to point out that a number of them got divorces; while the old partnership agreement had held, they couldn't afford divorces. They bought mansions in the Hamptons, some larger than Billy's; they bought BMWs; they bought co-ops on Fifth Avenue and Park Avenue; some bought cocaine. Dickie Rosenthal bought the plane in which he later died. Ken Lipper went into politics, first as deputy mayor for Ed Koch, then as a self-financing (failed) candidate for president of the City Council. Michael Bloomberg had seed capital for his electronic publishing company; James Wolfensohn, Harold Tanner, Ken Lipper, Morris Offit, and Bobby Bernhard would sooner or later start their own banking enterprises with the proceeds of the Salomon sale.

Many made significant charitable contributions. Wolfensohn became chairman of Carnegie Hall and later Kennedy Center, too. Henry Kaufman endowed a chair at New York University and funded a number of scholarships for graduate study. Morris Offit became a major support and eventually chairman of the Jewish Museum; Charles Simon became vice-chairman and a major contributor to the Museum of the American Indian. Tom Strauss and his wife became patrons of the ballet. Ira Harris endowed an institute for the study of business at the University of Michigan and made large contributions to the Museum of Science and Industry in Chicago. William Voute, who headed the industrial bonds trading department and sat on the Salomon executive committee until he and Gutfreund had a falling-out in 1989, became what John Cardinal O'Connor, speaking at his funeral in St. Patrick's Cathedral in early 1992, described as the greatest benefactor of the charities of the archdiocese in the decade of the 1980s.

Some gambled, at Atlantic City and Vegas—and on the Salomon trading floor, where now the fruits of one's labors went not to one's partners (and somewhat to oneself) but to stockholders far away. At least one of the senior people who worked on the floor in the late 1980s warned that traders betting with each other was undignified or worse. And they all now made their own investments, mostly quite heedless of the dangers of conflict of interest that might arise when they had a stake in the profitability of the companies with which they did business.

Gutfreund acquired the world's most extravagant wife. Riding uptown in the limo with public relations counsel Mel Adams in 1979, he said, "Mel, I've met the most wonderful woman, but, boy, can she spend money!" Prior to Susan, Billy Salomon recalled,

Gutfreund had never drawn his full allowance for the year, always using some of it to build up his capital in the firm. He was also cheap as a manager. Billy remembered him coming to his office waving a piece of paper, a salesman's chit for $60 or so for dinner for two in the early 1970s at "21." "You may want to okay this," he said scowling to Billy. "I won't do it."

It may not have been entirely irrelevant to the sale of the firm that Gutfreund was under money pressure. Even before they were married, it was clear to people who knew him that he could not afford Susan while working for a company that was seeking to build capital from retained earnings. The banker-turned-novelist Michael Thomas remembered a post-Christmas party at what were then Gutfreund's bachelor digs on Park Avenue, where the feature was a giant Christmas tree entirely surrounded by empty Tiffany boxes. When they married, they bought a terraced high-floor apartment in River House, the swankiest of New York swank. Having irritated their River House neighbors, they bought a duplex on Fifth Avenue just north of the Pierre Hotel and had a cantilevered staircase installed to link the two floors. When Solly's Columbus Circle office tower was built, the Gutfreunds' apartment would command the city's best view of it. Susan had its design engraved in a pair of crystal vases that stood before the window through which the skyscraper would be seen.

Once on a whim Susan organized a party to be held at Blenheim Palace, a grateful British royal family's present to the Duke of Marlborough for winning at Waterloo. She sent out invitations that read: Mr. and Mrs. John Gutfreund, At Home, Blenheim Palace. ("Of course, we invited clients," Henry Kaufman commented.) The Gutfreunds were at all the charity balls and among the sponsors of many, including the famous party at the Temple of Dendur in the Metropolitan Museum. In Susan's favor was the fact that Joyce Low had walked out on Gutfreund before he met Susan, that Susan bore him a son (his third), and that at least some of the people who saw them socially liked her quite a lot: "A child of Fort Worth and a very straightforward person," a New Yorker said not without condescension (and somewhat inaccurately; she had been an Air Force brat brought up everywhere and had merely married into Fort Worth). One of the Salomon bankers grudgingly added, "She *did* bring in some business, too."

Corporately, Salomon used the new money to grow in all directions, especially in mortgage finance, investment banking, and international operations. In an atmosphere of declining interest rates, just about everything Salomon touched turned to gold. Miles Slater, taking over Bob Dall's function of raising the firm's short-term money, generated $50 million of profit a year through the first half of the 1980s, trading short-term money-market instruments as a necessary auxiliary of funding the inventory. Various nutty provisions in the 1981 federal tax act (notably the "safe harbor" section that permitted companies to sell the future tax credits they had earned by losing money) opened unique opportunities for the creation of new instruments.

Salomon's profits soared, passing the $400 million mark in 1983, as the economy came off its back while inflation and interest rates fell. But the disinflation that benefited Salomon pummeled Phibro, which saw the value of its inventories fall as commodity prices dropped. And Salomon's traders learned with astonishment that the Phibro traders not only didn't hedge the value of their inventories, they didn't have any notion that they *could* hedge. Trading in oil futures did not begin as a serious matter until 1982, and Phibro knew nothing about it; and while the firm did enter into forward contracts in the metals markets, these tended to be deals tailored for customers.

In an atmosphere where people were no longer working for their own partnership but for a corporation, Gutfreund came under pressure to make sure that his traders and salesmen and executives, who were making the largest contributions to the Phibro-Salomon profits, were paid at least as well as Phibro's people. Ludwig Jesselsen, who had managed Philipp Brothers in the 1960s and 1970s, had been notoriously tight with his bonuses, with the result that his best trader and protégé, Marc Rich, left and then over the years took a number of Phibro's people. Among the results of that trauma was a compensation system by which Phibro traders got a cut of the profits made by their desk, although Tendler said the head of the department—the chief oil or copper or gold or orange juice trader—was always on salary plus bonus in an effort to make sure the trader and his supervisor did not have an identity of interest in artificially puffing up the apparent earnings of the department.

While Tendler was co-chairman of Phibro-Salomon and essentially first among equals, Gutfreund had little chance to find out how Phibro ran. Ray Golden, who was delegated to be liaison with Phibro because he had been a classmate of Tendler's at City College, got to learn only what Tendler wanted to show him. Once Gutfreund had pushed Tendler aside in 1984, Gerald Rosenfeld went in with a mandate from the boss and got the details, which shocked Gutfreund. He proclaimed a commitment to rein in the Phibro system and assure that everybody working for Phibro-Salomon was working for the company rather than for himself.

But by 1985, as the service contracts the old partners had signed began to run out, the established compensation systems at Salomon were no longer viable. The year before, the most profitable part of the firm had been—or had seemed to be—Lewie Ranieri's mortgage finance department. Ranieri had just moved onto the executive committee. Inside and outside the committee he insisted that his people weren't reaping the proper rewards of their work. The day after Salomon's people were given their 1984 bonuses, the people in the mortgage finance department came to work in T-shirts identifying themselves as "Ranieri's Raiders"—and the fat was in the fire.

After all, why *not* pay people more? It was the stockholders' money now, not the partners' money. Employees could not be expected to have the same lifelong loyalty that partners had. Almost everybody of any prominence at Salomon had a standing invitation from Drexel Burnham Lambert to come work for Mike Milken for much more money than Salomon paid. People who made more money for the firm *were* worth more to the stockholders, too. It was wholesome—all those funny young people in their Adam Smith ties at the White House preached the gospel daily, and the message was magnified at *The Wall Street Journal*—to give people incentives.

Clearly there were some problems. The research department served the whole firm; the quality of the computer and telecommunications operation was increasingly important; the efficiency of the cage was not to be sneezed at as a contributor to profits. Even the lawyers and the accountants considered themselves worthy of bonuses. Salesmen had to be measured by volume, not profits. What did you do about the fellow who borrowed the stock or the bonds so Salomon could sell short? That's a highly skilled and indispensable task, but it's a cost center. There were still all the things that Bill Simon insisted on considering when he chaired the compensation committee in the early 1970s—trades by the industrial bonds people made possible because the utilities traders agreed to buy this customer's utilities bonds; underwritings that came in because the commercial paper people were in weekly contact with the company's chief financial officer. The clever treasurer who funded the firm at a profit when long-term rates were higher than short-term rates might be even more valuable in the year when he minimized losses even though short-term rates had become higher than long-term rates. The profitability of the trading operations was a function of how the committee decided to allocate the cost of funds. Government bond inventories were cheap to fund; common stock inventories and mortgage inventories required more capital and higher interest rates on the borrowing. "And," said one of the men who tried to impose some system on Solly in the late 1980s, "nobody ever worried there about capital allocation; the attitude was that there was always capital."

It was the nature of the business that profits varied from year to year within each department. Results were erratically related to how hard people worked or even to how good they were: "One year," Billy remembered, "equities would be duller than hell, but you could measure the effort people made." It was one thing to say, as Wall Street partnerships always had, that incomes were a function of how well the firm as a whole did in a given year. But to say that income would vary wildly department by department, so that some people in the firm would get enormous raises at the same time others got painful cuts, was to ask for more trouble than the incentives could be worth. Very few traders are geniuses over an entire market cycle.

Finally, there was the division within the firm created by the sale of the partnership. "What was done in the Phibro sale," said one of the younger people closest to Gutfreund, "permanently fractured the firm. It created a class warfare between haves and have-nots." Both Billy and Gutfreund had nurtured Salomon's growth over the years by adding partners, sometimes from outside, more often from within the firm. Now the new people and the old people would be on very different footings, but both, each in their own way, would see their fates as far less entwined with that of Salomon Brothers.

Those who were partners prior to October 1, 1981, had been made very rich, far beyond what Salomon could pay to anyone who joined the firm in any capacity after that date. "You monetized the wealth," said one of them; "you harnessed future earning power so you could get the money twice." They had major investments outside the firm, which might take more of their attention than the work they did for Salomon. The second tier of "managing directors," those who had not been made rich by the Phibro deal, had no more loyalty to Salomon than employees have elsewhere to their employers, and maybe less. Paul Mozer, who took over government bonds trading from Craig Coats in 1988, had said shortly before he played games in that market that he hoped soon "to take his chips off the table and live on a boat or move to Florida with his wife."[1] To avoid conflicts in the firm between those who didn't have to work anymore and those who relied on their salaries to become rich, Gutfreund essentially decided to overpay everybody. In Warren Buffett's first report to the Salomon stockholders after he took over as "interim chairman," he noted that "last year [1990] the securities unit [Salomon without Phibro] earned about ten percent on equity capital—far under the average earned by American business—yet 106 individuals who worked for the unit earned a million dollars or more."[2]

And then that didn't work, either, because the people who seemed to generate the highest profits were dissatisfied with any compensation scheme that left anything for anybody else. "In an environment where you try to garner short-term gains," said Henry Kaufman, "there is always the question of whether it's the firm that makes the gains possible or the individual's ingenuity. To trade high-grade securities doesn't take much capital, and you get the illusion that you could get the same results on your own, which is not true. There's an enormous information flow in a place like Salomon; you know what clients want to do. But managing directors become like ballplayers, they become commodity items, and they go where the pay is best."

In late 1989, two years after he quit the Salomon board in anger over Gutfreund's failure to consult him about major decisions, Maurice (Hank) Greenberg of American Insurance Group met with Salomon's Lawrence E. Hilibrand, the biggest money-maker in Solly's mathematically oriented government bond trading department. A mathematician turned not only trader but riverboat gambler, Hilibrand put enormous bets on emerging statistical discrepancies in that market and ran the firm's largest single profit center. Greenberg offered him, in effect, the opportunity to move this department of Salomon to AIG, a casualty-insurance company that was increasingly seeking a player's role in the money markets. Greenberg would supply the infrastructure and the capital, Hilibrand would supply the people, and Hilibrand would share the profits. Hilibrand, thirty-six, with the opportunity of a lifetime, went to Tom Strauss and said he was going to take Greenberg's offer. Strauss panicked and asked whether Hilibrand would stay if Salomon matched it. He then went to Gutfreund, who okayed the deal. Neither Gutfreund's in-house Salomon executive committee nor the Salomon, Inc., board of directors was consulted, although the board had a compensation committee, chaired, as it happened, by Warren Buffett.

Not realizing that Hilibrand's deal was a private arrangement among himself, Strauss, and Gutfreund, the accounting department routinely sent to the executive committee and the board its statements of who had been paid what for his work in 1990. Hilibrand's piece of the profits was about $23.6 million, about a tenth of the money Salomon had made in a poor year for Wall Street. One member of what Gutfreund had renamed "the Office of the Chairman" complained about it, and Gutfreund said, "Well, we had to do these things for Larry." The numbers leaked, of course, and resentment flourished throughout the house. Alhough Paul Mozer had started cheating on the rules of the Treasury bond auctions before January 1991, there were those who believed that his belligerent behavior in the following months was an expression of fury by a young man who thought he was every bit as good as Larry Hilibrand and was paid a paltry $5 million for his year's work in 1990.

What was wrong with the payment to Hilibrand, however, was less the number than the system that produced it. Once a partnership where everybody participated in the firm's successes and failures, Salomon had turned into a loosely structured group of departments separately managed and separately compensated. In

1992 only five of the sixty-two partners who had voted on the Phibro deal eleven years before were still actively involved with Salomon Brothers. The makers of the deal had not just sold the partnership, they had dissolved it.

It was hard enough in the corner-cutting 1980s for established firms to socialize their young to the rules and customs of Wall Street. In Salomon's partnership-turned-corporation, the attitude became one of every man for himself, and the seeds were sown for the bitter crop of 1991.

Chapter 5

THE MYSTERY OF BANKING

"IN THE CORPORATE FINANCE AREA," said Harold Tanner, a dignified and careful banker who was manager of that department for Salomon from 1980 to 1986 and later ran his own firm, "the biggest asset we had was John Gutfreund. He had a prodigious memory. He'd be sitting at the managing partner's desk in The Room, and you'd bring somebody down the escalator to be in The Room— clients liked that. He'd remember the guy, he'd remember his wife, his wife's name, he'd remember any deals they had done together."

Tanner recalled something else, too, from the year before he decided to join his fate to Salomon's, when he was with Blyth Eastman Dillon. "We had earned our way into a Hilton Hotels financing," he said. "We were going to do forty percent of it, Salomon was going to do sixty percent. Gutfreund called and said, 'If you're good enough to take forty percent, you're good enough to be our partners. We'll do the deal fifty-fifty, no backstabbing the other firm.'"

Miles Slater, later co-manager of "strategic risk" for Bankers Trust, supervised several financing departments for Salomon from 1980 to 1986 before he went to London to become president and

CEO of Salomon Brothers International and to see if anybody could control the London office. Slater remembered that "Gutfreund could walk into a room of fifty people, sense the mood of the room, and immediately pick out the man you wanted to talk to. He was the best calling guy I've ever seen. Once the governor of one of the oil states came to town—this was during the oil boom, and we were trying to sell him Salomon for his cash-management. We met him at the Regency Hotel. I had a presentation for him and began to lay it out, and I felt John's hand on my knee. 'Miles,' he said, 'the governor's not going to understand this. Why don't you let me explain it.' He'd never looked at the proposal, but by the time he was through, the governor signed on."

A man working for a Japanese-owned securities house once had a delegation from the home office to squire around New York, and among the sights that interested them was The Room at Salomon, and perhaps a chance to meet Mr. Gutfreund, the King of Wall Street. An appointment was arranged, and Gutfreund was graciousness itself, as formal as his Japanese guests. This was the sort of thing he hated, but the feeling among those who worked for him was that whatever he had to do, if it didn't involve choosing among people, he would do it well.

Although Gutfreund's reputation was that of the demon trader, controlling all the desks by force of personality, intimidation, and foul language, his dream for Salomon—it was Billy's dream, too—was always that the firm would become a major player in the world of investment bankers. And for those who went back as far as Gutfreund did, Salomon's tragedy was that never, even in the years when it was the largest underwriter of securities in the world, did it establish status in the world of investment banking. "We *never* had the acceptance of a Morgan Stanley or a First Boston," said Dale Horowitz, still executive vice-president in 1992, thinking back over thirty-seven years with Salomon. "We never had the relationships, we never had the confidence that people would stick by us." And that was true. General Motors hired Salomon to explore possible acquisitions, and it was Salomon that came up with the idea of buying Ross Perot's EDS; but when the time came to negotiate with Perot, others were consulted. Salomon, its clients felt, understood prices, not values. From 1962 when he went to Salomon's "syndicate department,"

Gutfreund put more time and work and hope into Solly's efforts to catch banking clients than into any other activity. In 1978, Felix Rohatyn of Lazard Freres said of Salomon that "they have the competence and the capital, but they may have to buy the three-piece suits."[1] In 1985 when *Business Week* anointed him, Gutfreund thought he had his three-piece suit, but the world stripped it from him; in 1991 he thought he had another. But in fact there was no three-piece suit: It was the emperor's new clothes.

Salomon's efforts to enter the investment banking business did not by any means begin with Gutfreund or even with Billy. The first time the firm came to public prominence was in connection with a securities offering as far back as 1935. The New Deal's Securities Acts were freshly minted, and the official position of Wall Street was that they were unworkable. All that disclosure, who needed it? And the rules about prospectuses and when you could offer what to the customer, not to mention the Glass-Steagall strictures that took the commercial banks out of the underwriting business. There was, in short, an investment bankers' strike. In 1934 no major New York investment house brought an issue to market, and the total issuance of bonds and notes nationally was only $456 million (as against more than $3.4 billion in 1932).

Quite apart from any questions of expansion following the bottom of the Depression, companies wanted to get out from under the obligations of outstanding bonds that had been sold when interest rates were much higher than they were in the deflationary 1930s. Some of these old bonds were "callable"—that is, the issuer could redeem them on a few months' notice at a price usually about $103 or $104 for $100 face value—but the companies couldn't raise the money. In 1935, Salomon's Ned Holsten made a deal with Swift & Co., then the largest meat-packing company in the country, to bring out a $43 million issue of 3¾ percent bonds to pay back Swift's outstanding 5 percent obligations. Salomon was not the "underwriter" as Wall Street understood that term—it did not buy and then resell these bonds to its customers. Instead, the firm was Swift's agent, promising only to sell what paper it could. For this service Salomon charged $4 per $1,000 bond sold, or four-tenths of 1 percent, by contrast with normal Wall Street markups of $40 per $1,000, or 4 percent, for underwriting services.

Soon thereafter the investment bankers halted their strike, and for 1935 as a whole bond issues went back over $2 billion. Salomon got another $50 million of this business when Holsten acted as agent for a Socony-Vacuum 3 percent bond issue, but the New Deal days were a time of government-approved price-fixing, and the established bankers brought a complaint of price-cutting against Salomon before the tribunal of the recently formed National Association of Securities Dealers. Arthur Salomon was dead, Herbert was ill, and Percy hated a fight (as did Holsten), and Solly got out of the investment banking business.

Still, Salomon was in constant contact with all the insurance companies and bank trust departments, and every so often the Wall Street houses that did underwriting found it useful to have Solly salesmen working for their "syndicate" when they brought out a bond issue. The decision to participate was made in a "statistical department," largely as a function of the price of the new issue with relation to the prices of other bonds the house was trading, although the salesmen would also be asked whether they scented any appetite for this stuff among their customers. Then a small "syndicate department" negotiated the commissions Salomon would receive for selling its piece of the deal to its customers. The head of the syndicate department was a dour Dutchman named Theodor van Glahn, a tiger in tearing apart salesmen's expense accounts ("I see your hotel bill includes an item for valet services. Do you think Salomon Brothers should pay you for pressing your pants?"). He had considerable time to think about such things, because the department participated in only two or three deals a month.

In 1962, Billy took Gutfreund out of the municipal bonds department and put him into this syndicate department. As Teddy Low's son-in-law and one of the more presentable younger people in the firm, Gutfreund would be good at working with the establishment houses. Salomon now had enough capital to participate not just in the selling groups but as one of the contributors to the pool of funds that bought a new issue and ran the risk of successfully distributing it. Generally speaking, the lead underwriter decided which firms should take which pieces, a decision expressed by the "bracket" in which the firm was listed in the "tombstone" ad announcing the new issue. Gutfreund's job was to negotiate larger pieces for Salomon on the issues Salomon wished to take and to get out of the syndicates on issues Salomon didn't wish to take, without upsetting the lead managers. What he was really doing, said someone who worked in that department, was "clawing nickels and dimes and quarters from the syndicate managers."

Not long after Gutfreund took this job, Salomon for the first time since Holsten's aborted venture became a major player in a major underwriting. AT&T had a $250 million issue pending, very large for that time, and two syndicates, one led by First Boston and one by Morgan Stanley, were competing for the business. Salomon was in the First Boston syndicate. The Cuban missile crisis struck, and the Morgan Stanley syndicate fell apart. There was some feeling at AT&T and indeed at Morgan Stanley that the issue should be withdrawn. Billy Salomon, who was in daily contact with the Federal Reserve Bank of New York, urged that the issue stay on track to avoid panicking an already nervous market, and offered to pick up $25 million—three times its budgeted share—for Salomon's account. In the end Salomon distributed $50 million and made a considerable profit as well as earning brownie points with the Fed and First Boston.

Wall Street houses wanted to do underwriting for the same reason Willie Sutton wanted to rob banks, because that's where the money was. Underwriters' markups on new securities issues (over and above the fees the investment bankers can charge for drawing up the issues) ran 1 percent on bonds for well-known issuers and 3 percent and up on stocks, both involving large chunks of money. Salomon had no expertise in drawing up securities issues and virtually no established relationships with borrowers. Seventeen big houses dominated the issuance of securities in the United States—collusively, the Department of Justice had charged in the late 1940s in a famous losing antitrust case. Salomon was a supplicant at their table.

What Salomon brought to the underwriting feast, obviously, was "placing power." The fight in the 1960s was over the share of underwriting profits that should be kept by the people with the friends in high places at the corporations that issued the paper as against the share that should be available to the people whose customers bought the stuff. The Public Utility Holding Company Act of 1935 authorized the SEC to require the nation's utilities to put their securities up for public bidding, and the commission did so in 1941. For such issues the leading syndicate manager became Halsey, Stuart & Co., a Chicago firm that was almost as much of a maverick as Salomon and that went from managing a 1 percent share of public offerings in 1940 to a 29 percent share in 1948.[2] Salomon did a lot of business with Halsey, Stuart. When Gutfreund made partner in 1963 and was put in charge of the syndicate department, his mission from Billy was to get Salomon co-manager status with Halsey, Stuart on issues where Solly distributed as large a share of the bonds as Halsey itself. Gutfreund tried this and failed.

Salomon was not alone in feeling that the distributors were being cheated of their fair share of the proceeds from underwritings. Merrill Lynch had an enormous franchise with people who bought lots of utility bonds and stocks; Lehman Brothers had institutional connections that Morgan Stanley needed but would not pay for; Blyth & Co., a San Francisco firm, had West Coast customers that the New York firms could not touch without Blyth's help. With Salomon these firms formed what Wall Street promptly called the "Fearsome Foursome," which pushed back the Halsey, Stuart franchise and began to infiltrate the negotiated-bid business of the established houses, claiming that because they were more closely in touch with the customers, they could price new stocks and bonds better for the benefit of the issuers. By 1964, Salomon was in the "bulge bracket"—the upper tier of the firms listed in the tombstone ads. With $874 million of new issues managed or co-managed by Salomon that year, it had become the sixth largest underwriter of corporate issues in the United States. Salomon now became the manager of a number of issues awarded by public bidding, and Gutfreund came into his own. "He runs syndicate meetings," a colleague said with awe, "the way the Shah of Iran runs Iran."[3]

Gutfreund's contacts were with his fellow underwriters and the customers; Salomon did not have relationships with corporate America. Indeed, the first place Salomon achieved status as an investment banker was Canada, and that was the work of one man—Richard Schmeelk, who had come to the firm in 1941 from high school. On returning from service in the Navy in World War II, he had worked his way through a range of clerical jobs until a vacancy in the sales department gave him a chance to see whether Canadian companies might be interested in short-term financing through the American commercial paper market. Careful, bulky, looking more like a prizefighter than a banker, slow of speech, a long-headed man sympathetic to other people's concerns, Schmeelk made a hit in Canada, where both corporations and the provincial governments were happy to find an alternative to the tight little island of the four nationwide Canadian banks.

The 1970s were a time when the province of Ontario was running a big-league deficit associated with the infrastructure needs of a very rapidly growing economy. The feeling in Toronto was that Drexel, Harriman, the province's American bankers, were not earning their large fees, and half a dozen American firms were invited to compete for the business. Schmeelk, who was already there on regular visits to organize commercial paper offerings, brought Sidney Homer and Henry Kaufman with him and won the business, partly by offering to do it for less. The tombstones paired Salomon with Wood Gundy, the largest of the Canadian houses, and it became an extremely happy partnership.

All the other business essentially sprang from the work with Ontario. Schmeelk understood, said one of his Canadian friends, that being the banker for the province was like being the banker for royalty: It wasn't important to make money on the government account, because the entree to other business was the profit. "Salomon's deals with Ontario," said a Canadian admirer, "helped the other provinces, too, because their bonds priced off Ontario's." And the private issues followed: First Bell Canada, then Canadian Pacific, Canadian National Railways, Imperial Oil, Ontario Hydro, Quebec Hydro, and five other provinces. Schmeelk won for Salomon the position as leading U.S. underwriter for the largest public and private enterprises in Canada, including in the end the national government itself. "We came of age as an investment banker in Canada," Schmeelk said proudly, "and we parlayed that to the United States and Europe."

Having established himself with price, Schmeelk maintained Salomon's Canadian position by relationships. "Morgan Stanley," said a man now retired from senior office in Wood Gundy, the largest Canadian brokerage house, "opened an office in Montreal headed by a good guy named Larry Parker. They couldn't do one, two,

The three original Salomon Brothers (left to right, Arthur, Herbert, and Percy) in their original office at 80 Broadway in 1911, with the indispensable tools of their trade—the telephone for taking orders, hats on head for making the rounds to fill them.

The elegant wood-paneled partners' dining room in 1968, in what was otherwise clumsy quarters in a scruffy building at 60 Wall Street. Billy Salomon, Percy's son, sits firmly at the head of the table; Sidney Homer, with mustache, the great historian of interest rates who gave the firm status and ideas, is second from the right.

Billy Salomon with trader Bill Brachfeld, in 1968, when prices were still
posted manually on a giant board.
By then, Salomon was the world's
biggest bond trader, and its PR man
was defining a "liquid bond" as a
bond on which Salomon would
make a bid.

"The Room"—the Salomon trading room—at One New York Plaza, the first
of its kind, in 1973. The paper Solly's traders bought and sold here each day
was worth more than all the stocks traded on the New York Stock Exchange.

5

John Gutfreund and Billy Salomon in 1978, after the announcement that
Gutfreund would become managing partner—a decision Billy would later
regret.

6

John and Susan Gutfreund at one of the many charity balls they attended in the 1980s. Gutfreund looked as indulgently on his wife's spectacular extravagances as he did on the tactics by which his often brilliant but not always scrupulous juniors made money for the firm.

7

James Wolfensohn, his five years as a Salomon partner behind him when Gutreund sold the firm to a listed corporation in 1981, found no task too small in a new role as chairman of Washington's Kennedy Center.

8

SOS, the Sons of Salomon, at Dick Schmeelk's 1990 party for the firm's alumni. Schmeelk, who had been head of the firm's investment banking, is at far left; Bill Simon, who had gone on from Salomon to be Secretary of the Treasury and progenitor of the scandalously profitable leveraged buy-out, is second from left; Charles Simon, the best bond salesman ever but also the intellectual who brought Sidney Homer and Henry Kaufman to Salomon, is at far right.

9

Players in the May notes caper and its aftermath: at top, trader Paul Mozer and his lawyer Stanley Arkin at the federal courthouse in New York; below right, Tom Strauss, Salomon's president, formerly the head of the government bond department, crossing the street from the new Salomon headquarters at the World Trade Center; below left, hedge fund operator Mike Steinhardt at his desk, perhaps contemplating coups like his hugely profitable position in the May 1991 squeeze.

11

10

After the deluge, Warren Buffett, the legendary investor and major stock-holder of Salomon Brothers, tells a Senate Committee how it all happened and argues that it won't happen again. At the government's insistence, he made a clean sweep; Gutfreund and company were out.

three in Canada despite their relationships with the U.S. parents of Canadian subsidiaries, because they couldn't beat Schmeelk. And all he would do was fly up for the day, never even take a hotel room overnight. We used to tease him that Canada got nothing out of him." William G. Davis, premier of Ontario from 1971 to 1985, remembered that Schmeelk "had more than just a business interest in what he was doing; he had an interest in Canada. It wasn't just a question of taking fees; he got to know the business community here, and he made friends."

The Canadians also came down to New York for meetings with the ratings agencies and for closings on deals that involved U.S. purchasers. Davis remembered being taken to a Jets game and Schmeelk's astonishment that he was a Dolphins fan. Gutfreund himself would sit in on the pricing sessions just before the paper was to be taken to market, and the Canadians came to feel comfortable with the Salomon organization. "When you're working for a large organization," said Ted Medland, who was with both Wood Gundy and the provincial government, "you learn to talk saying 'we,' not 'I.' To this day when I hear an individual saying 'I' can do this or that, I look at him strangely, wondering, Don't you know whose expertise makes this possible? Do you think we'd be interested if we thought it was just *you* making the promise?" By 1981, Salomon's underwriting of Canadian issues was running at a rate approaching $3 billion a year.

It took a long time for Schmeelk's accomplishments to register fully in New York, partly because Smutny shortly before leaving had made him a protégé. Recognizing the boom in Salomon's Canadian commercial paper business, Smutny gave Schmeelk what Smutny said was the largest raise anybody had ever received at Salomon. Schmeelk was nobody's rocket scientist, although he was a supporter of their work for the firm ("The quants," he said, "are value added"), but he was a source of unquestioned solidity within the firm and with corporate clients.

For five of the six years Schmeelk was head of worldwide corporate finance, Salomon was the number-one raiser of capital in the United States. Schmeelk was appointed to the Phibro-Salomon executive committee in 1981 and served his five years there with mounting concern "about the practices in Solly's growing mortgage finance department, the leadership in the municipals area, and the inability to make tough decisions at the top." He quit the firm in 1987, joining Peter Gottsegen, who had left Salomon's London shop, to start a merchant bank funded by both Canadian and U.S. pension funds to make investments in Canada. Before leaving Salomon, as his personal contribution to the cause of continued Canadian unity, Schmeelk donated a million dollars to start a Canadian foundation that would give two Anglophone Canadian college graduates a year's graduate study at a French-speaking university in Quebec, and two Francophone Canadian college graduates a year's graduate study at an English-speaking university in Ontario. Some forty-four fellows have gone through the program.

In 1990, Schmeelk invited seventy of his former partners no longer with the firm to a party he called a reunion of the "Sons of Salomon," and led by Billy, virtually all of them came. "You must remember that most of these were people who owed everything they had to Salomon," said someone who was there. "You should have seen the camaraderie," said Billy. It was an epiphanic experience for even the most cynical of them, and Billy himself tried to make a tradition of it the next year, but the spontaneity was gone and the party by all reports was far less sparkling.

THE GUERRILLA GROUP AND THE FINEST HOUR

There was another area where Salomon had relationships that earned money year after year after year: municipal bonds. From the mid-1960s to 1987, Salomon was the nation's largest underwriter of municipal bonds. Through almost all that period the leader of the department was Dale Horowitz, a Columbia Law School graduate (not the expected background for a trader), a man with faith in friendship. The invasion of the municipals underwriting market had begun as an effort to copy Gutfreund's success with corporations, through the formation of what Bill Simon and Horowitz called a similar "Guerrilla Group" in bidding for municipal bonds: Merrill again, Simon's old employer Weeden, and First National City Bank of New York (later Citibank). The values here far exceeded immediate profit, because the same public officers in charge of marketing a state or municipal debt issue were usually involved in investing the money of the state's or the municipality's pension funds. Salomon's best customers for bonds were often Salomon's clients in the tax-exempt markets. Horowitz, an organization man who related to other organization men, was splendidly suited for the work. He was a founder and later the chairman of the Public Securities Association, and was serving as the chairman of the Securities Industries Association in 1991 when the firm was hung out to dry for misbehavior in the government bonds market. Despite the skittishness of the industry in the face of Salomon's problems, there were no calls for his resignation and he completed his term.

Salomon's finest hour came in the New York City financial crisis of 1975 when everybody else left the burning bridge. The cowards were right, too. The city had been seeking to defraud the public by selling so-called tax anticipation notes that supposedly were a kind of bridge loan to keep the city going until unpaid taxes were collected. There was no backing at all for some tens of millions of dollars of those notes, because the taxes for which they were supposedly a temporary substitute had in fact been paid, and the city was selling notes on the grounds that, after all, it needed the money. Horowitz chaired the committee that was the liaison with the city administration. Not without trepidation, he committed Salomon to be manager with Morgan Guaranty of the first issue of notes by the Municipal Assistance Corporation that Governor Hugh Carey and Felix Rohatyn of Lazard Freres had put together out of cardboard and glue to sustain the city's falling financial structure. The bonds were not salable even at a 9 percent yield triply tax exempt, and Salomon took a $5 million loss. Both Billy and Gutfreund supported Salomon's close identification with this expensive assist in the effort to rescue the city, although the firm never got much public recognition of its altruistic loyalty.

Horowitz was close to Gutfreund. They had come to Salomon at just about the same time, almost the only people their age in the firm who had been to good colleges, and they had both worked in municipals. In the mid-1980s, Gutfreund asked Horowitz to handle various problems with the bright juniors—from Lewis Ranieri's impenetrable bookkeeping to the disruptive arrogance of the young banking department head Lee Kimmel. These were tasks Horowitz was temperamentally quite unsuited to perform.

The other side of this coin was that he and the younger people he was supposed to control became and remained friends, to the fury of the members of the executive committee who had brought the complaints against them—but perhaps to the satisfaction of Gutfreund, who probably had turned these personnel matters over to Horowitz precisely because he didn't want to do anything about them.

Horowitz claimed his rewards in the form of managing directorships and good salaries for what was generally considered his municipal department, even after he had turned over its day-to-day management to someone else. The corporate bankers were furious because they felt he had blocked a directorship for one of their best young people (David Schulte, who departed Salomon to start his own shop and later did ventures with the vulture investor Sam Zell) unless a far less able man in the municipals department was also made a managing director. Trading results in municipals were mediocre, and competition pushed down the spreads on municipal bond underwritings. The department bloated, began to carry excessive inventories, and its earnings ceased to justify the capital it consumed. In the end the municipals department would disappear, but Horowitz himself would remain; indeed, Horowitz, still the apostle to the Gentiles in the world of Treasury policy-making and trade associations, remained after Gutfreund was gone.

STAR BANKERS

Billy first reached out for star players in banking in 1968 when he lured Ira Harris away from Blair & Co. Born in the Bronx, Harris was a graduate of the University of Michigan and came to deal-making from stock brokerage; he credited his liberation from that trade to a cold call he made to a customer, an older man who turned out to be one of the great stock pickers of his time. When he was twenty-five, Blair sent him to head its office in Chicago, where he found a home. ("Harris was never really *Salomon*," Billy sniffed. "He was always more *Chicago*.") He took a considerable pay cut to come to Salomon, because he thought Blair was going nowhere and Salomon was on the march.

Harris liked to make a splash and lived high on the hog. Among his promotions for the firm was an annual Salomon golf tournament for the Chicago financial market; at one tournament he was observed blasting a ball out of a sand trap while talking into a telephone hung over his shoulder. (He says a photographer trapped him into the picture.) A man of great charm with a fine talent for discerning what other people wanted out of a relationship, he liked to say that the investment banker's role was to absorb the hostility the parties felt for each other in the negotiations, so they could come to their agreement and remain friends. Gutfreund put Harris, too, on the executive committee—and, of course, eventually made him the negotiator of the deal that sold the firm.

One man came out of the sales department to major status in the banking area: Jon Rotenstreich, who had joined Salomon in 1965, and in 1975 became the first head of what was called corporate finance, the department that structured new kinds of securities issues. He was paired with Schmeelk as head of underwriting, and the two men got along easily. Rotenstreich's insight was that with the end of fixed commissions in the brokerage business, activities that had once been frowned on as poaching other people's customers would come to be regarded as marketing to increase one's market share. He thought the vice of the sale to Phibro was that Harris had sold 100 percent of the firm, leaving the former partners who had lived and died by Salomon's success with no great reason to care how well the firm did. Rotenstreich built Salomon's relations with several of the truly giant corporations, especially IBM.

Billy's and Gutfreund's drive into banking outside Chicago had begun in 1969 with the hiring of Daniel I. Sargent, a banker who had been a vice-president of the Philadelphia & Reading Corp. Sargent brought in a number of railroad clients and (with Kaufman) won leading positions with Manufacturers Hanover and Bank of America, neither of which, however, was issuing many securities at the time. Sargent also, with help from Gutfreund and Billy, brought a number of young people from other firms—Ken Lipper from Lehman, Peter Gottsegen from Kuhn Loeb, Warren Foss from First Boston, and Lee Kimmel straight out of the training program at Smith Barney.

By far the most important of those who came from outside the firm in the 1970s was James D. Wolfensohn, an Australian-turned-Englishman recruited by Billy from the Schroeder Bank in London in 1976 at the age of forty-two. Edgar Aronson, the head of Salomon's London office, had known Wolfensohn since he was with Darling & Co. in Sydney; then or later, the two seem to have developed a certain antipathy, which persists. Billy had known him in New York when for six years, while still in his thirties, he had been head of Schroeder's New York bank. Wolfensohn had also done some work for Laurence Tisch, who through Ira Harris was a major Salomon client. The top job at Schroeder in London was up for grabs and wasn't going to go to Wolfensohn ("It's hard to know which was the worse handicap," said Aronson, "that he was Australian or that he was Jewish"). Wolfensohn came to Salomon "with impeccable credentials," he said, under an extraordinary guarantee from Billy and from Gutfreund that he would be put on the firm's executive committee soon after he received his partnership (which pro forma was delayed a few months). He also said that his arrangement with Billy was that "I would come either for five years or forever, and I would make that decision later." Nobody else knew about this arrangement, and when Wolfensohn disappeared immediately after the sale to Phibro, his five years up and his large partnership share being cashed in, there was a certain amount of resentment around the office.

Wolfensohn did wonders for Salomon's image in London. In June 1977, when England celebrated the Queen's Jubilee, Solly held London's best party, with a trio of Vladimir Ashkenazy, Itzhak Perlman, and Lynn Harrell playing chamber music for three hundred invited guests at the Covent Garden Opera House, followed by a black-tie supper on the balcony-level bar. Both New York and Washington have reason to be grateful to Wolfensohn, a cellist good enough to have studied with the late Jacqueline du Pre, for his support of their musical institutions. In New York he also chaired the original committee that preserved the splendid old Customs House, no longer needed by the government, from demolition for the construction of what would have become yet another unoccupied downtown office building. And he did one large and extremely important piece of work for Salomon (and the government): the Chrysler bailout, into which he put, he said, two whole years of his life. It involved negotiating with unions, two national governments, state governments, creditors, and indeed other automobile companies (Wolfensohn's first plan was for a merger with Ford), and at the end "raising $2 billion at a time when a couple of billion dollars looked like a lot of money."

But he had been hired to manage a department. "The reason we brought him in," Gutfreund said at the time, "was to manage and organize our corporate finance effort. The fact that he had a world-wide presence was of value to us, but it was an extra."[4] And managing, he didn't do. A rather fey presence, soft-spoken and apparently shy, Wolfensohn was generally regarded at Salomon as a better salesman of himself than of the firm. "You went to a meeting," one fellow banker recalled, "and Wolfensohn never said a word. But at the end he'd go up to the client and say, 'There are some things I'd like to talk with you about, but I didn't think this was the right forum. I'll call you later.' " It was Wolfensohn who first proclaimed in the United States, in 1977, an end to relation-ship banking. "Mr. Wolfensohn," Ann Crittenden reported in *The New York Times*, "suggests that personal client relationships are far less important in investment banking than they once were, and Salomon's rapid emergence in world finance tends to bear him out. To a much greater extent nowadays the best deal available— rather than old loyalties—determines who gets a client's busi-ness."[5]

Wolfensohn was always an adviser more than he was a banker. In 1992 when he and Jacob Rothschild of England joined to form a small mid-Atlantic bank (of which Wolfensohn's partner Paul Volcker would be chairman), the *Financial Times* rather unpleas-antly noted that Wolfensohn had finally decided to be a decision-maker and commit money for which he was responsible rather than just ideas. He and Harris were friends, but had different styles; indeed, he said later that if Harris had not been based eight hundred miles away, he would never have gone to work for Salomon. In any event he was gone on the day after the Phibro deal closed. In effect he was never replaced. Talented bankers came to work for Salomon in the succeeding years, but there was never again anyone in New York with Wolfensohn's status and access. Billy Salomon thought that Gutfreund considered Wolfen-sohn a possible rival and got rid of him for that reason. Others agreed, seeing Wolfensohn's departure as a template for the removal later in the decade of men their followers might consider better leaders than Gutfreund.

THE SECOND WORST LEVERAGED BUY-OUT IN HISTORY

The event of the 1980s in banking, from Salomon's point of view, was Rule 415, by which the SEC in 1982 approved what was called "shelf registration" of securities issues. Prior to Rule 415 a corporation wishing to sell stocks or bonds to the public had to prepare a registration statement specifically for this issue and distribute a "prospectus" based on that registration statement to every purchaser before selling it. The underwriter's name was part of the prospectus, and the underwriter was the man who planned the issue. These prospectuses were issued as "red herrings" with a warning printed in red that the SEC had not yet agreed they could be used as selling documents; within thirty days of the SEC's announcement that the registration statement had been declared "effective" (which did not mean they vouched for the *accuracy* of the statement), the securities had to be priced and sold, or the entire process had to be started all over again.

Now, under Rule 415, the SEC would accept a registration statement for this *kind* of security for this issuer, requiring only that the financial statements be updated as necessary, and the issuer could at any time sell to the public. The work of drawing up the terms of the issue and the registration statement could be separated from the work of underwriting the paper, and the issuer could simply solicit bids from underwriters whenever it wanted to come to market. Everything would be pricing.

Although Rule 415 would mean that firms such as Salomon and Merrill Lynch, which still had limited relationships with corporations, would get much more business than they used to have, Gutfreund stood with the industry in opposing the new rule. "The so-called need for instant access to the market," he said in a statement to the SEC, "what I call the window philosophy, is a confusion of priorities. The question is not whether an issuer pays a little more or less for his capital. The question is whether he has a sound business venture."[6] Rule 415 was undoubtedly calculated to be most helpful to firms such as E. F. Hutton, where Reagan's SEC chairman John Shad had been a relatively unsuccessful solicitor of underwriting business. But it was essentially an extension of the principles Salomon had advocated since the 1960s. The Fearsome Foursome was down to a Daring Duo, but they had won.

Except that what they had won, as Gutfreund saw, wasn't worth much. Even before Rule 415 was adopted, Rotenstreich on his way out to be treasurer of IBM gave Gutfreund a four-page analysis of what open bidding for already registered securities issues would mean for the markups that investment houses could charge on bond underwritings for already established companies. The margins on plain vanilla underwriting of bond issues would not yield enough return to pay the salaries, the rent, and a return on the capital that would have to be allocated to hold the bonds during the selling period.

There were ways around the problem. One was to concentrate on Harris's sort of mergers-and-acquisitions practice, where the investment bankers earned fees without committing capital. Another was to be inventive in adding bells and whistles to the bonds. The last would be to compete with Drexel Burnham in the "high-yield" or junk bond business, structuring "leveraged buyouts" and mergers where the acquirer paid cash for the acquired, raising the cash by mortgaging its future earnings as heavily as the market would bear.

Harris continued to be a success in the M&A business and Salomon did a lot of it, but outside Harris's Chicago shop the success ratio was only fair. Twice the firm was in the middle of disastrous takeovers, once when Solly (and counsel Martin Lipton) okayed the Getty Museum's decision to sell its shares of Getty Oil to Texaco despite a prior agreement in principle to sell to Pennzoil, and even more dramatically when it advised William Agee of Bendix on strategies in his bungled bid for Martin Marietta, which responded by making a bid for Bendix. When the dust settled, Salomon was out of the picture (although it received $3 million for its labors) and Agee was out of a job (although he had a golden parachute of $825,000 a year for five years). Paul Hoffman quoted an anonymous banker as saying, "The whole thing doesn't make any great point except: Don't hire Salomon."[7] Salomon's point man in the Bendix affair was Jay Higgins, who was later (on Martin Lipton's recommendation) appointed to Gut-freund's Office of the Chairman after all the stronger people in the underwriting department had left or been removed.

The bells and whistles business, on the other hand, came nat-urally and was a great contributor of clients. Salomon's areas of expertise in bond trading had always included convertibles and bonds with attached warrants, which permitted their owners to purchase the stock of the company that had issued the bond at what could be a bargain price. Homer's book, *Inside the Yield Book,* was a treasure trove of suggestions for "adding value" to debt instruments. Europe especially needed such instruments, al-though it wasn't necessarily easy to sell the Europeans. Salomon's Peter Gottsegen, number two in the London office, liked to say that selling financial innovation on the Continent was like selling shoes in Africa: There were lots of people who needed shoes, but they didn't *want* shoes.

In 1980, thanks in part to Bobby Bernhard's and Edgar Aron-son's personal connections—which were reinforced by Gut-freund's flying trips on his best behavior to cultivate the socialist government—Salomon won a mandate from Sweden to under-write the first "jumbo" Eurodollar bond, $1.2 *billion*. The plan Salomon sold the Swedes involved the use of warrants to reduce interest rates. Rates were high in the Eurodollar market in 1980 and were expected to come down. The warrants Solly attached to the Swedish bond would be rather like the old domestic convert-ible bonds in that they would give the purchaser of the bond the right to buy another security. This of course would not be stock (you can't own stock in a country) but more bonds, at any time, at the 1980 rate. For those who believed interest rates were com-ing down, this option was worth money. To get the option, buyers of the Swedish bond were willing to accept a lower rate on the initial issue, just as the buyers of traditional convertible bonds were willing to pay with lower rates because they were also buy-ing an option on the stock.

Thereafter Salomon put its full resources of cleverness into constructing hybrid securities that could yield the banker more than a simple markup. Zero-coupon bonds and their variants, floating-rate notes, interest-rate swaps, currency swaps, zoos full of strange financial instruments, cross-breedings of warrants and

options and futures and bonds flew from the drawing boards on
the forty-fifth floor of One New York Plaza to amaze both corporations and institutional investors. "We were very good at what
we did," said one of the young veterans nostalgically. Robert Scully
and Warren Foss were particularly fertile with these ideas, many
of which came from spending some part of every day in The Room
and studying what the traders were doing. Salomon salesmen became masters of the art of marketing these things. Scully and Foss
became the head of the firm's private placement division, which
marketed such paper directly to institutional investors without
the cost of going through the registration statement requirements
of the SEC.

But the profits from even the most difficult to understand of
such instruments were nothing like the profits Mike Milken was
making for Drexel (and for himself) in the junk bond business.
The youngsters in the firm were envious and felt their elders had
lost their balls because they had made so much money selling the
firm. William Voute, the chief bond trader, and president Tom
Strauss, who liked to be up to date, thought Solly should not miss
the informing market of the time. But most of the executive committee was lined up against junk bonds: Kaufman didn't like this
business, Schmeelk didn't like it, Ranieri didn't like it, Harris didn't
like it. Foss, supported by the apparently conservative Harold
Tanner, finally convinced Gutfreund—provided, Gutfreund said,
that he wouldn't have to meet these people.

The first junk bond deal Salomon wrote and marketed was an
LBO for Revco drugstores by the management of the company.
LBO, or leveraged buy-out, means that insiders buy up the company's stock from existing stockholders, financing the deal with
the proceeds of bank loans and bonds issued by the company
itself. Because there is little cushion of stockholders' equity between the claims of the bondholders and the value of the company, the bonds can be sold only by offering a very high interest
rate; they are thus called "high-yield bonds" by the Mike Milkens
of the world and "junk bonds" by outside observers. The insiders
not only pocket the payments for their own stock in the company,
they become its sole and exclusive owners. If it turns out the
business can service the debt taken on to buy-out the stockholders, the insiders can then take it public again, selling some fraction

of the 100 percent they acquired in the buy-out and pocketing *those* proceeds. Meanwhile, the investment bankers and the lawyers who put the deal together receive millions of dollars in fees paid out of the deal.

Revco was the result of a number of mergers that had created a group of retail operations (mostly but not entirely drugstores). The leveraged buy-out was the least defensible of its kind, having no purpose other than to enrich the officers of the company (and the stockholders: the "insider trading" scandals of the 1980s grew out of the enormous jolt that LBOs and acquisitions gave the stocks). Bankers defend such business with the argument that the officers of the company who are buying it will be better managers if they reap all the rewards of their labors. But this argument could not be offered in the Revco LBO because, as reported to the examiner in the bankruptcy that followed the deal, the judgment of Salomon was that the officers were poor managers and would fail.

The deal was eighteen months in negotiations, during which time the operating performance of the Revco stores fell further and further behind projections. No changes were made in the projections for the future even though past performance had made the numbers impossible. In the original plans a number of subsidiaries were to be sold prior to the buy-out to reduce the amount of debt the deal would have to carry, but when it turned out that they couldn't be sold for anything like the projected prices, Salomon simply increased the total debt in the deal—to $1.7 billion. The Revco deal closed on December 29, 1986, and the new Revco was in bankruptcy less than two years later. By general agreement in the trade, the Revco LBO was the second worst junk-bond deal in history, pride of place being retained by the Interco merger scheme organized and touted by Bruce Wasserstein and Joseph Perella of First Boston. The report of the Revco bankruptcy examiner told a convincing story of near-total incompetence.

Solly developed a computer model to analyze this LBO but left out seasonality factors—the company's need for additional working capital to stock the stores for the Christmas season. One of the bank lenders to the deal—Marine Midland—did an analysis that indicated the firm would not have the money to stock the stores, because all its revenues would have to go to service the debt. "An internal memorandum of Marine," wrote the examiner appointed by the bankruptcy court, "shows that twice as much had to be realized from divestitures as originally had been projected to cover required debt service, and that Salomon had projections that showed a similar need."[8] The examiner concluded that Salomon's deal had sold the public a bankrupt company and that Salomon among others could therefore be sued for "fraudulent conveyance." In the end Salomon paid an admitted $39 million to the Revco creditors, which looked like a relatively low penalty considering that its fees on the deal had been $38 million. In fact, counting lawyers' fees and settlements with others who had lost money in this mess, Salomon's costs were probably half again that figure.

In 1987 the Salomon investment bankers planned a buy-out for the owners of Southland Corp., proprietors of the 7-Eleven stores, with the result (after the initial issue failed) that Southland, too, wound up in bankruptcy court. Then the investment bankers pushed Gutfreund a step further, into "merchant banking," a then-fashionable activity in which bankers closed deals by putting up large pieces of their own money, hundreds of millions of dollars, as "bridge loans" that would later be bought out by other lenders after the deal crossed its early hurdles. The first of these was for TVX, a chain of television stations based in Norfolk, Virginia. Salomon put up $320 million of its own money, and Michael Zimmerman, who took over the merchant banking division after Foss left, was lucky to get it back without interest after TVX racked up heavy operating losses and was unable to service the loan. The company that bought the stations from Zimmerman later went bankrupt itself.

In 1988, Gutfreund gave approval to a crazy plan by which Salomon would acquire up to $1 billion of stock in RJR Nabisco to earn its place at the table in the buy-out deal that company's chairman Ross Johnson had launched because he was bored.[9] The plan had to be aborted when Kohlberg Kravis Roberts upped the ante on the company before the markets opened the next morning. A year later, according to Richard Clurman, the former editor of *Time* magazine, Salomon bought 150,000 shares of Time, Inc., after the announcement that Time was going to make a deal with Steve Ross of Warner Communications. Morgan Stanley, Clurman reported, also tried to get a piece of the deal. Clurman reported further, revealing Salomon's image problems, that when Time's Dick Munro called the two firms to complain, Morgan Stanley's chairman Parker Gilbert said, "If I need your advice, I'll ask for it," while Gutfreund "told me to stick it up my ass."[10]

Billy Salomon liked to say that the people who worked as investment bankers at Salomon Brothers and left would make the greatest investment banking house the world had ever seen, and it's hard to disagree with him. Richard Schmeelk, Ira Harris, James Wolfensohn, Jon Rotenstreich, Harold Tanner, Ken Lipper, Miles Slater, Kennard Wilson, Peter Gottsegen, Lee Kimmel, Ronald Freeman, David Schulte, Gerald Rosenfeld, Richard Grand-Jean— all were or grew into names of major substance, and by 1991 there were few such names left at Salomon. The senior banker, the member of the executive committee, was Jay Higgins, architect of the Bendix "Pac Man" strategy by which two companies bought up each other's stock as the way to fight each other off.

Gutfreund had made himself the representative of the firm to corporate America, but for all his capacity as a salesman he had never been a banker, an adviser to businessmen on their financial needs. Morgan Stanley, Goldman Sachs, Lazard, and First Boston had clients who relied on them for advice and paid them mostly by following it; Salomon still had only customers, with whom it traded. In conversation Gutfreund sometimes spoke of an underwriting as "a trade." Bankers Trust once commissioned a report on why stock in Bankers Trust and Salomon sold for a much lower price-earnings ratio than stock in J. P. Morgan and Morgan Stanley, and the answer came back quickly: The Morgans made money on their relationships, Bankers Trust and Salomon made money on trading, and earnings from relationships were worth more than earnings from trading.

THE RETURN OF *CAVEAT EMPTOR*

"Revco," said a man who was high in the councils of the firm at the time, and on the investment banking side, too, "was classic Salomon Brothers. The people who did it weren't bankers, they were bond traders. They had so little appreciation of the business, I don't think they could have found their way around a Revco drugstore. As long as they could sell the paper, they would do the deal."

What was wrong with these deals, apart from the faulty analysis, was Salomon's willingness—nay, eagerness—to sell its customers dubious paper, knowing the stuff was dubious. Bad as Mike Milken was, he always maintained at least a façade of concern for the S&Ls and pension funds and insurance companies (some of them very solid insurance companies) that bought the junk bonds Drexel brought to market. What got Milken into hopeless trouble, finally, was his felt need to support the price of the junk he had issued and the market-manipulating games he played to maintain the pretense that people wanted to hold the hot potatoes. Billy had always believed that Salomon's true strength was its customer relations. Now these were sacrificed on the trading desk to the mathematical games, in the corporate finance department to the fancy options that could be overpriced because nobody understood them, and in the banking department to the huge fees that could be generated by the leveraged deals. Several people who held high office at Salomon argued that what crippled the firm in the 1980s was Gutfreund's willingness to shrink the customer base.

Bob Scully said it would be wrong to blame Salomon, that what now seems most distressing resulted from "an evolution that customers demanded and competition compelled. The customers were looking for executions; they didn't want anybody who was Mr. or Ms. Relationship." The rise of the chief financial officer at the client corporation inserted a layer between the banker and the people who had overall responsibility for the company and its future, just as the rise of the general counsel placed a barrier between top management and the lawyer, and the rise of the marketing director blocked communications between the CEO of even a packaged-goods company and its advertising agency. The CFO was supposed to buy financial services as cheaply as he could buy them, to fund the company's activities as cheaply as he could fund them, and to make the greatest return on any spare cash that might happen to be in the till. To make a judgment that over time all these tasks might be best accomplished by dealing with people who felt some loyalty to his company (or to him) would be to diminish his job.

Meanwhile, the institutional investors who had always been

Salomon's customers were growing great in their own right and hired teams of money managers to give them the advice they had once sought from Salomon's salesmen and their rivals. The money managers were judged not by their performance over a span of years (although the pension funds and the insurance companies in fact had long-term liabilities) but by what they could squeeze out of their investments each quarter. Like the CFOs, they were expected to pay the minimum for simple transactions—but they could be sold fancy goods. In this atmosphere an adversary relationship grew up between the "buy side" and the "sell side." Firms such as Morgan Stanley and Goldman Sachs and even Merrill Lynch, which continued to hold themselves out to the public as *agents* who would act in the interests of their customers, began to make up for the declines in their commission revenue by trading against their customers.

Salomon's glory before the 1980s had been the essential *cleanliness* of its relations with its customers. Solly had never held itself out as their agent; Solly was a dealer and made its bread and cheese by selling to someone else for more than it paid you when it bought. When the firm *was* your agent—when you put in a bid at the Treasury auction through Salomon—it was understood that its price would be your price, though once the auction was over, you were on your own in the aftermarket, and Salomon might sell its piece for more than you would get for yours. In the 1980s, under both Mozer and his predecessor E. Craig Coats, it became a common experience for customers to find after the auction was over that they had paid more than Salomon had paid in its purchases for its own account. "I'd have people come storming in to me," said a man who was for some years in charge of customer relations at another firm, "and say, 'I'm never going to do business with those bastards again.' And then you'd find in a few weeks or a few months that they had taken their business back to Salomon, because they felt they had to be in touch with The Room."

Gutfreund remained personally sensitive to the question of the people with whom Salomon did business. In the mid-1980s the firm was approached by Thomas Spiegel of Columbia Savings & Loan, the closest but also the most paranoid of Milken's customers. Columbia had an office in the same converted Beverly Hills store that housed Milken's office, and Spiegel himself had his office encased in metal as part of his protection against terrorist raids. Spiegel shrewdly saw trouble ahead for Milken and wished to shift some of his business to Salomon. Gutfreund very reluctantly okayed taking Spiegel as a customer, provided he could be completely insulated from contact with the man. Similarly, he gave Foss the go-ahead on Revco only after assurances that he would never have to meet with anybody on the client side. But in the end, if there was money to be made, he would not stand in the way.

Scully was right that the moral disaster at Salomon had causes larger than the greed of a few people on Wall Street. In the 1980s the practice of all professions in the United States—banking, law, medicine, accountancy, advertising, athletics—moved from a context of relationships to a context of transactions. The new generation of businessmen was taught in school to manage by objectives, that after each transaction one can draw a bottom line and then proceed to the next transaction as if the last one had never happened. This is not the real world, and if it were the real world, one would wish to change it. But there was money to be made that way, for a while—and even more money if you took the further step from transactions to products, from the organized market where the recognized players enforce codes of conduct to the primitive market where the buyer must beware. In perspective that was the step Salomon's Treasuries dealers took in 1990–91 when all their fellow traders who were not in their loop became just customers, and it was okay to fuck customers.

Chapter 6

RANIERI'S RAIDERS

AT THE BEGINNING, the vast new capital the merger with Phibro brought to Salomon was almost as much bane as boon, because there was a shortage of ideas about what to do with the money. Phibro had bought Salomon because it needed a place to spend retained earnings, and the $300 million or so actually paid out to the partners—Salomon's own money, anyway—had taken little of the honey out of the pot. But stockholders in an enterprise with the risk characteristics of Phibro-Salomon would expect a greater return than they might require from an industrial company. In the 1970s boom in commodity prices, one could invest virtually any amount of money profitably in growing inventories of raw materials, but Phibro had bought Salomon because its officers saw that this boom was ending. The Salomon partnership had since the days of Smutny put its capital into special situations and run the business on borrowed money; thanks to its status with the Fed, Solly had little need for a liquidity reserve. But there weren't enough special situations around to absorb several billion dollars.

This problem never did go away, and the difficulty of generating sufficient return on so much capital in a financial services enterprise would eventually tear Salomon apart, leaving John Gutfreund at the mercy of people who promised to make the firm a lot of money with junk bonds, oil futures, market manipulation, ultimately customer abuse. The crisis was delayed into the late 1980s, however, by the sudden arrival of a new way to make money on Wall Street. From 1982 to 1985 by far the greatest piece of Salomon's unexpectedly high profits was contributed by the packaging of mortgages into various kinds of investment paper and the trading of the paper after it was sold. Salomon—specifically, Lewis Ranieri—invented this business, perfected it, milked it, and until 1985 very nearly owned it. Nobody expected that this very marginal operation would become so significant an activity. Tendler reported that when his people did their due diligence prior to Phibro's purchase of Salomon in 1981, they did not even mention the mortgage department.

The story of Ranieri and his fat traders, so brilliantly told by Michael Lewis in *Liar's Poker,* was significant not only in the ill-fated journey of Salomon Brothers but in the development of American economic policy. The integration of housing finance with the securities business multiplied the losses to the taxpayer from the misbegotten government deregulation of the savings and loan industry in the 1980s.[1] Combined with government-approved accounting gimmicks, many of which the federal banking regulators have perpetuated for the banking industry, the eruption of Wall Street into the financial space previously fenced off for housing deprived American monetary policy of perhaps its most important weapon both in the restraint of inflation and in the encouragement of recovery after a cyclical downturn. And the securitization of commercial real estate, which became Salomon's crusade once others had learned the tricks of skimming the cream off home mortgages, was among the factors that produced both the huge building spree of the late 1980s and the building bust that frustrated all efforts to get the economy moving again in the early 1990s. Congress and the regulators having decided that reforms to the government securities business must wait until after the next big scandal, Salomon may figure most prominently in future histories of American finance as the house that compelled the ancient dog of mortgage finance to learn a whole series of new tricks.

AN ENGRAVED INVITATION

Salomon was able to make so much money in the mortgage business in part because The Force was with it. The government for a long time had hoped that *somebody* on Wall Street would do what

Solly did in the mid-1980s. The New Deal legislation that established the Federal Housing Administration included the seeds of the idea that someday mortgages would be held by financial institutions other than those that made the original loan. FHA created the level-payment fixed-interest thirty-year mortgage that built the American suburbs, simply by placing a government guarantee behind the repayment of the mortgage. That guarantee made the paper salable to investors who knew nothing of the property or its occupant. As early as 1934, when the program was brand new, Carl Bimson of Valley National Bank in Phoenix put his bank into the business of writing government-insured mortgages that were to be sold to insurance companies anywhere in the country, and by the end of World War II about a fifth of all American home mortgages were held by insurance companies.

Title III of the National Housing Act of 1934 contemplated the creation of private companies that would sell bonds and use the proceeds to buy mortgages from their originators, providing additional money for housing, but during the Depression nobody in the private sector had the guts to start such institutions. In 1938, to get the ball rolling, the government had to charter its own Federal National Mortgage Association ("Fannie Mae"). Like everybody on Wall Street, Solly underwrote and traded Fannie Mae paper, which was an interesting hybrid of a government issue but not terribly important.

Then Lyndon Johnson's 1968 Housing Act put an afterburner on the demand for mortgage money. The insurance company share of the nation's mortgage holdings had dropped from one-fifth to something less than 5 percent, because gas pipeline companies and office buildings paid better interest on their borrowings. The nation's existing banks and S&Ls were stretched to their limit financing about 1.5 million new homes a year. The Housing Act promised 2.6 million new homes. Where was the money to come from? It had to be Wall Street. Fannie Mae was privatized, and a new Government National Mortgage Association ("Ginnie Mae") was formed to package subsidized mortgages. The S&Ls were given authority to launch the Federal Home Loan Mortgage Corporation ("Freddie Mac"), which would package and sell *their* mortgages. Among them, the three "Government Sponsored Enterprises" financed $46 billion worth of mortgages between 1970 and 1975.

Both Ginnie Mae and Freddie Mac were something new under the sun. Instead of selling bonds and using the proceeds to buy mortgages, they would package mortgages into "pass-through" certificates that simply shipped to their purchaser the payments homeowners made on the mortgages in the package. Ginnie and Freddie stood behind the homeowner: If he missed his payment, the agency would pay the certificate holder for him. If the home-owner sold his house or refinanced his mortgage, the owner of the certificate got back his share of the repayment and then had to find a new place to invest his money.

Salomon underwrote the first Freddie Mac pass-through in 1972, but Bill Simon and Sidney Homer both hated it, because the uncertainty about when the principal would be repaid meant it didn't fit anywhere in the yield book. The ratings agencies—Moody's and Standard and Poor's—did not accept the validity of the concept and refused to give the paper a rating, which multi-plied the risks of the underwriter. And from Salomon's point of view the fact that the government itself was packaging the instruments limited the profits a Wall Street house could make.

All this changed in 1976 when Bob Dall had lunch with a young Bank of America vice-president named Alan Rothenberg, who had been on loan to Governor Jerry Brown to look for ways that financial institutions could help California. He thought the mort-gage finance business needed reform. There was a large gap be-tween the interest rate homeowners had to pay for mortgages and the interest rate corporations had to pay on their bonds, and the nation's savings were moving increasingly from a depository chas-sis (banks and S&Ls) to a contract chassis (pension funds, insur-ance, mutual funds). The contract thrifts would be happy to hold mortgage paper at rates only a little higher than bond rates if that paper could be easily resold.

Fannie Mae had no incentive to bring down mortgage rates, because it operated entirely with existing mortgages and profited by the spread between bond rates and mortgage rates. The banks and S&Ls, by contrast, made money by originating and servicing mortgages. If they could expand those operations by selling off the mortgages as they were written—reducing the amount of capital that had to be devoted to the business—they would be a force for expanding mortgage credit at lower prices. And Roth-enberg found a way around the worry that mortgages would be paid off early: Bank of America would "overcollateralize" the mortgage bonds—in other words, pledge to the payment of principal and interest mortgages with a face value that totaled more than the face value of the bond. When one mortgage was repaid, Bank of America would simply substitute another mortgage being held in reserve for just that purpose.

These would be Bank of America mortgages. Would Salomon sell the paper? And Dall said yes, which took guts because such mortgage paper was not a legal investment for institutional investors in many states and would not be until Congress passed the Secondary Mortgage Market Enhancement Act in 1984; but Salomon underwrote the Bank of America issue in 1977. Before the ink was dry, Dall had done another such, for First Federal Savings & Loan in Chicago, and Salomon placed the whole issue itself.

Like any securities issue, these "conventional mortgage–backed securities" (CMBS) required a market in which the purchasers could later sell the paper if they wanted the money for other purposes. Salomon, of course, would have to make that market as part of its services to the issuer and purchaser of the securities. Dall was occupied with trading government paper, and there was a question whether uninsured mortgages fit into the governments department. A study was commissioned from some mid-level traders and salesmen; government bonds salesman Thomas Strauss, who had become close to John Gutfreund, was its chairman. William Brachfeld, the partner in charge of governments trading, knew that a study on how the mortgage business fit into Salomon was in the works, but he probably did not know how broad the committee's mandate was. Shortly before the report was delivered, Brachfeld was offered a newly created job as a roving "supersalesman of American investment products in Europe." Then he learned that Strauss was recommending *all* mortgage trading, including the government-guaranteed instruments, be removed from his orbit.

This happened at about the time Gutfreund was taking over from Billy as managing partner. When the dust settled, Brachfeld had left on bad terms with everybody (and without getting what he considered his rightful share of the profits on the inner-circle oil investment that had been made for the partners), Strauss had overall supervision of governments trading, Dall was running a new mortgage department, and an overweight, bearded utilities bond trader named Lewis Ranieri was Dall's trader on the mortgage desk.

SOME PART OF A GENIUS

Ranieri's was the last of the magical Salomon stories. Born into a family that owned restaurants, he had expected to be a chef and was working in a restaurant while going to college until an accident awakened an asthma condition that made it impossible for him to tolerate kitchen fumes. He became a night mail clerk at Salomon, which earned his eternal loyalty by paying for an expensive operation his wife needed, though he had been with the firm only three months and did not qualify for health benefits. His rise from the mailroom to the trading desk was in the old-fashioned Salomon pattern, except that it took longer (ten years) and involved a remarkable stop in the operations department, where at the age of twenty-five, with no training in the field, he was put in charge of the firm's fledgling computer operation. Moving from there to the trading desk involved a pay cut, which he took partly because he was a Salomon man and Salomon men were traders, and partly because he wanted out of computers. By 1977 he was a vice-president, and the next year he was a partner. Four years later Dall was gone for health reasons, and Ranieri was the head of the firm's fastest growing department.

Ranieri worked at least fourteen hours a day. He was in the office before Gutfreund, in the partners' dining room; he was at the trading desk; he was in Washington; he was at the S&L conventions. He socialized more in the office than outside it. Gutfreund called him "Sonny," and he called Gutfreund "Pops." (The only other person at the firm who had a similar relationship with Gutfreund was the banker Lee Kimmel, who called Gutfreund "Pappy," being from Fort Worth rather than Brooklyn.) Enormously overweight, Ranieri moved gracelessly, and his manner was awkward. His deep voice spoke in a rather plaintive New York accent, and he talked slower than one would expect from a man who had to move as quickly as Ranieri had to move. But he was more serious-minded than most of the people at Salomon in the

1980s, a reader and an aficionado of opera and theater. He did not spend his money on private planes or dope, although he did treat himself to a Rolls-Royce; after the failure of his first marriage (to an older woman who was a friend of his mother), he remarried and started a suburban family.

The difference between science and art, someone once observed, is that anyone could have found Planck's constant, because it was there to be found, but only Beethoven could have written Beethoven's symphonies. Ranieri's relationship to the securitized mortgage business fit somewhere between the two. He was not, could not be, just a trader: Many of the instruments he traded did not exist before he got to work, and the customers for them were few and far between. On the other hand, the social need for mortgage-backed securities was there, and others were working on ways to create them. What is beyond doubt is that from 1978 to 1986, when the mortgage securities business went from a standing start to a market that traded *almost a trillion dollars'* worth of paper a year, Lewie Ranieri was far and away its dominant figure.

Unlike Bill Simon, Ranieri did not stand at his desk—people as overweight as Ranieri are far more comfortable sitting down—but he screamed into the phone and at the desks around him to his ever-growing cohort of myrmidons, young men who owed their life-styles not to Salomon but to Ranieri. In 1986, deliberately or otherwise, Gutfreund severed him from the source of his strength, summoning him to work upstairs in the Office of the Chairman. As a member of Salomon's executive committee and then as vice-chairman of the company, he was in title for about two years the head of all the firm's fixed-income trading and real estate operations. It was Ranieri who chose John Meriwether to be the hands-on trader for all Salomon's proprietary accounts.

Ranieri was an inventor, a salesman, a political operator—and a gambler. "A great new-business man," one of his partners said. It was Ranieri who jumped on a single sentence in the financing section of the Report of the President's Commission on Housing in 1982 and created the instruments that got rid of the problem that weighed down the securitized mortgage business. Unless heavily overcollateralized, the pass-through certificate couldn't guarantee the steady income stream the pension fund or insurance company wanted. The report suggested that the pass-through be divided into "'fast pay–slow pay' pools in which one group of certificate holders received all payments of principal until its certificates were retired, thereby insulating the second group from early retirement of its investments."[2] "Fast pay" would be a speculative instrument, money returning to investors in an unpredictable stream; "slow pay" would be conservative. Different strokes for different folks. The spirit of Sidney Homer rode again.

Marcia Meyerberg of Freddie Mac designed and marketed the first such "collateralized mortgage obligation" (CMO) in early 1983, and Ranieri promptly hired her. Young and slender and not interested in the games the mortgage desk played, she would find her role inventing a corporate finance function in mortgages, spinning off mortgage banking subsidiaries that Salomon could sell at a profit, until the politics of the firm drove her off to Bear Stearns. From Meyerberg's simple CMO much could follow. Within a year or two there were "synthetic" mortgage bonds, "inverted floaters" (if the interest rate on Treasury paper went up, the interest rate on these mortgage securities would go down), and all sorts of fancy variations on "segmented" mortgage instruments, most notably "strips," one of which got only the homeowners' principal payments (POs), the other of which got only the interest payments (IOs).

If interest rates were expected to go down (which meant people would refinance their old mortgages), POs would be expected to pay off fast, and IOs would lose much of their anticipated return (because the pool that paid the interest would shrink). If interest rates were expected to go up, holders of POs would have to wait a long time for their money (because people would hang on to their old homes to preserve their low monthly housing payments) and holders of IOs would get a larger total return. Before Ranieri's departure in 1987, Salomon was splitting mortgage packages into as many as twenty-seven different "tranches." The lowest tranches of these certificates—the Z-bonds, so called because they came last in getting money out—were among the most speculative instruments ever offered to American investors. But there can be no question that this "toxic waste," as the traders called it, was sold not only to speculators but also to money managers for insured banks and for pension plans.

What put Ranieri into orbit was the horrendous interest rate spike of 1981–82—the same collapse in the bond market that gave Salomon its two losing months before the Phibro deal—and the remedies to that disaster found by the Federal Home Loan Bank Board that supervised or failed to supervise the nation's savings and loan industry. (The Bank Board also owned and operated the Federal Savings & Loan Insurance Corporation that so carelessly insured the deposits.) The nation's S&Ls as a group lost money in both 1981 and 1982, because they had to pay depositors higher interest rates than they were earning on portfolios of mortgages written in a time of lower interest rates. Savings and loan CEOs walked around at their conventions with little cards in the breast pockets of their shirts announcing the month their thrift would go broke if interest rates stayed where they were.

Among the accounting changes approved by the Bank Board to keep the S&Ls looking as though they were solvent was a rule that permitted them to sell their old mortgages, claim the loss for tax purposes immediately, but write it off on their books over a period of forty years. Every time an S&L sold a low-interest-rate mortgage to Ranieri at a loss, the taxpayers in effect gave it back about half the losses. And it could then invest the money Ranieri paid, plus the tax bonanza, in new high-interest-rate mortgages, showing a great improvement in its bottom line. Salomon itself bought cheap, then sold dear on the chassis of the collateralized mortgage obligation. These transactions may have provided as much as two-fifths of the total earnings of Salomon Brothers in the period 1982 to 1985. To put it bluntly, the profitability of the leading investment house in the world was built in the 1980s on a conspiracy against the taxpaying citizenry of the United States organized and perpetrated by a regulatory agency and in effect confirmed by the bipartisan Garn-St. Germain Act of 1982.[3] When Ronald Reagan signed the bill, he said, "I think we hit a home run." But it was not "we," it was Salomon Brothers that got the home run.

To handle the volume of business generated by the S&Ls, Ranieri developed an almost entirely separate firm within Salomon Brothers. He had his own traders, his own salesmen, his own bankers, his own back office, his own funding operation; at one point in the game he even tried to hire a separate public relations firm to represent the Salomon mortgage department. (He did not have his own research department, because Henry Kaufman wouldn't permit it, but there were people assigned exclusively to mortgage research, and Ranieri had a hand in choosing them.)

The easiest thing for the S&Ls to do to take advantage of the government's largess was to replace the old low-rate mortgages they sold to Salomon with mortgage-backed securities that Salomon would package for them. On an ordinary day in 1984, Salomon would have as much as $5 billion, more than twice its capital, tied up in illiquid mortgages waiting to be securitized— and nobody in top management even knew it. If interest rates rose, that inventory of mortgages could lose its value very quickly; if interest rates fell, the department would be hugely profitable, far beyond any profits that could be made from just packaging or trading the paper. As Ranieri ran it, the entire Salomon mortgage department, which eventually commanded the services of a thousand people, was a gigantic bet on the movement of interest rates.

And the government had structured the situation so that whatever Ranieri and Salomon won on these bets, the taxpayer would lose. The 14 percent mortgages the S&Ls wrote when interest rates were at their peak would be refinanced by the homeowners when the rate peak passed, and the income from such mortgages would no longer be available to balance the losses the S&Ls still had to write off, 2.5 percent a year for forty years, on the mortgages they had sold to Salomon. If they had simply held on to their old 8 percent mortgages through the crisis years, they, not Salomon, would have been the gainers from the reductions in interest rates the Federal Reserve System organized from 1982 to 1985. But Salomon had the mortgages, bought at a steep discount, and Salomon had the profits, and in the end the taxpayer paid the losses.

Meanwhile, Salomon also benefited from the fact that Ranieri and his cohorts were dealing with very poorly informed people at the S&Ls. The market for mortgage paper was not a public market—an S&L chairman didn't know what prices other people were paying for paper similar to the paper that was being offered to him. No other Wall Street house had a Ranieri or anything like him; indeed, they all got into this business, mostly not until 1985, by stealing people from Salomon. Salesmen from Salomon learned how to persuade S&Ls to double their bets through repurchase agreements by which a previous investment could be turned into cash to permit the purchase of more of the same. If the paper was going up in price, this was a cheap way to buy more of it. If the paper was going down in price, "doubling down," which reduced the average price of the investment on the S&L's books, was (or looked like) a way to recoup losses even if through some freaky bad luck the original investment never quite made it back to its original price. "Really, when you think back on it," said Bob Dall, "it was just a classic form of pyramiding." Meanwhile, Salomon was able to charge the customer an interest rate on the repurchase agreement that might be more than a percentage point higher than its own cost of funds. The fact that you could turn your CMO into cash so easily became a selling argument for the CMO itself. "By swapping mortgages for securities," a Salomon pamphlet explained, "thrifts open up an important source of short-term financing."[4]

Salomon became the largest writer of repurchase agreements for the nation's S&Ls; its profits on such activity may have run as high as $100 million a year. Once, when there was reason to fear American Savings & Loan of Stockton, California, might go under before buying back the bonds it had sold to Salomon under its repurchase agreements, Ranieri was able to persuade the Federal Home Loan Bank Board to guarantee American's borrowings so that American could borrow some more. Joe and Judy Depositor wouldn't put their money into an S&L without government insurance; why should Salomon be disadvantaged, especially when the Bank Board needed Salomon so badly? In fact, Salomon nearly had to claim that guarantee: The regulators were planning to close American on the Monday that the stock market break drove bond prices so high that American looked potentially viable again.

What Salomon was peddling to the S&Ls once the interest rates approached normal again in 1985 was a trick called "risk-controlled arbitrage," by which a customer clever enough to follow the advice of a Salomon salesman could guarantee himself a profit by taking long positions here and short positions there in the different tranches of mortgage instruments. And Salomon, of course, would arrange the money necessary to purchase the instruments in these risk-controlled arbitrages by doing repurchase agreements. These things were sold as investments even safer than straight mortgages, which was not true although the salesmen may have thought it was.

(I was a speaker in the spring of 1987 at the annual convention of the Florida League of Financial Institutions, and I found myself preceded on the program by a young man from Salomon who smilingly peddled risk-controlled arbitrage. It was the week after Howard Rubin, who had been one of Salomon's best traders but recently moved to Merrill Lynch, lost no less than *$350 million* in trades involving the division of mortgage securities into interest-only and principal-only pieces. I thought I owed my hosts some mention that this loss on a trade on a single instrument, the largest in all recorded history, had occurred in one of the instruments the Salomon salesman was recommending as safe. What was going through the young man's mind, I don't know; but his smile never wavered.)

Other supposedly safe arbitragelike investments were designed in the Salomon brains department for sale to S&Ls, such as a "utility model" that came to light when Lincoln Savings & Loan failed in 1989. Salomon had put together a package that bought the utilities a computer said were 8 percent or more undervalued in the market and sold utilities the computer said were 8 percent or more overvalued in the market. Presumably, if the market rose, the undervalued would rise more proportionately and the overvalued would rise less; if the market fell, the overvalued would fall most and the undervalued would fall least. Charlie Keating of Lincoln bought $40 million of this package in April 1987, and by July 1988, when the bank examiners came around to look at what was in the vaults, he had lost more than $5 million of his stake.

Donald Shackleford of State Savings Bank in Columbus, Ohio, is a small midwest type with a Skeezix shock of graying hair and a deadpan manner that conceals a major comic talent. After all this was over and sanity returned, he became president of the League of Savings Institutions, and the first ever to be asked to serve a second year. In 1988 he told the Senate Banking Committee that "what Wall Street is doing out in the open is almost indecipherable to the typical guy sitting in Ohio or Illinois or Kansas, or someplace, trying to get risk arbitrage, or mismatched LIBOR-funded hedges, and the only guy that's going to make money on that thing in the long run is the salesman, because you can't figure out what you're doing."[5] The phrase "out in the open" was crucial here. Someone who was a member of the Salomon executive committee in Ranieri's glory days said, "What was going on in that department . . . and you think what they do to some poor ghetto kid who steals $45."

Every so often Ranieri bit off a bit more than he could chew, most notably in 1986 when he led a crusade to bar the Government Sponsored Enterprises from the issuance of REMICs—Real Estate Mortgage Investment Conduits—which the Congress was about to make the instrument of choice in mortgage finance by relieving it of certain tax and accounting burdens. David Maxwell, chairman of Fannie Mae, hoped and expected to dominate that business, and he was not amused when he learned that Ranieri was pushing to reserve the bonanza from underwriting such paper for firms in the private sector. (Fannie Mae is a Government Sponsored Enterprise with five presidential appointees on its board. Maxwell, who in 1990 was awarded a $28 million bonus on the occasion of his retirement from Fannie Mae, was among the inventors of hardball in policy disputes.) Helped by other Wall Street firms, Ranieri won a partial victory in the Congress, requiring Fannie to get approval from the Department of Housing and Urban Development to issue its own REMICs. When Ranieri sought to follow up by lobbying HUD to refuse Fannie Mae's requests, Salomon was excluded from the syndicates that sold Fannie Mae paper to the public. In a speech to the Mortgage Bankers Association, Maxwell accused Ranieri of being "anti-housing" and of "trying to drive a wedge between mortgage bankers and thrifts."[6]

When *The Wall Street Journal* asked Fannie Mae about Salomon's exclusion from its dealer list, CFO Bruce McMillen said, "I can tell you emphatically that our decision is not based on the fact that Salomon is opposing us" on REMICs but "because of our perception that they do not give us any indication that they value our business very highly."[7] Three months later Ranieri was fired, and two weeks after that, Salomon was restored to Fannie Mae's good graces with a $200 million underwriting assignment.

Among those Ranieri recruited to his department were people of considerable distinction, such as Bernard Carl, a soft-spoken, compact young lawyer who had been a partner in Edward Bennett Williams's law firm and a member of the National Commission on Housing—and who would move on to run Robert Bass's Castine Partners, one of the nation's most successful investors in real estate and S&Ls. Most of the salesmen who went out to visit the S&Ls were from the smart but gray cadre of recent MBAs who formed the bulk of the young folk who joined Salomon in the 1980s. They were bought away by other Wall Street firms inserting themselves into the mortgage markets and went on to head the mortgage departments in the large, old-line firms. But several of the men Ranieri appointed to trading posts on the mortgage desk were versions of himself: fat, Italian, uneducated graduates of the mailroom. They established a raucous "culture" of practical jokes and enormous fast-food eating frenzies at their trading desks. For people like Dick Schmeelk, it was to die; the bankers avoided that corner of The Room when they took their clients to visit. For those who worked for Ranieri there were larger questions: "He had a reputation as a bully," one of them said, "and he didn't *look* right; but he was a loyal guy." For John Gutfreund it didn't matter as long as the department made lots of money.

Richard Pratt—who as chairman of the Federal Home Loan Bank Board from 1981 to 1983 wrote the regulations that puffed up Ranieri's balloon, and then moved on to be vice-chairman of Merrill Lynch Capital Markets, specializing in mortgage finance—said that three-quarters of all the money that was made in mortgage securities from 1972 to 1990 was made in the period 1982–85. So it certainly can be argued that Ranieri's record as a genius was made at a time when anybody in his shoes would have been a genius. People close to the top at Salomon Brothers have been heard to say that the Ranieri success story merely reflected the fact that he was in a fixed-income business with virtually unlimited authority to build inventory through the years when such inventories were constantly rising in value. In the second half of 1986 interest rates rose, and Ranieri's inventory lost money; Dale Horowitz was assigned to ride herd on the mortgage department and find out what was going on, which he couldn't do. In the summer of 1987, in Martin Lipton's office, Ranieri was canned. Q.E.D.

Their suspicions made worse by the secrecy with which he ran his department, some Salomon partners claimed that Ranieri moved his profits into the current fiscal year and pushed his losses off until next year until the skullduggery caught up with him. But it was also true that Ranieri, appearances to the contrary notwithstanding, was some part of a genius. He had a talent for calculating the value of mortgage bonds and could do the often rather elaborate math accurately in his head. On a utilitarian level it may well have been that he understood what he was doing better than anyone else in the market or in government. After shaking his uncomprehending misery at his eviction from Salomon, he went on to multiply his wealth and his status by becoming an operator of S&Ls that the government had raised from the dead and an adviser to the Robert Bass interests on mortgage financing and real property investments. In mid-1992 he was a partner with Larry Tisch and the Reichmann family in an effort to salvage Britain's moribund Canary Wharf project, the huge real estate development once touted as the future financial center of Europe and perhaps the world. Others would defend Ranieri even more strongly. "In the Salomon world," said someone who worked with him both in New York and as the firm's delegate to London on mortgage matters, "the time horizon was five minutes. And Lewie was building a long-term business."

Especially when confronted with situations where an S&L showed a loss on his trades, Ranieri was highly defensive about his involvement with the thrifts. He considered himself a keeper of the Salomon torch ("the *covenant*," he liked to say), and he understood what that torch was. While he was the boss of the sales force, he never permitted people to sell junk bonds to S&Ls, a restriction that was dropped immediately after his departure. And he made a number of speeches to S&L gatherings, warning people not to buy things they didn't understand and to be especially wary of mortgage derivatives that were touted as safe. "I used to tell my people," he said, "that the salesman is responsible for the relationship. I would tear up deals where I found the trader cheated the customer. I never did a dishonest thing in my life."

The collapse of the S&Ls and the rapid loss of values in the property market shrank the Salomon mortgage operation by two-thirds, but the trading of mortgage-backed securities remained an enormous business. The government's method for cleaning up the

S&Ls and the banks that kept going bust through the early 1990s was to seize them, buy their bad assets at what the S&L or the bank had claimed they were worth, and then sell the institution as a "clean" thrift to purchasers who wanted access to a lot of cheap money. (And it was cheap money: People acquiring a thrift or bank from the regulators who had seized it were given and usually exercised the right to cancel their depositors' old high-rate CDs and issue new CDs at lower rates.) The acquirers needed something to do with all that cash, and mortgage-backed securities were a perfect place to spend it.

NationsBank, as it eventually called itself (it was originally NCNB, for North Carolina National Bank, known in Texas after its takeovers in that state as "No Cash for NoBody"), went from owning virtually no mortgage-backed paper to becoming the nation's largest investor in such things in the six months after it acquired First Republic Bank of Texas from the Federal Deposit Insurance Corporation. Many of these newcomers to the market were willing to buy the riskier tranches of the mortgage paper, which offered higher interest rates. Solly was happy to oblige— until the Office of the Comptroller of the Currency looked at what some nationally chartered banks had in their vaults and cried, Hold! Enough! Meanwhile, the Resolution Trust Corporation, set up by the Bush administration to exorcise the S&L horror, hired both Salomon and Ranieri—separately, of course—to be major advisers to their people. After all, who would know better what these portfolios of peculiar mortgage paper might be worth?

GOOD RESEARCH, BAD DECISIONS

As in the rest of its activity, Salomon gathered a crackerjack research team for the mortgage department, headed by real estate professor Kenneth T. Rosen of the University of California (who alternated terms between Berkeley and New York). A young man with pale curly hair and splendid promotional talents, Rosen had built his department of the U.C. business school into a powerhouse by establishing an "advisory board" with a $10,000 annual entry fee. For its membership on the advisory board a company (developer, insurer, S&L, investment banker) got the right to send one person to a business meeting in San Francisco in the winter and a pair of people, mayhap husband and wife, to a long conference at Pebble Beach in September, complete with free golf for member and spouse.[8] The profits from the advisory board paid for research at the university. Salomon got no special access to the university by hiring Rosen; indeed, the university benefited more by its access to what Salomon was doing.

Thanks to Rosen and to the firm's need to protect its own immense investments, Salomon did develop authentic expertise in real estate. On Rosen's recommendation, his fellow academic David Shulman was hired to be full-time head of a real estate research staff. Shulman accepted in 1986, telling Ranieri and Gutfreund that their invitation to him to come to Solly "is the most convincing sign I have that this market has topped." Shulman may well have protected Salomon from huge losses in this business, especially after the figures on the Columbus Circle headquarters that Mort Zuckerman was to build for the firm reached a rental of $75 per square foot as the requisite for the building to break even. Nobody except their hairdressers knows the deal Salomon and real estate developer Larry Silverstein struck for the space at 7 World Trade Center that Salomon occupied instead, but anything above $23 a square foot would be surprising. The building was standing vacant, with no tenants even in prospect after the collapse of Drexel Burnham, and Silverstein absolutely had to rent it.

Shulman was unremittingly bearish through the 1987–89 period when American banks blew tens of billions of dollars into the great bubble of American commercial real estate. The fact that he was knocking the deals made it impossible for Solly to do much of that business. Shulman then multiplied his unpopularity by taking his "absorption models" to London and Paris, where Solly's hopes of making a major impact on real estate finance were not furthered by the reports of this convincing Cassandra. Salomon's Houston office raised hell when Shulman refused to believe the conventional wisdom that said the Houston market had turned around. But before anybody could even look sideways at Shulman (who was in any event still protected by Henry Kaufman), the two biggest builders in Houston, Gerald Hines and Trammel Crow, sent letters to Solly saying that Shulman had got it right.

"Real estate finance," Shulman recalled, "was $50, $60 million of gross revenues when I came. We put out reports that hurt deals, killed deals—and I was always backed up by Henry. We had un-believable freedom, freedom we wouldn't have had in any other firm. Elsewhere, real estate research is part of the real estate de-partment; here, it's part of the research department." As the deals ran down, Salomon became more of a broker, introducing devel-opers to Japanese banks, and the people on both sides of such transactions being what they are, they soon eliminated the broker. The Salomon real estate program dropped from eighty profession-als to two dozen. Nevertheless, recognizing his solid reputation with finance professionals ("Everything you would hope a Sal-omon man would be," said James Grant of *Grant's Interest Rate Observer;* "brilliant, informed, in touch with the markets"), the new Salomon management in early 1992 made Shulman overall director of Solly's economic research. And Shulman said of Ranieri that "Lewie's vision will come to pass: commercial and residential mortgages will trade like stocks and bonds. Lewie was a revolu-tionary. Revolutions are messy."

On the other hand, a high fraction of the commercial mortgage deals for which Salomon was the catalyst turned out very badly indeed. "Real estate development," an Atlanta builder said near the bottom of the last real estate cycle in 1977, "is a function of the availability of money. And the availability of money is a func-tion of the stupidity of lenders."[9] Salomon's "innovative financing" was among the reasons that new stupid lenders were attracted to commercial real estate, especially the pension funds that did other business with Salomon, long after such investments were folly.

Ranieri had always been attracted to the idea of securitizing commercial as well as residential mortgages, but in fact the two activities are entirely different. Especially when the homes are scattered throughout the country, mortgage lending is an actuar-ial activity: The lender can predict how many of his mortgages will become delinquent in a period of years almost as precisely as a life insurer can predict how many of his policyholders will die in that time. But commercial real estate is not actuarial at all: The security of the mortgage is a function of the value of one or two or three large buildings, and that value is on a yo-yo. What was wrong with Salomon's approach to commercial mortgage securi-tization became obvious with the name of the client that gave Salomon the most business: Olympia and York.

What Salomon designed for Olympia and York was a scheme by

which the Canadian real estate empire could take its profits out of its New York properties and leave the risks with American institutional investors. Because real estate prices can fluctuate wildly, banks in lending to developers may try to impose elaborate cross-default provisions and guarantees so that the developer's business, not just the building on which the mortgage is taken, goes on the hook for the loan. And the banks may look for a piece of the tax breaks the government gives to investors in real estate. Salomon's customers were happy to leave the tax breaks with the developers, because they were themselves tax exempt, and the developers were therefore willing to give them what looked like a somewhat sweeter deal than they could get from corporate bonds. But the mortgages Salomon securitized for O&Y were "nonrecourse" mortgages, which meant that if O&Y stopped paying on the paper, nothing stood behind the repayment to the bondholders except the building itself.

In the case of 55 Water Street, the largest office building in downtown New York, which O&Y had acquired in 1977 for something like $100 million, Salomon commissioned an appraisal which said that in 1986 the building was worth $786 million. This meant that the $548 million mortgage Salomon sold to customers was a conservative investment. Among the disadvantages of this mortgage bond, from the purchaser's point of view, was the fact that it left O&Y with the power to siphon "excess" revenues from the building even as its future earning power deteriorated. The bonds were tailored so completely to the borrower's rather than the customer's needs and desires that they were hard to sell, and the issue became known around the firm as "55 Underwater Street." But the losses Salomon took on selling the bonds in 1986 were as nothing compared to the losses the bondholders took in 1992 when the appraised value of the building dropped near $100 million again.

The Alabama Public Retirement System put $158 million into the 55 Water Street bonds that Salomon sold the pension fund. The loss on this investment approached nine figures in 1992, and to avoid admitting it, the investment managers of the retirement system agreed to take over the whole building, spending another $120 million or more to make a 1960s structure (complete with asbestos) attractive in the 1990s. This deal was brokered by L. F.

Rothschild; somebody there said, "Well, the Alabama Public Retirement System is still light on real estate investments, and it made sense for them to increase their weighting in real estate." Some 40 percent of that building was vacant in early 1993, and there was lots more attractive space available in downtown New York. It is by no means impossible that these investments will reduce the living standards of retired Alabama schoolteachers into the next century. And for what? To increase the supply of stupid money that could be put into real estate development. And to make a buck for Salomon Brothers. And, of course, for Ranieri's people; he insisted on going to the mat for the people who worked on his mortgage desk, demanding that they get their "fair" share of the profits they generated. In the end, that insistence on money, money, money for "Ranieri's Raiders" would trigger not only Ranieri's personal removal from the firm but a reorganization that took from Salomon Brothers the few elements of cohesion that remained from the days when Billy had made all the decisions himself.

Chapter 7

THE HOLE IN THE HEART

IN MAY 1992, Salomon Brothers consented to an SEC order imposing a fine of $290 million on the company and enjoining it not to do again a whole series of naughty things that the company, in the tradition of these "consent decrees," did not actually admit ever doing. Most of these naughty things involved misbehavior in the government bond market, but one of them related to an apparent effort to cheat the Internal Revenue Service. In late 1986, the SEC contended, Salomon had arranged with other Wall Street firms to make fake sales and repurchases of government securities and options associated with them. The purpose of these fake sales and repurchases, said the SEC complaint, was to reduce Salomon's 1986 income for tax purposes by $186 million, thereby postponing tax payments to future years.

Asked about these allegations, the Salomon public relations department retreated to its standard posture that if such things had happened (and we neither affirm nor deny that they did), it was because individual employees acted on their own without the knowledge of top management. This explanation was printed as offered in *The New York Times,* but other papers seem not to have carried it. What would be the incentive, after all, for individual employees to create $186 million in losses on their ledger in a firm that rewarded people according to the profits it got from their labors? Nevertheless, the SEC story was at least as peculiar as the Salomon defense, because such tax straddles are zero-sum games: If Solly had made such arrangements, the houses on the other side of the deals (rumor accused Goldman Sachs and Morgan Stanley) would have had to show increased profits in 1986 at the expense of reduced profits the next year—which would mean they were out of pocket a whole year for taxes paid prematurely.

Congress was going to pass a new tax bill at the very end of 1986, and it could have been that Solly's partners in crime, if such they were, had reason to take profits in that year because they could offset them with tax losses (particularly real estate shelters) that would be gone in 1987. Still, the fact was that only Salomon on all of Wall Street reported bad results for the fourth quarter of 1986—results that dragged the pre-tax profits of what had shaped up as a record-breaking year some $150 million below the totals for 1985. And the fourth quarter of 1986 had been a miracle trimester for the rest of the investment banking community, the best it would know until the Federal Reserve made the profitability of financial intermediaries its major policy objective in 1991.

Solly's bad fourth-quarter report for 1986 was a turning point in the history of the firm. Salomon was "leveraged" more than forty to one—that is, its inventory of financial assets was more than forty times its capital. The most basic immediate reason Salomon made money was not the talents of its traders or the inventiveness of its brains but its ability to borrow from banks and in the commercial paper market at rates below what the banks and the markets charged other borrowers. When the report on the fourth quarter of 1986 was released, the credit rating services sent polite investigators to call, and the banks that had been funding Salomon asked what the hell was going on. If the bad news from the fourth quarter of 1986 had been the tax dodge, presumably a wink and a nod would have reassured the banks and the ratings services. But everything that happened at Salomon after the publication of that bad quarterly report indicated that there was no such easy explanation, that nobody at the company knew what the hell was going on.

Salomon's front-office systems in the 1980s were state of the art and fantastically informative, with bottomless data to retrieve, charts and graphs and historical data, stochastics, analytics programmed into the machines to trigger simultaneous arbitrage transactions in several markets. By the 1980s the great quote board at the front of The Room had lost its importance because the information came off the screens. Most traders, indeed, could not see the board because the screens were built high on the walls of the cubbyholes around their desks. But the back-office systems had remained primitive, in part because so much of Salomon's growth derived from the size rather than the number of its trades. Don Howard, who came to Salomon as chief financial officer in 1988, said that he found a general ledger "designed primarily to produce individual tax returns for the partners" of the firm as it had existed before 1981. This was a considerable exaggeration, but it *was* true that at a time when Salomon had major offices in Tokyo and London as well as New York, and its traders "passed the book" around the globe in the government debt and foreign exchange markets that were a large part of its livelihood, management had no way to find out what was going on other than the goodwill of selected employees.

Salomon had been run for years as a mom-and-pop store where you looked in the cash register every day (marking to market), every month, every quarter, and every year to see how much money you had made. Billy had had goals, John had had ambitions, but neither had had anything resembling a plan. They couldn't, really: Planning was antithetical to the trader's temperament. In early 1987, only a little more than a year after John Gutfreund had been anointed King of Wall Street and his firm had been acclaimed the four-hundred-pound gorilla that sat wherever it wanted to sit, Salomon Brothers had to figure out what it was, what it was doing, and where it was going. What went wrong in the government bonds department in 1990–91 was merely one illustration of the fact that no answers were found to any of those questions. As one of the key participants in the meetings put it a few years later, Salomon's agitated self-examination of 1987 generated little guidance to anybody because "if you don't know where you're going, any road will take you there."

MANAGEMENT BY ANECDOTE

Rupert Murdoch liked to say that you manage by walking around. Certainly that was Billy's philosophy. He took and made his share of phone calls, but most of the time he was walking around the floor, peering over people's shoulders at their scratch pads (later at their screens), drawn to where the noise was. Some of these visits would turn into brief discussions with the head trader on the desk about where the markets were going. Usually, traders had full discretion to take positions with Salomon's money—after all, they were going to be in and out of their positions in a matter of hours, ideally a matter of minutes. Every so often, however, a trader would have a position he thought he would like to hold for a while ("designated office account" was the term), and he would consult Billy about it. Stocks and bonds in that account would be held for thirty days and then either put into the back of the book as part of the firm's capital if the investment looked profitable (taxes did not have to be paid, of course, until the investment was sold) or put back into the market if there was a loss (which could be deducted from income for tax purposes). If there were disagreements among traders or departments, Billy would listen and make decisions. Virtually none of these decisions wound up on a piece of paper. Trading was an activity conducted *viva voce;* so was managing at Salomon.

Vincent Murphy arrived at Salomon in 1962 from Johnson & Johnson, where he had been export manager; he was hired to impose some system on what Billy recognized as chaos. He was another of Charlie Simon's introductions; his sister's husband worked for J&J and greatly admired Murphy, an ex-Marine with decorations from World War II who had made the export department shape up. Salomon badly needed a new operations chief, the incumbent being elderly and behind the times. Simon set up a dinner for the Murphys with Billy and Virginia "in this fancy joint on 57th Street. Billy in those days was drinking a lot of wine. By the end of that dinner Murphy was no longer my friend but Billy's devoted follower. There are damned few Irishmen I trust," Simon continued, "but Vinnie turned out to be Billy's right arm."

Murphy was a lean man with a long head and a narrow jaw. He considered himself a professional manager, and he was. When the rest of Wall Street got into severe operating problems in 1968–69, with lost stock certificates and miscredited accounts and bankrupt brokers, Salomon stayed current and clean. Murphy especially admired Billy's way with disagreements within the firm: "If you and I had different opinions, we'd say, 'Let's go to Billy.' He was always available. He'd listen to you and then to me, and he'd say, 'I like Vinnie's approach better; let's give it a try. If it doesn't work, we'll try it the other way.' When John got into that position, he'd make snap judgments—not on the logic but on who was the speaker. He'd do it in two seconds—this is the answer, and that's how it's going to be."

Murphy was responsible for keeping the firm's books, and on the advice of Harry Brown, he snooped. He opened people's mail. Nobody could hide a ticket from Murphy; he stayed late every night "to close off the day." When the other partners were break-fasting, Vinnie was meeting with Billy. If he had any doubts, Billy would come around at the end of the day and tell the trader to sell his position—"and you find out in an instant," Murphy said in satisfied recollection, "whether that was a realistic price he said it was worth." (A banker who was at Salomon in the Billy days said that is the definition of management in a trading house—a leader who can go up to one of the traders and say, "Leroy, sell your fucking position.") Not surprisingly, Murphy was unpopular ("uni-versally hated," one of his successors said). When Billy turned the firm over to Gutfreund, his advice was to rely heavily on Murphy and Wolfensohn. "So, of course," Billy later said, "the first people he got rid of were Murphy and Wolfensohn."

Murphy moved over to the operations end of Merrill Lynch and made a new career, which involved representing that firm to some major clients, among them the Vatican. In 1992 he called Charles Simon for lunch and presented to him—for Simon's subsequent presentation to the Museum of the American Indian, of which he was an active vice-chairman—an ornamented contemporaneous silver relief of Chief Joseph at the ceremony of surrender of the Nez Percé Indians. It had come up for auction, and Murphy bought it for $25,000. He wanted Simon to have it as his gift to his beloved museum because, he said, he owed his career in the securities business to Charlie. That was the old Salomon, resur-rected briefly at lunch: a firm of relationships.

Murphy's time at Salomon ended when the firm still had about fifteen hundred employees and the traders' positions were almost entirely long or short. It was by no means clear that his system would have tracked the firm's activities when there were eight thousand employees on six continents and the positions were a tangled mass of options, futures, swaps, and exotic off-balance-sheet items. But Paul Mozer certainly could never have got away with the fakery that made the trouble in 1991 if he'd had Murphy hanging over his shoulder.

Murphy, moreover, although he told Carol Loomis of *Fortune* as late as 1970 that he didn't use a computer to calculate positions because it was too slow, was supportive of Bloomberg's efforts to get the firm's records into retrievable form. He had been in charge of data processing for his end of J&J, and he had some sense of what could be done. Billy himself was much less interested; when Bloomberg told him that "the time will come when we can determine the value of all our business with Morgan [Guaranty], Bankers Trust, everybody we do business with," Billy said, "Why would you want to do that? If you're not doing enough business, try harder."

Billy had one confidant in running the firm (Murphy) and one in running the business (Gutfreund), and otherwise all partners were equal. Even when space was cramped, Billy gave department heads a great deal of leeway in hiring the people they said they needed—or just wanted, because Salomon often hired people whom partners had met in the course of business and thought would be useful; as Birinyi noted, it was not uncommon for people to be hired at Salomon and told to find out what needed doing. And then Billy liked to meet everybody who was doing anything of interest. When there was a banking deal, the man who did it would probably keep the head of the banking department informed, but he would also go directly to Billy; ditto for governments trading; ditto for block trading, although Billy might want Gutfreund's involvement in the price Salomon would offer. That was the other side of accessibility: Billy had direct personal relations with everybody over a relatively low status. He was equally imperious—courteous, but imperious—with everybody. He did form an "administrative"—later "executive"—committee in the early 1960s, but the committees were discussion groups. Billy made the decisions, and Billy walked around to see how well they were carried out.

Apart from the all-powerful compensation committee that decided people's bonuses, the only strong committee—and this held true until the junk bond agitation of the Gutfreund days—was the credit committee, which decided whether Salomon wished to recommend an underwriting to its customers. Among the things that happened at executive committee meetings was the decision that someone should or should not be made a partner, and much might depend on who the candidate's rabbi was. In later years department heads on the executive committee would say to John Gutfreund, "If you're making a partner for *him*, you have to make a partner for me, too." Nobody said that to Billy.

Taking over in 1978, Gutfreund retained the system of direct reporting, with no pieces of paper to confirm what was said. But he had no Gutfreund at his side to know what the boss thought of the business, and no Murphy to keep the fences mended at the corral. Murphy's successor, Allan Fine, let Solly's back office fall some distance below the state of the art in automation—CFO Don Howard reported himself shocked by the inadequacy of what he found at Salomon when he came over from Citibank in 1988. "Well," Fine said, "we had a situation where every week they were inventing a new instrument, and it might trade a handful of times. Automated programs have to be repetitive and stable; and we didn't have that."

Henry Kaufman said that however primitive the systems may have been, "Fine kept the records straight." Fine was a member of Gutfreund's executive committee and thus in a position to defend his people when they came under attack, but he was dependent for his information on clerks whose chances of promotion were in the hands of the traders who could promise them rewards for keeping their mouths shut. In the increasingly elaborate world of the late 1980s when mathematicians, who didn't know about the morality of markets, were creating and trading the firm's positions, computerized compliance procedures were a must—and Salomon didn't have them.

Billy made decisions according to a logic that was Billy's own. Gutfreund seemed to make them according to the views of the people who spoke with him most recently—which heightened the problem that he clearly had favorites. He saw Ranieri, Warren Foss, Lee Kimmel, and John Meriwether a lot more than he saw other people of their generation. "We had management by anecdote," said one of Gutfreund's favorites. "Somebody went to John and told him a story, and if his instincts didn't contradict it, that would be the next thing to do."

Gutfreund had risen through the firm in large part because he was smarter than other people and knew it. In a business that has always rested on character (because everything is done on the spoken word and the handshake), Gutfreund rewarded only brains—and profitability. Some of the old-timers felt that people of enormous potential were ruined by Gutfreund's indulgence to them. Kimmel, the banking department's expert on financial institutions, was the most cited example. Dismayed and enraged by the breakup of his marriage, he behaved offensively in the office; people left because they couldn't take it. But he had what one of his superiors described in an old-fashioned way as "the best wits in the firm. He could have been made to stop. But John kept rewarding him, which meant he only got worse."

None of this mattered in the first years after the sale to Phibro when Salomon was on an astonishing roll. The mortgage business kicked in $100 million a year and more in earnings. The government kept pushing interest rates down, automatically pushing up the value of the Salomon inventory. The backing of the Phibro capital allowed Solly to multiply its borrowings, apply an immense weight of money when it wished to move prices, and bid for the lead position in any underwriting for any corporation. The whiz kids kept designing new instruments that could be sold at terrific markups. The futures and options business blossomed, opening opportunities to guarantee a profit from trading for a big customer even before the trade was done by using in these "derivative" markets information about what the customer was going to do in the real market.

And Phibro's profitability collapsed. The 1970s had been the time of the New International Economic Order. The producers of raw materials saw the terms of trade change in their favor for the first time since World War II, and Phibro as a dealer in oil and metals and tropical products saw the prices of its inventories rise dramatically. The 1980s, however, were to be the decade of the resurgent industrial West, as commodities prices dropped and the heavily indebted countries of the Southern Hemisphere had to produce all-out to pretend to pay the interest on their loans. Phibro's profits began to fall. Ray Golden as Gutfreund's delegate to Phibro was stiffed when he tried to find out why, because the Phibro people worked for David Tendler, but he learned enough about how Phibro ran its relations with its Third World suppliers to want no part in that business. "If you're dealing in oil offshore," Henry Kaufman said rather sadly, "there are all those people involved."

The contrast between the ballooning numbers at Salomon and the shriveling numbers at Phibro, coupled with some of what Golden had picked up on his travels, gave Gutfreund the chance to go to the board and demand that he be made chief executive officer of Phibro-Salomon. Asked recently what issues Gutfreund raised to drive him out, David Tendler said, "He told the board he could run the company better than I could, and they believed him." For a while Hal Beretz from Phibro continued as president of the joint company, but then Gutfreund turfed him out, too, meanwhile throwing the "Phibro" out of the corporation's name to make a holding company called, simply, Salomon, Inc. Ultimately the Phibro commodities businesses other than oil were spun off as an independent company, and Salomon kept control of what was called Phibro Energy, an oil trading, storage, and refining operation.

In charge all by himself after 1984, Gutfreund expanded Solly's international reach. Tokyo was becoming the world's leading source of capital, and the easiest way for the Japanese to show that they weren't really trying to keep out foreign competition was to let Solly make some money in ten-year Japanese government bonds and the Japanese bond futures market. Splendid office space was acquired in the Ark Hills office-cum-hotel-cum-concert-hall complex near the U.S. embassy. London was preparing the Big Bang that was in theory going to make it the financial center of the European Community. Salomon built over the railway hall of Victoria Station an unbelievable trading floor, ceiling forty feet high, more square footage than a football field, twice as large as The Room in New York—and filled almost two-thirds of its seats. ("This," said Peter Gottsegen defensively, "happened to be a big box where you could move in a lot of wires.") In October 1986 when the British deregulated their securities markets in what they called a Big Bang, Salomon was more than ready: There were almost a thousand people working at the Victoria office, up from less than two hundred only three years before.

"We believe at Salomon," said Charles McVeigh, who was running the London office then as he does now, "that if you put enough people in one place, you get something more than the sum of its parts. If you're going to operate in many markets, you're only as strong as your weakest link. The fact is that North American corporations today raise more money abroad than they do at home, in marks and yen and Swiss francs, at various interest rates. It's unacceptable for Salomon not to have capacity in each of these markets. Despite the size of that room, if you look at dollar bond trading, it's six men—four seniors and two juniors. Can six people actually maintain two-way markets in all these issues with great liquidity? Only with great difficulty. If a hundred-million-dollar issue is well received here, that issue is very hard to trade, because it's locked up for eight years in Luxembourg and Belgium. These guys don't sell on volume." Salomon was going to luxuriate in wide margins, in short, because there weren't many competing traders. But in reality the margins weren't and never would be high enough to support the extravagance of the London office.

When the 1986 fourth-quarter numbers were in, it became apparent that both Tokyo and London were losing bundles, that the profitability of the mortgage and municipals departments was way down, governments trading had fallen off as a source of revenue, and the firm was heading into trouble.

CREATING GUILLOTINES FOR THE HEAD COUNT

Early in 1987, Gutfreund summoned a meeting to consider the fundamental economics of the firm. The participants included Tom Strauss, recently elected president of Salomon Brothers, up from governments; Dale Horowitz, up from municipals; William Voute, up from corporates; Lewis Ranieri, up from mortgages; David Stockman, recently arrived from the Reagan administration; Gerald Rosenfeld, who had worked at McKinsey & Co. and at Bankers Trust, had cleaned out the mare's nest at Phibro, and was being given the title of chief financial officer; consigliere Donald Feuerstein, who was the secretary of the corporation as well as being general counsel; and Henry Kaufman. One of the participants said, "There was no great secret about what had gone wrong the previous year. The head count was up thirty-eight percent in one year. More than five hundred people in the firm were making more than one hundred thousand dollars a year. And if we did nothing, our payroll costs for the next year were going to be up twenty-two percent from 1986. London was hemorrhaging money —we had lost at least a hundred million dollars in London the year before. But London was Tom Strauss's baby. He believed there were going to be eight or nine great worldwide banks in the 1990s, and Salomon would be one of them; and he was heir apparent. He said, 'Well, that's the price of entry'—and boom! we were off to the next topic. Which was buying a piece of a German merchant bank, for fifty million, and boom! that was done, too."

There was some consolation for the people who had been upset about the fourth-quarter numbers and the banks' reaction to them. The previous summer Strauss had sent money-market trader Miles Slater to London to take over that office and do something about its expenses. (He had accepted, against the strong advice of Ranieri, Voute, and Kaufman, all of whom said, "Tom is your friend, but if you succeed, he'll take the credit, and if you fail, he won't be your friend.") Slater, Strauss insisted, would get a grip on the expenses problem in London. But it was agreed that the firm should do a major self-study, with task forces for each "strategic" area of business, seeking a "new Salomon."

A hundred-odd managing directors were summoned to the firm's annual spring retreat—again at Arrowhead Lodge in Tarrytown—to hear Gutfreund outline his hopes for the new Salomon and his reasons for having reorganized the old executive committee into a new Office of the Chairman that would be more compact and would allow him to shed some of his responsibilities. But if you're going to manage by walking around, which Gutfreund still did—the walks now extending to London and Tokyo—the others in the Office of the Chairman are not going to have time to run their departments. In fact, the most obvious first result of Gutfreund's new organization was that people who once had more or less lived in The Room virtually disappeared from the trading desks. They were busy making policy, usually under the leadership of Strauss, who was always game for another meeting.

The first Office of the Chairman was very small: Vice-chairman Ranieri, who would be, as he described it, "head trader," responsible for all the firm's "proprietary" trading in bonds, notes, and mortgages; vice-chairman Voute, who had sided with the youngsters in pushing Salomon into underwriting junk bonds, would be in charge of all customer relations; Tom Strauss for international; and Feuerstein, ex officio as secretary, to the horror of business theoreticians who regarded putting the general counsel in the chain of command as an appalling confusion of staff and line functions. (Given what happened to Salomon in 1991 and why it happened, the business theoreticians may be right.) Kaufman, who had been on the old executive committee (since 1972), was not part of this new Office, although Gutfreund asked him to continue as a vice-chairman of the parent holding company, a request that he refused. Operations chief Allan Fine was also eliminated from the top management level. Neither Kaufman nor Fine was a profit center for the firm.

The dignity and importance of being at Gutfreund's elbow would soon make others clamor to be part of his Office. It expanded with traders and salesmen and bankers who demanded this recognition of their contributions to the firm's profits, until it grew larger than the old executive committee, becoming, as one wag put it, "the Auditorium of the Chairman." Neither Kaufman nor Fine was asked to become part of it, and in the spring of 1988 both of them quit Salomon. Fine felt that if he didn't have Gutfreund's ear on disciplinary matters, he could not serve the compliance functions that were part of his job. Kaufman flew off to Germany after telling the board he was leaving. Mel Adams, still helping the firm with its public relations, learned of Kaufman's defection through a terse memo from Gutfreund, who said no announcement would be made. He reached Kaufman in Frankfurt and pointed out there was still time for him to reconsider, but Kaufman didn't want to reconsider. Nor would he make a statement. Even today the closest he will come to criticizing Gutfreund is a laconic "In the final analysis, we are what we are. I'm not so sure that people basically change."

ACTIVITIES VERSUS BUSINESSES

Salomon presented an almost insuperable management problem because of the kind of business it was. The basic management tool in other businesses is the budget and the allocation of corporate capital to specific uses. But Salomon couldn't budget. The firm's largest expense item was its cost of funds, which swung widely from year to year (even month to month) as the Fed changed its policies, and varied from department to department according to business opportunities that could not be forecast. And the very concept of the allocation of capital was foreign to Salomon Brothers.

Salomon was not like a commercial bank. Capital had an obvious function in a commercial bank—or did, before deregulation confused everybody—because the kind of assets it could hold were limited by the bank-chartering laws. Therefore, the capital of a bank meant that some part of every loan was made with the money invested by the owners of the bank. And banking is a *business,* with calculable return on assets and more or less apparent relationships between return and risk. The fact that the relationship is apparent does not mean that bankers see it. From Third World debt to leveraged buy-outs to real estate deals, the twenty-year record of the world's largest banks argues that commercial bankers lack not only vision, but eyesight. But there are rules of thumb by which bankers can if they wish measure what they call the risk-adjusted return on assets (RAROA).

Trading securities, on the other hand, is more like an activity than a business. The return on assets will vary enormously from month to month and year to year, and different assets become risky at different times. Billy said he could not remember a year when Salomon did not have at least one losing month, and in some years there were two losing months. Until after the Phibro deal, capital had never been allocated to the various activities at Salomon because, in fact, the partners' capital was largely absorbed by the partnership's long-term investments: Most of the day-to-day trading and just about all the position-taking associated with underwritings were done on borrowed money. And virtually all the money was borrowed short, overnight, for a week, thirty days, maybe ninety days, possibly six months. One of the things Don Howard did when he came over from Citibank was increase the fraction of Salomon's borrowings that were long-term; this may have saved the firm in 1991, because it meant that fewer loans had to be renewed in the weeks right after the disaster.

The Federal Reserve, it was argued, backstopped the borrowing needs of its primary dealers. To the extent that the inventory carried with those borrowings was long-term (bonds or mortgage securities), a cost allocation that charged the trading desk only for the out-of-pocket interest payments on such short-term borrowings guaranteed huge returns when short-term rates were much lower than long-term rates. But such cost allocations were folly, because they ignored the risk that the inventory would suddenly lose value if long-term interest rates rose, and the P&L would suffer if short-term rates rose more than long-term rates. Marking to market after the positions had been acquired was not a substitute for costing the risks before the fact.

In 1974, under Vince Murphy's prodding, the firm did its first desk-by-desk cost accounting and laid out at monthly partners' meetings the gross profits and expenses of each department. This was primitive and not very helpful, because the common costs of the firm were, in fact, allocable quite differently to different departments—and also because desks so often worked together at a salesman's behest, one of them taking a loss on a trade with a customer so the other could make a larger profit on a different trade with the same customer. The people who were salesmen for the municipal bonds traders were also salesmen for the municipal bonds underwriters, and the commercial paper desk was the point of entry for the corporate underwriters. And Billy wasn't very interested in accounting procedures. In 1984 for the first time, under pressure from Kaufman, Schmeelk, and Slater, Gutfreund established an "assets and liabilities" committee of the kind that had been routine for a generation in other financial services enterprises. "Then," said Schmeelk, "he staffed it entirely with traders, who refused to accept the idea that the desks should be charged with the costs of the capital they used. It was a joke."

Which left open the question of what a stockholder bought when he bought shares in Salomon, Inc. There is no brand name like Oreo cookies, no factory, no distribution network. Capable traders no doubt come out ahead most of the time, but the modern investor who wants a predictable stream of quarterly earnings cannot get that from traders. What investors actually bought in the 1980s when they bought stock in Salomon was that portion of the firm's future earnings that the managing directors (many of whom still considered themselves "partners") could not figure out how to keep for themselves. One of the few things that came out of the self-study was a decision by Gutfreund's kitchen cabinet (slightly different from the Office of the Chairman: Strauss, Voute, Feuerstein, and Kimmel) that a trading house could keep its autonomy only if the money behind it was very patient capital.

"Japs," said Strauss, "they're patient."

"No," said Kimmel. "The most patient capital in the world is flight capital. If we're going to take a major institutional partner, it should be a Swiss insurance company—Zurich Re or Swiss Re." Very secret negotiations were indeed begun with Zurich Reinsurance, but in the end the Swiss wanted to pay less for a piece of Salomon than Salomon wanted to charge.

HOW MANY BONDS DO WE HAVE TO TRADE TO MAKE $38 MILLION?

The highlight of the managing directors' meeting at Arrowhead in the spring of 1987 was a presentation of "the Revco model" by Warren Foss and Ronald Freeman, Solly's walking delegate to the oil industry (he had broken in at the firm in the 1970s as Ray Golden's assistant; his client was ARCO). This was an easel show of how much money Salomon had made on the Revco deal—all of it, incidentally, in the last days of 1986, which would otherwise have been even more disastrous. There was a markup for Salomon as underwriter on the paper, a merger-and-acquisition fee, a setup fee, a dealer/manager fee—total, $38 million. Freeman, who would move on in 1991 to the European Bank for Reconstruction and Development where he became Jacques Attali's number-two man in planning assistance to Eastern Europe, was especially vehement about the need to convert Salomon from a bond trading house to a Drexel-like creator of deals and junk bonds. "How many bonds do we have to trade," he asked repeatedly, "to make thirty-eight million dollars?"

The new Salomon was going to be housed in Mort Zuckerman's billion-dollar project at Columbus Circle, and it fell to Ranieri as the man in charge of real estate to spread the glowing spiel about the combined retail-hotel-office complex that would tell the world the greater glory of Salomon. Part of the work of the task forces set up following the Arrowhead meeting to study the various departments was related to the space utilization planning for the new building, but most of it was devoted to the construction of enormous reports, three and four hundred pages long, full of accountants' footnotes, on the future of various aspects of financial services and Salomon's role in that future.

One of the most enthusiastic supporters of the task force venture was Ranieri, who was convinced that it would show his operation as the firm's premier engine of profitability. It didn't. The mortgage department was a devourer of capital, and its required support staff was large and expensive. There were too many people on the sales staff, and they were overpaid. "There was never enough management reporting in that business," said Henry Kaufman. "There was always this question of *what was going on there.*"

On the more sophisticated accounting basis that Gerald Rosenfeld introduced as Salomon's new chief financial officer, even the repurchase agreements with the S&Ls were less profitable than the mortgage department had thought. As interest rates climbed in 1987—and as more and more of the people Ranieri had trained were competing against Salomon at other firms—the mortgage department simply stopped making money. Ranieri, now in the Office of the Chairman and wearing a tie to work every day, knew that a lot of his old trusted lieutenants were gone, but he did not realize that his base in the firm had been eroded. He also did not know that David Maxwell, as chairman of the Federal National Mortgage Association, one of Salomon's biggest clients, had visited Gutfreund to complain—possibly in a threatening way—about Ranieri's lobbying in Salomon's name against Maxwell's plans for Fannie Mae to dominate the REMIC business. Ranieri was totally surprised when in July 1987 he was asked to come to a meeting in Lipton's office, with no word of the agenda. Gutfreund, whom he had called Pops and who had called him Sonny, fired him on the grounds that "nobody likes you anymore." (In the summer of 1992, a much-chastened Gutfreund invited Ranieri to lunch and expressed his regrets.)

When the task force reports were finished, an "internal board" of Salomon, eighteen managing directors appointed for this purpose, began what became a series of interminable meetings. There was a gag line in the house that Salomon was losing money in August and September 1987 because the revenue generators were closeted with one another making policy. And the firm's priorities were changing. In the year from mid-1986 to mid-1987, none of Salomon's trading desks had made much money on conventional customer business of the kind that had once supported the firm. Freeman and Foss had won: Gutfreund bought their argument that trading had become or would become a commodity business and that the future lay in hugely profitable deals like Revco. Salomon was going to take on Milken and show him a thing or two.

Indeed, there was another such deal already in the works—Southland, the 7-Eleven chain of stores. And after that TVX, the television chain. Both were badly thought out and poorly executed—in every way, exemplars of "the Revco model." Meanwhile, Solly should narrow its customer base, eliminate customers and desks that weren't profitable, give up the sort of trading for nickels and dimes that had built the firm. "The Salomon I joined," Laszlo Birinyi noted wryly soon after he left, "was a firm that wanted to do as much business as possible with as many customers as possible. The Salomon I left was always looking for the big score."

The traders fought a rearguard action. Both William Voute and governments trader Craig Coats demanded additional capital or authority to go after even bigger bank credit lines, to hold heavier inventories. Freeman thought the best bet was to get out of customer service entirely and trade only for the firm's own account. For that purpose Salomon would need much less inventory and less capital, and Freeman advised Gutfreund to buy out the shareholders and take the firm private again. Meriwether objected that he needed the firm to be the broker for the big buyers of Treasury securities, because the orders from the customers gave him the information he needed in proprietary trading.

Two of the trading areas, however, had been left defenseless: municipal bonds and commercial paper. Dale Horowitz had built municipals into a department with more than 130 employees, well paid because Horowitz had been a good rabbi. Foss had pointed out effectively in an internal board meeting that the average underwriting for corporate clients was $200 million, while the average municipals underwriting was $20 million; and although spreads are wider in the public securities business, the fees on a $200 million corporate issue were a lot larger than the fees on a $20 million muni issue. The new cost accountings showed the department losing money.

Bill Simon, who started a municipal bonds trading company (William E. Simon & Sons) after Salomon closed its municipals operation, said he made bundles of money on this activity with about thirty people and that Solly's department could have been made profitable by pruning. "The real issue," Henry Kaufman said, "was whether we had competent management for the department." But the internal board, while assuring the Salomon staff that management had no plans to fire anybody, set a numerical target for reductions in force. They brushed aside concern that the loss of contact with the state and municipal treasurers would reduce the salesmen's effectiveness in placing paper with public pension funds, because the decision had been made to reduce the customer base, anyway. "Closing the muni business," said one of those who participated in the decision, "was a swipe at the head count."

Commercial paper dealing went back to the origins of the firm. Schmeelk's entire Canadian operation had grown from contacts made while placing commercial paper for businesses. "You take out the basic genes of the firm," Miles Slater said, "and it loses something." Henry Kaufman said, "There was many an entree to corporate finance work through the commercial paper route. The abandonment of that business broke relationships that had started with services, with accommodations. It was not understood in the firm how important that relationship was. If the question is cost-effectiveness, reduce the costs—don't get out of the business."

One of the investment bankers who left Salomon shortly after this decision said disgustedly that "you should be willing to run a commercial paper department as a loss leader, because it means you're in the CFO's offices every week, you know what he needs." There was also a contrary argument, that in an age when transactions have displaced relationships, the CFO buys the services of an investment banker separately for each job, and the commercial paper contacts are worth little. One of the decision-makers said, "There was a lot of discussion about the value of having that department. If Henry had fought for it, it probably could have been preserved." But arguments from Kaufman might not have carried much weight. As few at the firm then knew, he had already decided to resign from the board of the parent corporation, and he was making his plans to resign from Salomon Brothers, too.

The elimination of the municipals and commercial paper departments was handled abominably. The people involved were to be notified October 12 in as civilized a manner as possible, with assurances that they would have the inside track for other jobs at Salomon, if available, and unusually generous severance arrangements, if not. On Friday, October 9, somebody leaked the story to *The New York Times,* and several hundred people learned in the Saturday paper, when they had nobody to call who could tell them whether or not the story was true, that they were about to be fired. By then the politics at Salomon had become so Byzantine that rumors swept the firm about who had done the leaking. All the rumors still hover in what Shakespeare's witches described as the foul and filthy air.

On arrival Monday morning, people were herded into an auditorium for their mass dismissal and were told to clear out at the end of the day, which was probably not part of the original plan. Historically, people fired by Salomon Brothers had been given office space to use while finding another job; it was only the people who quit who were ordered off the premises immediately. But there was precedent in the Ranieri execution, which had occurred outside the office and included a ban on his coming back even to pick up his personal effects. The Wall Street community was ablaze with horror stories from these firings: Women having babies were told in hospitals that they no longer had a job. A young couple on a honeymoon, two Salomon people who had met at the office, received a telegram on the cruise ship telling them not to report for work when they returned to New York. Part of Gutfreund's reputation had been cruelty; like many shy people, he could seek to dominate meetings by humiliating the people with whom he disagreed. "He would kick my cat if he was sure nobody was looking," said Charlie Simon, "because he knows I love my cat." Thanks to that reputation and incompetent management, Salomon was given no credit anywhere for the $67 million spent on severance for the eight hundred people (an average of more than $80,000 per person) dismissed in 1987.

In the end what the task forces and the internal board did was divide the firm into insulated compartments. Each little section was to be separately audited and its profitability separately assessed. As the examples of the municipals and commercial paper departments illustrated, a skeptical eye would be cast on any claims that this department helped with the profitability of another department. Some of this was undoubtedly driven by outside forces. "There was a shift in the business," said Miles Slater. "Where once there had been generalists who had to know what was going on in other markets, now there was a technology that pigeonholed professionals. You had to refine your capabilities. Picture a box. The more vertical lines you have, the more rigid the box." But a lot of it was deliberate management policy. The separations became even worse after Gutfreund, frustrated by the task force effort, called in McKinsey & Co. in 1988 to structure a system of management by objectives. This provoked a rebellion of the traders, led by Voute and Craig Coats, who left in late 1988 to form their own firm with two other veteran Salomon traders.

And management never did get control. Part of the new system was periodic audits of accounts, department by department. When the auditors came to visit Paul Mozer, Coats's replacement as head of government bonds trading, he threw them out—and got away with it.

MR. PERELMAN AND MR. BUFFETT AND MR. GREENBERG

Meanwhile, the reorganization activities of the "internal board" had been shockingly interrupted. Among the items left over from the Phibro purchase was the ownership of 14 percent of Salomon's stock by the South African mining conglomerate Minorco. Henry Slack of Minorco, Sir Harry Oppenheimer's son-in-law, had courteously told Gutfreund in early 1987 that he was shopping the block, but the price of the stock had been dropping precipitously since 1986, and Gutfreund apparently thought they would want to wait until they could get more for it. Suddenly, in September 1987, they agreed to sell it—to Ronald Perelman of Revlon, one of the classic Milken clients. Perelman announced plans to acquire a controlling interest in Salomon. A week after this announcement, Gutfreund met with Perelman, who indicated that if his bid for the firm succeeded, he intended to change management. There wasn't any serious danger that he would bring in Milken, who liked life in Beverly Hills. But Perelman was also a customer of Bruce Wasserstein, who was leaving First Boston and looking for a home.

Gutfreund panicked and went to Warren Buffett, commander of a $4 billion pool of investment capital built from a few thousand dollars at a firm he called Berkshire-Hathaway. A legend in his lifetime who lived in Omaha, Buffett wrote a brilliant annual report to his stockholders and said folksy things when asked questions. Gutfreund and Buffett seemed an odd couple, but they had met a dozen years before when Salomon was the sole underwriter of a $400 million issue of preferred stock that was a necessary element in the rescue of Government Employees Insurance Corporation. GEICO would become Buffett's best investment ever, the largest single source of his wealth, but in 1976 it was a basket case of a casualty insurance company that had written automobile policies for too many bad drivers. Despite their very different views of finance (Buffett disliked securities trading and had once called for a confiscatory tax on the profits from the sale of stocks held less than one year), the two men had become friendly if not close: Gutfreund never became a participant in the Nebraskan's elegant two-day biennial clambakes for his friends and advisers.

To beat off Perelman, Gutfreund made Buffett an offer he could scarcely refuse—a special $700 million issue of preferred stock with a 9 percent dividend (more than nine-tenths of it tax-free to Buffett's company, because dividends to corporations from their stockholdings are exempt under the tax code—but by the same token not an expense deductible from taxable income for Salomon). The Buffett deal was further sweetened by an option to buy Salomon stock at any time in the next nine years for $38 a share, a price the stock had in fact surpassed, although in 1987 it was back in the twenties. Buffett and his buddy, the lawyer Charles Munger, would join the Salomon board. With Buffett's money, Gutfreund could buy the Minorco shares, and he did.

Gutfreund called a special meeting of the Salomon board of directors and presented the Buffett deal on a take-it-or-leave-it basis. All the inside directors were now the people he had promoted (Kaufman had resigned), and in any event their jobs were threatened, too. The outside directors who had come in with Phibro, especially Maurice (Hank) Greenberg of American Insurance Group, were appalled at the sacrifice of Salomon's stockholders' interests to Buffett's interests. Preferred stock issued by a company with more than $3 billion in stockholder equity, earning $300 to $700 million a year, was a very safe investment. Why should Salomon have to pay a punitive dividend rate? In the end, in protest partly against the deal itself and partly against Gutfreund's failure to tell the board what he was doing until he had done it, Greenberg resigned. He didn't like Buffett, anyway. In his Berkshire-Hathaway annual report two years before, Buffett had criticized the accounting procedures of a casualty insurance company that was obviously Greenberg's, and Greenberg was known not to appreciate criticism.

"Warren doesn't do due diligence on his investments," said a Salomon veteran who knew Buffett well. "Warren does trust. John misled him." Even so, it was surprising that the friendship of the two men survived Buffett's experiences on the Salomon board as chaired by John Gutfreund. The reason relations remained good was probably that Buffett had very little notion what Gutfreund and Salomon were doing. On a visit to New York a couple of years after he joined the board, he had breakfast with Bankers Trust chairman Charles Sandford and said with a sigh, "It's very difficult to know what's going on inside a financial services company."

In point of fact, certain alarm signals were sounding quite soon after Buffett's arrival on the board. Early in 1988, announcing the poor results for 1987, Gutfreund said he had taken no bonus that year. But in fact he had won the approval of the board to reduce the exercise price of his options to buy 544,000 shares of Salomon stock, from as much as $38 all the way down to $19.95, a gift worth $3 million on the day it was made. Long-term investors like Buffett have defended the use of stock options as a compensation plan for corporate CEOs on the grounds that it gives them a stake in increasing the price of the stockholders' shares; but if the price at which the CEO can exercise the option keeps getting reduced, there is no benefit to the shareholders. Buffett was on the board that okayed this bit of deceit—and delayed its revelation from the 1988 proxy statement, which asked for the issuance of another 4.5 million shares for executive stock options, to the 1989 proxy statement, which accompanied good news. When that proxy statement came out, revealing this, Charlie Simon sent Gutfreund a note asking if he could get some of those options himself, and Gutfreund sold him ten thousand options at $19.95, for $1.00 a share. But when Simon dropped Gutfreund a note after his departure from the firm and asked for the options, he learned for the first time that Gutfreund's long letter of confirmation of the sale, doubtless written by Feuerstein, had contained a clause saying that Simon's purchase was valid only while Gutfreund remained Salomon's CEO.

Gutfreund had been brought up in a partnership context, and it was never really solidly in his head that he had obligations to the stockholders or board of a listed company with stock traded on the New York Stock Exchange. When Tendler was co-chairman and dominant figure on the Phibro-Salomon board and Gutfreund had to report his and his "partners' " activities, his mood was described as "morose." Once Tendler was gone, he kept the board at arm's length. The board was not involved in the task forces and was not kept informed of the decisions that were being made by the "internal board" that worked over the task force reports. Twice in 1988 and 1989, Lee Kimmel was involved in major efforts to find Salomon a partner who would pay for the restructuring of the firm to face the new millennium. Once, as noted, it was Zurich Reinsurance. And once it was Reuters because, as Kimmel put it, "information about money is now more important than money itself." Neither time was the board informed that such contacts had been made, although in the Reuters case there were several meetings.

The board had a compensation committee; Buffett sat on it. But nobody told that committee about the deal that yielded Lawrence E. Hilibrand $23.6 million. (Of course, nobody told the other members of the Office of the Chairman, either. The news got out because the accounting department, not imagining that such information was supposed to be kept eyes-only for the chairman and the president of Salomon Brothers, distributed the compensation sheets to the vice-chairmen as a matter of routine.) When Paul Mozer's forged bid in a Treasury auction was revealed to Gutfreund and Strauss, they discussed telling the government about it—but it seemed never to have occurred to them to tell the board, although in fact they had a duty to do so. Discussing Buffett's status on the board in his early 1991 interview with Gutfreund, Gilbert Kaplan of *Institutional Investor* asked, "What role does he play in decision-making?"

And Gutfreund answered, "None."[1]

Chapter 8

THE HAND IN THE COOKIE JAR

EIGHTY-ODD TIMES A YEAR the U.S. Department of the Treasury auctions short-term bills, medium-term notes, and long-term bonds, a total of $2 trillion a year, borrowing money to fund the current budget deficit and to roll over the expiring portions of the nation's $4 trillion debt.

How can Salomon make money from these auctions? Let me count the ways:

1. Salomon can buy the Treasury's paper at the auction and sell it to customers at a higher price: the old-fashioned way, although some of the tricks of this trade are very newfangled—like buying the whole bond from the Treasury and then selling the stripped coupons and the principal payment on expiration as separate securities. The bidding process itself is still astonishingly old-fashioned. The auction occurs at 1:00 P.M. sharp, and bids must be submitted on a one-page aqua-blue form to one of the twelve Federal Reserve Banks scattered across the country. The bid must be for at least a million dollars' worth of whatever is being auctioned. Buyers can put in as many bids as they wish at different prices, but there is only one round of bidding.

Bids from the Wall Street houses are pushed over a counter on the banking floor of the rusticated stone fortress of the Federal Reserve Bank of New York on Liberty Street. Salomon's clerk, like the others, hangs on one of a row of telephones across from that counter, and at 12:59 P.M. gets the numbers from Solly's chief bond trader. The numbers he now writes on the form are the total amount of bonds for which Solly is bidding, for itself and its customers, and the interest rate ("yield") to two decimal points that Solly and the customers demand if they are to buy that amount of paper. In 1991 the customers whose orders were included in Salomon's bid did not have to be mentioned on the bid sheet; Salomon simply promised a "list to follow." The Fed's clerks take this bid sheet and compare it with some dozens of other sheets submitted by other firms. The winners of the auction are those who bid to charge the government the lowest interest rate.

In this sort of once-for-all instant auction, of course, the total amount of the bids at different interest rates will be greater than the total face value of the paper being auctioned, usually four or five times as great. If the bidders at the low rate had bid for more than the total auctioned, under the system in use in 1991, the Treasury prorated the award so that each bidder got the same fraction of his bid. (With $20 billion of winning bids for $10 billion of paper, every bidder received half of the total he had bid for.) If the bidders at the low rate had bid for less than the total offer, they got all they bid for, and the bidders at the next rate up then got their turn—and they were prorated on the same principle. Before any proration occurred, the Treasury allocated part of the issue to "noncompetitive tenders" that could be submitted by small purchasers ($1 million and under) who agreed to take the average rate accepted by the winners of the auction. Of the $12.25 billion offered in the May 1991 two-year note auction that made all the trouble for Salomon Brothers, only $11.3 billion was available for sale to the competitive bidders.

In the May 1991 auction for two-year notes due in May 1993, Solly's winning bid was for an interest rate of 6.81 percent. Nobody else had bid to take that low an interest rate, so Solly and its customers got their full order of $10.6 billion. After the auction the note would carry a fixed interest rate (in this case, 6¾ percent), and its price (initially set just below one hundred cents on the dollar to bring the yield to maturity up to the bid 6.81 percent) would be determined by the interplay of buyers and sellers. The usual expectation would be that if interest rates on Treasury paper went down, the note would sell at a higher price; if interest rates went up, the note would sell for less. But usual expectations relate to usual occurrences, and what was to be bought and sold here was not some proxy for interest rates in general but a very specific note to be redeemed in May 1993. It was conceivable that the price of this note could vary independently of the general movement of interest rates.

2. Salomon can make money in the auctions by selling the Treasury's paper before the Treasury actually auctions it, in a "when-issued" market formally approved by the government in 1981 but not supervised by anybody. What is traded in the "when-issued" market is a contract to sell or buy a bond or note the Treasury has announced but not yet actually issued. This anonymous market (there are no public records of who bought or sold or the prices paid) runs from the day the Treasury announces the size and maturity date of the issue it will auction to the day the winners at the auction pay for and receive their notes or bonds. The seller of such a contract makes money if the interest rate on these bonds or notes when they are issued is higher (which means the price of the bond is lower) than the rate specified in the contract. The theory of the "when-issued" market is that it helps participants "discover" the right price for the paper the Treasury wishes to sell. They then can bid at the auction with more confidence, which should mean lower rates for the Treasury.

The existence of this when-issued market made possible a kind of baby arbitrage, which is the way many dealers make their profits. Buyers tend to be more eager than sellers in the when-issued market for two-year Treasury notes. Dealers will need the new notes (the "on-the-run" or "benchmark" issue) because that will become the trading vehicle in the market. The two-year note is the most popular Treasury issue in the trade. Its rates tend to be considerably higher than the rates on the three- and six-month bills, but the prices don't move violently in response to interest-rate changes because the owner of the note will get his money back relatively soon. There are a number of insurance companies, especially in Japan and Germany, that follow a strategy of always owning U.S. paper with two years to run. They are risk-averse and want to know ahead of time what interest they will be paid on their holdings. Before each auction they sell their holdings from the previous auction and "roll over" into the new notes.

In general, borrowings for a shorter period of time can be done at lower interest rates than borrowings for a longer period of time. Thus paper with less time to run before its redemption usually offers a lower yield than paper with more time to run. The interest coupon on a two-year note is of course set for the entire two years at the time of the auction. As time goes on and the effective length of the note diminishes, the price of the note tends to rise. All other things being equal, the note auctioned last month will sell for a slightly higher price than it did when brand new. This means that the "roll" itself—the sale of last month's notes to get the money to buy next month's notes—is usually a source of modest profits.

Coupled with the fact that only professional dealers are on the selling side before the auction, automatic demand for forthcoming notes from risk-averse institutions tends to produce higher prices (lower interest rates) in the when-issued market than after the Treasury has distributed the notes. And the fact that the Treasury has just increased the supply of notes with its new issue tends to depress the price of that issue on the day the auction settles. At a number of banks and securities houses it became routine to sell the upcoming notes "when issued" and close out the short position by purchasing them in or just after the auction, clearing perhaps two or three cents per hundred dollars (two or three hundred dollars per million dollars, two or three hundred thousand dollars per billion dollars) on the two transactions.

On the other hand, the when-issued market is a form of futures market, in which traders buy and sell contracts for future delivery of a commodity. The problem with such markets always is that anybody can create contracts to sell a commodity, but only God can make a tree or a wheat crop, and there's a limit to how much copper the miners can take out of the hills in a year, and the Treasury presets the amount of the notes and bonds to be bought at this auction. If sellers in the futures market sell more of the commodity than will, in fact, be available on the day the contracts fall due, those who own the commodity can "squeeze" them, compelling them to pay any price to live up to their contract. As old Daniel Drew put it in the nineteenth century, speaking of short squeezes on the stock exchange, "He who sells what isn't his'n,/Must buy it in or go to prison." The penalty for failure to deliver is that the seller owes the buyer every day the interest that is accruing on the bond or note he has not yet delivered.

The key word in the description of a squeeze is "available." Bunker and Nelson Hunt, then Texas billionaires, drove the price of silver from about $7 to about $50 an ounce in 1980 by buying and warehousing the real silver while scarfing up contracts on the New York Commodity Exchange. Traders who had contracted to deliver real silver to the Hunts in satisfaction of their futures contracts simply couldn't find any silver to buy because the Hunts already owned it all. In the end, the government had to change the rules at the Comex to break the stranglehold (which also, as the price cascaded down, broke the Hunts). In some ways the danger of a squeeze is greater in the Treasury markets than it is in markets for real commodities, because all wheat or copper or silver is acceptable in one way or another in satisfaction of a futures contract, while the contracts in the when-issued market are for one description of bond or note only, and no other Treasury paper can be substituted.

Natural behavior by the traders who arbitrage the bond market can make a squeeze worse. The computer screen shows a graph, which is the "yield curve." It is normally a smooth curve—that is, the interest rate on a note with twenty-one months to run is a little but not much lower than the interest rate on a note with twenty-two months to run, which is a little but not much lower than the interest rate on a note with twenty-three months to run. (See Figure 1.) Suddenly the traders' screen shows that the interest rate on a twenty-three-month note has become *lower* than the interest rate on the twenty-one-month note. (See Figure 2.) The twenty-three-month note is clearly overpriced (in the language of the business, it is "rich"), and the arbitrageur, having spotted this anomaly, rushes to sell the note short, planning to buy it back at a profit when the yield curve returns to normal. He usually doesn't have to worry about selling a Treasury note short—the world is full of ways to borrow a Treasury note and deliver it to the buyer. At the same time he buys a two-year note in the normal part of the

GOVERNMENT YIELD CURVE, 13 TO 24 MONTHS
Date: July 2, 1992

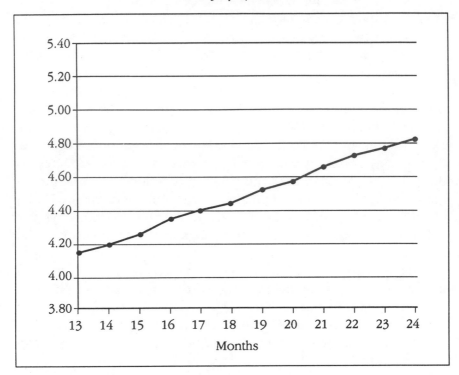

Figure 1 shows the prices on July 2, 1992, of two-year Treasury notes with 13 to 24 months before maturity. The horizontal axis shows the length of time that must elapse before the note is paid back, and the vertical axis shows the effective interest rate that will be earned on this note if it is held to maturity. This graph displays the "normal" yield curve: The longer the time before the note is paid, the higher the interest rate, and the slowly rising line is quite smooth.

curve to make sure that a change in the general level of interest rates won't take away his sure profit on the mispriced twenty-three-month note. This is what bond traders at a place like Salomon do all day long, sitting at their telephone and computer consoles and yelling at each other over the screens that separate them from each other.

If there is a squeeze on the note with twenty-three months to run, however, and it is driving up the price because the squeezers have created a shortage of those notes, the impossible dip in the

GOVERNMENT YIELD CURVE, 13 TO 24 MONTHS
Date: July 1, 1991

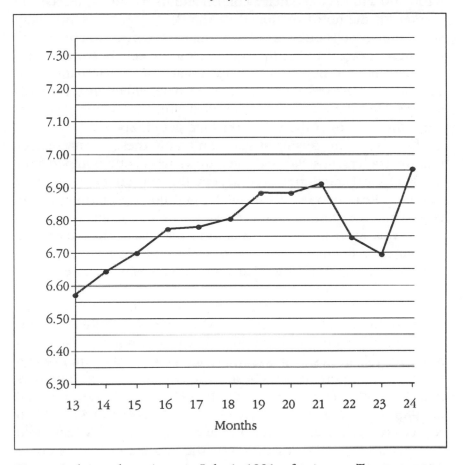

Figure 2 shows the prices on July 1, 1991, of two-year Treasury notes with 13 to 24 months before maturity. The hedge funds and Salomon were visibly squeezing the market. Note that the April and May notes (those with 22 and 23 months to go) both yield much less than traders would normally expect. This means that these notes are selling for much higher prices than they would have commanded without the squeeze, creating profits for their holders and losses for those who had sold them short.

yield curve will not merely continue, it will worsen, with enormous losses to the trader who does not see that—to use the language of the trade—"the shit is on." A *Wall Street Journal* article in late October 1991 told the sad story of a young trader recently hired by Boatman's National Bank in St. Louis who lost $400,000 and his job when Salomon and its friends squeezed the market for the notes auctioned in May 1991.[1] As the supposedly smart money sells more notes, waiting for the price to come back to where it ought to be, the squeeze on the sellers worsens and the demand for notes to borrow escalates. "Their natural instincts," said a former trader, looking back affectionately at his fellows, "led them right into the meat grinder." When that happens, the players of the baby arbitrage get clobbered.

There was some feeling at Salomon that in these circumstances it *is* the traders' mistake, and the fellows who got whomped after the May 1991 auction should accept the consequences of their mistakes. Real men don't eat quiche and don't go tattling to the cops when they lose money because they read the market wrong. There was even more feeling among the losers that Salomon's acclaimed mathematical modelers were and are squeeze artists who can use the firm's knowledge of who owns what note to take the "wrong" side of the trades (buy up everything the traders are selling to push up still further the price of the already "rich" issue) until those who know only what they see on their screens close out their positions at a loss that is Salomon's profit. Compiling for the SEC estimates of how much money the firm made in the auctions where Mozer cheated, Solly came up with numbers that did not in any way justify the huge bonuses Mozer was paid in 1988, 1989, and 1990: $2,850,000, $3,850,000, and $4,600,000 respectively, over and above a salary of $150,000.[2] What could justify those bonuses, however, was the information Mozer could contribute to the firm's proprietary traders on the basis of his department's client contacts.

Normally, serious squeezes do not occur in the Treasuries market because the notes and bonds are available for lending and then for lending again. The seller in the when-issued market who can't buy the notes or bonds he needs for delivery to the buyers in the when-issued market can buy the notes through a "repurchase agreement" after the settlement day. This just shifts his obligation to deliver the notes from the buyer in the when-issued market to the seller in the repurchase arrangement, but it gives him time: He can worry later about finding notes to close out the repurchase agreement. The buyer in the when-issued market now has his notes and can lend them to another short seller to use in satisfaction of another contract. Thus a relatively small quantity of notes or bonds that can be recycled through borrowings or repurchase agreements will relieve the squeeze.

There remains what the market calls a "floating short," which will not be cleared up until some holders sell for good, because the suppliers of the borrowed notes can always take them back. But the problems that come up in the trading of two-year notes can usually be resolved in a month or less, because the purchasers of these notes who want to own only the most recently issued paper—the "on-the-run" or "benchmark" note—will sell their holdings from the last auction to get the money to buy in the next one. Still, those with notes to lend can make quite a lot of money lending them while the squeeze is on.

3. Salomon can also make money at the auctions, then, by becoming the owner or the controller of bonds or notes that the sellers in the when-issued market must borrow because they can't buy what they need to fulfill their contracts. These borrowings take the form of "reverse repurchase agreements."

The straightforward garden-variety "repurchase agreement" has become the basic system for financing the government and government-guaranteed securities business in the United States. The owner of bonds or notes needs cash to pay for what he has bought, and in essence he borrows the cash by pledging his bonds or notes. He can borrow something very close to 100 percent of his purchase price. The formal structure of the loan is that the lender "buys" the bonds or notes from the borrower, who agrees to buy them back ("repurchase") at the same price at the end of a specified time, paying interest for the use of the money during the period the agreement runs. Because the loan is very safe—if the borrower fails to buy back the bonds or notes, the lender owns them, and these are easily salable securities—the "general repo" interest rate is very low, often below the "Fed Funds" rate that banks charge each other for interbank loans.

Thomas Russo of the law firm of Cadwalader, Wickersham & Taft, who had worked on market regulation problems for both the SEC and the Commodity Futures Trading Commission, estimated the total value of all repos outstanding in 1991 at $4 *trillion* with over $300 billion changing hands daily.³ Salomon was and is the largest writer of repurchase agreements; its typical "book" of such contracts ran $25 to $40 *billion* a night in 1991. Because Salomon's market power and resourcefulness were so great, it could borrow cash at less than the Fed Funds rate, profiting by charging the Fed Funds rate or a little more to other dealers and brokers who needed financing to carry their inventory. This was a straight banking business, with Salomon as intermediary between people who wanted short-term use of money and people who wanted short-term income from assets, with Salomon making a "spread" on the difference between the interest rate it paid the lenders and the interest rate the borrowers paid Solly. But in this process Salomon also acquired the key to the mystery of who has control of what notes today.

The "reverse" repurchase agreement may offer additional possibilities for profit. When there is a squeeze in the market for a note, the short seller looking to escape his pain can find balm only in one very specific asset. If he can put his hands on this asset through making a "reverse repurchase agreement," the interest rate he demands on his money will have little or nothing to do with the Fed Funds rate or any other market rate for borrowing money, and everything to do with the scarcity of the note or bond. Such reverse repurchase agreements for scarce notes and bonds, initiated by the lender of the money rather than the borrower, are said to be at "special" rates, and indeed they are. In 1986, when a bunch of Japanese brokers and insurance companies cornered the market for U.S. Treasury bonds due February 15, 2016, people who had those bonds could do reverse repurchase agreements with people who needed them and borrow money at rates as low as one-eighth of 1 percent a year.

There are tales of holders of long-term bonds who have been *paid* to borrow money on a reverse repurchase agreement because somebody desperately needed those bonds. If Mozer controlled the lending of $10 billion of a two-year Treasury note for one month, he could easily negotiate "special" repo rates that would cut Salomon's cost of funding its inventory by $15 million. And that's pure profit. At Salomon *most* of the profits of the governments trading desk were made in the repo market, in little pieces or big ones, and among the responsibilities of the chief trader—in 1991, Paul Mozer—was control over the lending of the notes and bonds. Salomon's self-serving lowball estimate of its profits on the May 1993 notes was "approximately $16.7 to $18.4 million."[4]

4. Finally, Salomon can make money on the Treasury auctions through its customer relations—financing their purchases or charging them a commission for its services as agent or just knowing what they plan to do. The world of securities trading is a world where information, not knowledge, is power. Information about forthcoming shifts in customer demand for Treasury paper of different maturities is irresistible weaponry for those in the firm who arbitrage the markets and trade the firm's existing position. That's why the dealers are forever on the telephone with each other as one o'clock approaches. "You know, we all spend the last fifteen minutes before the auction bullshitting each other about who's bidding and what's likely to win the notes," said a veteran of the business. "But the only real information you have is what your own customers are going to do. You work with customers, tell them what you think, but the customer hears rumors about what Solly's doing. That's the information everybody wanted—what's Solly doing. People wanted to be customers of Salomon to find out what Salomon was saying. Even when Solly was cheating them."

CHILD'S PLAY IN THE BOND MARKET

Salomon's public relations director, Bob Baker, said that an internal investigation after the disasters of August 1991 showed that Mozer's strategy was the baby arbitrage. He was typically short in the when-issued market, having played the market through the week to sell at the highest possible prices, and he bought at the auction mostly to close out his short positions. He would then finance the purchasers' positions, making a little money on that leg and sharing his information on who owned what with John Meriwether as Salomon's trader for its own account and with Lawrence Hilibrand as the mathematics maven. To make any substantial amount of money on the baby arbitrage, he had to be a very big buyer at the auction, and he was inconvenienced by the

Treasury's system of prorating the notes and bonds sold at auction among all the bidders at the winning interest rate.

The trouble for Salomon began in 1990 when Mozer found the cute trick of bidding at one interest rate for more than 100 percent of what the Treasury was offering, to maximize what Solly would get in a proration. The Treasury found this undignified and childish because if it worked once, everybody would do it next time. Michael Basham, Deputy Assistant Secretary of the Treasury for federal finance, called Mozer to remind him of a Treasury rule that had always been more like a gentlemen's agreement, that no purchaser would bid for more than 35 percent of any given issue, and to tell him that in the future the rule would be enforced. Mozer was used to throwing Salomon's weight around. He warned Basham not to get in Solly's way, noted that John Gutfreund was buddy-buddy with Treasury Secretary Nicholas Brady, and said he would have Gutfreund call Brady if Basham interfered with him. He then complained to the press that Basham was costing the government hundreds of millions of dollars by driving the Treasury's best customers away from the market.

Basham was a compact, handsome, matter-of-fact young man raised in this market at South Carolina National Bank. When he left the Treasury a few months after the Salomon explosion, he went to one of the most interesting jobs at Smith Barney, developing that house's relations with the emerging markets of Eastern Europe. He remained unperturbed by Mozer's threats, and the next time Mozer put in a bid for more than 100 percent (which he did), Basham had the Fed simply correct it to 35 percent of the offering. Mozer decided he knew a trick worth two of that. There was no ban on Salomon's buying from a customer what it had bought in the auction as the customer's agent, although it was forbidden to arrange for such transactions in advance. As that prohibition was on the honor system, Mozer saw no *real* as distinct from *formal* reason why Salomon could not simply fake a bid for a customer and keep the notes for itself when the bid won.

Mozer was not one of the firm's quants, having graduated from Whitman College in Walla Walla, Washington; he picked up a business degree and started commercial life as a salesman in Salomon's Chicago office. But he considered himself at least as clever as any of the mathematicians. He liked to handle big customers himself, eating dinners with them at the very best restaurants, on the Salomon expense account, shunting aside the salesmen assigned to the accounts. Unlike his predecessors who liked the theater of the auction and played to a gallery of executives and other traders while chatting up the competition on the phone in the fifteen minutes before the bids closed, Mozer preferred to be alone, a preference that could not always be satisfied. After the scandal broke, the party line at Salomon was that nobody in senior management tracked Mozer's bids for billions of dollars of bonds, but the story was simply not plausible. Gutfreund had been involved in these things for too many years to be frozen out by some thirty-six-year-old former bond salesman, and others had to approve the borrowings in billions that were necessary to fund Mozer's positions.

The SEC consent decree in the case that grew out of its Salomon Brothers investigation said that Mozer as early as 1989 had arranged with another broker to acquire a larger than permissible position in a Treasury auction of nine-month cash-management notes as part of an arbitrage Salomon was running between short-term Treasury yields and the interest rate for dollars in Europe. (For this service Solly paid about $300,000 to the other broker, Daiwa Securities.) The first instance of Salomon's submission of an *unauthorized* bid in another firm's name was in July 1990, and the customer chosen was Mercury Asset Management, a branch of S. G. Warburg & Co. This was a truly spectacular piece of arrogance, because Warburg was the most powerful if not the largest securities house in Britain, and its chairman, Sir David Scholey, was the most influential individual in British finance. Moreover, Warburg was a "primary dealer" in its own right, doing business frequently with the Federal Reserve Bank of New York. Mozer entered the fake bid himself, concealing it from the Salomon salesman who dealt with Mercury as well as from Mercury itself. He instructed the order clerks to show no salesman's number on the order and to enter the order in the computer with instructions "do not confirm" so that Mercury would not know it had purchased the bonds. After the auction he entered a false trade, showing the sale of the bonds from Mercury to Salomon, again with instructions to the computer not to confirm the transaction to Mercury.

Having got away with it in July 1990, Mozer followed the same procedures in August, this time with Warburg's own name on the bid. And again in December, now for "Warburg Asset Management." And in February, when Salomon bid for $3.15 billion of five-year notes, 35 percent of the total auctioned, first in the name Warburg, later corrected to Mercury. Also in February, Mozer entered another unauthorized bid of the same size in the name of Quantum Fund, an offshore investment vehicle (Americans are not allowed to own shares) operated by the Hungarian savant and panjandrum George Soros. In this auction, in other words, between its bid for its own account and the two fictitious bids for others, Salomon was seeking 105 percent of what the Treasury was selling. But now, quite by accident, Mozer was caught. Unluckily for him, Warburg had entered its own $100 million bid in the same auction.

If Mozer had contented himself with a bid for something less than 35 percent in Warburg's name, it is possible that his deceptions would never have been uncovered. But Warburg's modest $100 million bid for its own account, added to the Salomon bid allegedly for Mercury, had put *Warburg* over the 35 percent limit, and the Treasury asked Salomon to explain why Mercury and Warburg should be considered different entities. Through his assistant, Thomas Murphy, also a managing director of Salomon, Mozer argued that because Warburg owned only 75 percent of Mercury, a Mercury bid should not be lumped with a Warburg bid. At that moment Mozer was on very thin ice. Barbara Walter, vice-president for dealer surveillance at the Federal Reserve Bank of New York, had nothing in her files about the relationship of S. G. Warburg and Mercury Asset Management, and Kurt Eidemiller, the Treasury's financing analyst on the case, made a direct call to Larry Leuzzi, one of the directors of bond trading at Warburg, to ask for information. It never occurred to Eidemiller to mention that the reason for his call was a very big bid for February five-year notes by Salomon allegedly for Warburg; he could not have imagined that Leuzzi wouldn't know that.

In April, seven weeks after the auction, the Treasury rejected Murphy's argument that Warburg and Mercury were separate entities. Michael Sunner, a deputy assistant commissioner in the Treasury's Office of Financing, courteously informed three directors of Warburg and Mercury (and Mozer, as Mercury's presumed agent in that auction) that the Treasury had decided Mercury and Warburg were a single entity for bidding purposes and therefore bound to keep their total bid under 35 percent of what was being offered. Salomon received its copy of the letter from the Treasury on April 19. Mozer saw it on April 24 when he returned from vacation. He and Murphy called the three people at Warburg who had been been sent copies to assure them that a simple clerical error at Salomon had been the cause of the Treasury's problem and to ask them not to embarrass Solly by telling the Fed they had never heard of this bid. And, indeed, Warburg did not embarrass Solly. Its letter of reply to the Treasury was, Assistant Secretary Jerome H. Powell told a House committee, a noncommittal "thank you very much."[5] One of the Warburg executives was unavailable, however, and there remained a risk that he would ask the Treasury what it meant by that letter. That same day, April 24, Mozer told Salomon vice-chairman John Meriwether, who was in charge of all the firm's fixed-income trading, what he had done to increase Salomon's share of the take in the February auction.

Meriwether reportedly chewed him out. He had no reason *not* to chew him out, of course, because acquiring a heavy position in the February notes had been a mistake. Soon after that auction, American forces beat up the Iraqis in Kuwait and interest rates rose, meaning bond prices fell in the expectation that happy days would soon be here again. Someone who was once Meriwether's boss could not understand how Meriwether was able to keep Mozer in his department after the revelation of the concealed bid: "He's a control freak; he's even more anal than I am. When people who worked on his desk went to the bathroom, he had to know why they were leaving their chair." Nevertheless, on April 25, the very next day, obviously unchastened, Mozer bid for Salomon and for Tudor Investment Corporation in a five-year note auction, adding an extra billion dollars for Salomon to Tudor's genuine bid of $1.5 billion. Tudor was not informed, and Mozer kept for Salomon some $600 million from the $2.1 billion allocated to Tudor in the auction, once again forging a sale from Tudor to Salomon, with no confirmations to the customer.

(Some months later, testifying before Congress and perhaps recognizing how damaging this coincidence might be, Salomon's new CEO, Warren Buffett, would suggest that this transaction had been by prearrangement with Tudor. On the remonstrance of Paul Tudor Jones himself, the James Bond-y proprietor of this huge futures-market speculator, Buffett later put out a statement of apology, admitting that he had no reason to believe anyone on the outside had been Solly's partner in this deception. Plaintiffs' counsel in the class action suit against Salomon and others for manipulating the bond market believe Buffett may have been right the first time. Basing their argument on internal Salomon documents, they claim that Salomon, Tudor, and others had a plan to manipulate the market for the April five-year notes which Mozer aborted the day after the auction because in the light of the Treasury letter about the Warburg bid he got cold feet.)

On April 25, while Mozer was preparing his fake bid for Tudor, Meriwether met with president Tom Strauss and general counsel Donald Feuerstein to tell them what Mozer had done in the February auction. Gutfreund was out of town, and Strauss knew that Gutfreund liked Mozer's aggressiveness. Although he had for years been Salomon's contact man with the New York Fed and knew how straitlaced that institution was, Strauss decided he should wait until Gutfreund's return before taking any action on Meriwether's report. Gutfreund heard the news at a meeting on April 27—and did nothing: He did not dismiss or discipline Mozer, or tell anybody else to do anything. Four weeks after that meeting, Mozer structured Salomon's Götterdämmerung in the May auction of two-year notes.

THE PLOT AND THE PLOTTERS

The tale of the disaster of the May auction began in the very early spring with a meeting of a dozen or more warlocks of the securities business in the offices of Bruce Kovner, a bearded trader who was general partner and boss of Caxton Partners. A $1.2 billion "hedge fund," trading whatever securities looked hot today, Caxton was empowered by its charter to buy or sell short or play futures contracts or do anything else its managers might want to do. The Federal Reserve had made government notes hot by lowering the interest rates on very short borrowings (the kind people like Kovner used to carry their positions) well below the rates on medium-term notes. The interest payments the purchasers of those notes would receive from the government on their holdings were considerably higher than the interest payments they would have to make to the banks that lent them the money to buy the notes. Thus the government would in effect pay the traders to buy and hold Treasury paper they might later sell at a profit. And there was less competition than there had been. Drexel Burnham, which had been the second or third largest trader of governments in the past few years, was bankrupt and departed from the market.

Among those attending this meeting were Caxton's bond trader, D. Scott Luttrell, George Soros of Quantum Fund, and Michael Steinhardt of Steinhardt Partners, a $1.5 billion private partnership with a remarkable record of profits through good markets and bad. Steinhardt, who was graduated from the Wharton School at nineteen, was an overweight, charming Wall Street type in his early fifties, with thinning hair and a wonderful German beer-hall mustache. (When he first went out on his own in the 1960s, a little less overweight and sans mustache, as the senior of three kids in a firm then called Steinhardt, Fine, Berkowitz & Co., the chief ornament of the office was a snooker pool table.) There was a lot of savvy money here: Among the original investors still in the partnership was Larry Tisch of Loew's, CNA Insurance, and later CBS. When William Salomon retired from Salomon Brothers, one of the first things he did was put money into Steinhardt Partners.

Although Steinhardt was one of Salomon's largest customers, Salomon's president Tom Strauss and its chief equities trader Stanley Shopkorn were also large investors in the partnership. There were other connections, too: Steinhardt's chief government bonds trader, Ernest Theurer, was a recent alumnus of Salomon who kept in touch with his old friends. Steinhardt's was probably the best known of the limited partnerships, largely because its general partner and maximum leader couldn't resist the call of a little publicity now and then. But his affection for publicity had its limits. Until 1990 his partnership was licensed by New York State, which requires such partnerships to file periodically at the county courthouse lists of the partners in such operations and of all infusions and withdrawals of money. It is a Class D felony to remove such papers from the county clerk's office, yet Steinhardt's papers (except for the very first list from the mid-1960s) have all disappeared from the files. Paul Roth, his attorney, took the position with the author that filing the papers now missing was the extent of his client's obligations to the public record.

Limited partnerships like Steinhardt's were speculators in all the markets, but until the meeting in Kovner's office they had never been significant players in government bonds. Participants in this meeting when approached by *The Wall Street Journal* did not deny that the meeting occurred and that Luttrell, who led it, spoke encouragingly about the prospects for the two-year notes that would be auctioned in April. But they wished it understood that everybody made up his own mind about whether to participate in the market for April 1993 two-year notes, and there was no conspiracy or collusion.

Someone from Salomon was at Kovner's meeting, but Solly did not make large-scale purchases of the April two-year notes, perhaps because a squeeze of these dimensions by owners rather than financers of a new issue had never been tried before and looked rather risky. The big buyers were Caxton and Steinhardt. A lawsuit by another limited partnership called Three Crown, losers in both the April 1993 and May 1993 two-year notes, alleged that between their purchases in the when-issued market and their purchases through brokers at the auction, Caxton and Steinhardt either owned or had contracts to buy no less than $16 billion worth of a $12 billion auction. The financing of these positions was spread all over the Street: Bear Stearns, Shearson Lehman, Greenwich Capital, and First Boston were involved, as was Salomon. They in turn were making reverse repurchase agreements with the short sellers, at only slightly reduced interest rates.

But the original repurchase agreements through which Caxton and Steinhardt had borrowed the money they needed to carry their position were of very short duration. In late May, Steinhardt yanked the notes away from the other big Wall Street houses and financed its whole bundle, something more than $6 billion, through repurchase agreements with Salomon alone, under an unusual arrangement whereby Steinhardt retained control of where *Salomon* might offer the notes when making its own repurchase agreements. Under these instructions, Salomon refinanced Steinhardt's position with institutions that would not make the April notes available for the shorts to borrow—state and local pension funds and money-market funds that are forbidden to lend their assets, Japanese and European insurance companies that buy and hold.

Added to the normal reduction in the floating supply that occurs through the month after the issuance of notes, because dealers sell some of them every day to retail customers, the shift of holders under repo created a severe squeeze in the April issue. So many of the April notes were placed with institutions which did not lend them that they did not come into anything like reasonable supply for five months, and they were still candidates for "special" rates in the repo market as late as September. "Given unfriendly financing that keeps the collateralized issue off the market," C. Barndt Hauptfuhrer of Three Crown explained in a submission to the SEC the following February, "concentrated ownership of the issue results in control over financing rates that sellers must pay to borrow the issue to cover short positions. Manipulative profits are derived from the control of financing rates."[6] Big profits, tens of millions of dollars, made almost entirely on borrowed money, some of them in this instance to Steinhardt and some of them to Salomon.

Steinhardt's and Caxton's success with the April 1993 notes came to the attention of Julian Robertson of Tiger Management, another major-league hedge fund, who decided to take a piece of this action in the May auction. His usual brokers were Morgan Stanley, who wanted no part of the cowboy stuff going on in the governments market, so he turned to Salomon. Two nights before the auction, Tiger's senior traders, David Gerstenhaber and Tim Henne, had dinner with Mozer at Le Refuge, an intimate box of a French restaurant on a side street in the East 80's. Mozer told them Salomon would finance their purchases, and they might be able to participate in the profits from reverse repos at "special rates." Another lawsuit seeking compensation for losses in these auctions alleged that Mozer told Robertson's traders that "there might be some pressure from other dealers and even from the SEC, but he would take the heat for that."[7] They agreed to buy $1.5 billion; and Mozer two days later put in a $2 billion bid for them, buying back the unauthorized $500 million immediately (on the usual "do not confirm" instructions), and later buying the other $1.5 billion at a small profit to Robertson, who quickly decided he had seen as much action as he wished to see. (Plaintiff's counsel in the lawsuits growing out of the squeeze claim Robertson's trader kept in touch with Mozer and returned to the market later to help keep the squeeze going.)

Caxton was out of the May auction, but Quantum was definitely in, for a full 35 percent of the offering—with Salomon as broker, on an agreement that Salomon would finance the position with repurchase agreements, which meant Solly would control the notes. And Steinhardt was in with both feet, having bought at least $6 billion and perhaps as much as $10 billion of May 1993 notes in the when-issued market.

Mozer himself had sold Steinhardt $1.85 billion of those when-issued contracts but had bought at least $2.3 billion worth from others, and Salomon's "net" when-issued position going into auction day was $485 million in the black. Salomon failed to report that position on its bidding form, as the rules required, and that failure became part of the SEC's case against the firm. Solly's explanation was that it had not come to auction with a long position in years and years, so everybody had forgotten about the rule.

The rumors around Wall Street the day before the auction, especially among Salomon's customers, were that the institutions, upset about the market after the April auctions, were not bidding for the May notes, and the winning bid would be a high rate. Solly salesmen were telling people that it might be 6.84. It is generally believed that Mozer was active in the market the morning of auction day, judiciously selling (which may have been why he did not realize he still had a long position in the when-issued market). Just before one o'clock the when-issued market was trading at 6.83 percent. And Solly came to the Fed with a bid of 6.81 percent, which meant that Solly and its customers got everything they bid for. On the day the May notes auction "settled" (the Treasury issued the notes and collected its money), Solly controlled no less than $10.6 billion of the $11.3 billion available to competitive bidders after the noncompetitive bidders had taken their piece. Out there in the wilderness were all those traders and banks playing the baby arbitrage, who had sold short at least $4.2 billion to Steinhardt, and $2.3 billion to Salomon. They were well and truly squeezed, and they were going to lose many tens of millions of dollars.

Among the squeezed shorts was Robert Hickey of Hickey Financial in Chicago, a conservative banker and a worrier who looked older than his forty-one years and who managed several risk-averse funds that traded Treasury securities and nothing else. Salomon was his leading dealer, and he did about $20 billion a year of trading with Mozer and Murphy, who would buy him a dinner on their semiannual visits to Chicago. "We had been doing business with these people so long, we trusted them," Hickey said. "We were very naive. We were short coming into the May auction. I told them I thought the notes were pricey and we didn't want to trade up [that is, make a bid to yield less than the 6.83 percent price in the when-issued market]. About twenty minutes after the auction, Mozer called and said, 'We bid eighty-one.'

"I said, 'Do you expect them to stay tight?'

"He said, 'I have no reason to believe they won't free up.'

"The price kept going up, and some days later I called again. He said, 'Well, they're in very strong hands.'

"The third time I called, about three weeks after the auction, I said, 'I think you're manipulating the market.' And Mozer said, 'Our counsel tells us that everything we've done is legal.' "

Mozer had gone to John Macfarlane, Salomon's treasurer, before the auction to tell him that he wanted $15 billion of financing to handle Salomon's position and customer positions and Steinhardt's position in the May notes. Feuerstein apparently heard of this request from one of his assistants and told the assistant he thought it would be a bad idea; he also told Strauss that he thought Mozer had "an attitudinal problem."[8] By Salomon's version of the story, Macfarlane was in London and didn't like what he heard. He asked for Meriwether's opinion, and at a meeting on May 28, Meriwether recommended financing the full $10.6 billion that Salomon was buying or financing for itself and George Soros's Quantum Fund, leaving Steinhardt to find his own money. The rest of Wall Street, having been stung by Steinhardt in the April notes, was still reluctant to help him again at the low rates he expected, and Mozer went back to Macfarlane to request Macfarlane's help in finding someone else to fund Steinhardt's May position. Mozer thereupon, presumably with Meriwether's approval, took over the financing of Steinhardt's position in the *April* notes to free up Steinhardt's credit for use in his plan to buy the May notes.

Word of the squeeze was everywhere. As early as May 23, one day after the auction, Hauptfuhrer of Three Crown was on the phone with Peter Sternlight at the Federal Reserve Bank of New York to alert him to the dangers from Salomon's extraordinary capture of the May 1993 notes. Hauptfuhrer was the man who had built much of the Salomon repurchase system in the late 1970s before going out on his own as a trader under the name Three Crown. As Hauptfuhrer hung up, Michael Basham was on the phone from Treasury with a similar message. As late as May 28, Salomon still had not provided the "list to follow" of purchasers who should be recorded as having bought the notes auctioned on May 22. Anyone looking over the chronologies later provided by the various government agencies to Congressman Edward Markey's House subcommittee on telecommunications and finance would think it fair to say the thing stank to high heaven.

On May 29, two days before settlement day, Michael Basham at the Treasury called William Heyman, director of Market Regulation at the SEC, to discuss what looked like manipulation in the when-issued market for these notes, and the Treasury's assistant general counsel called the SEC's Division of Enforcement to ask for a formal investigation. *The Wall Street Journal* for May 31 had an article about the jump in the price of the May notes, which had generated profits of about $30 million since auction day for the lucky holders of the notes. (Mozer was among those the *Journal* reporters had called, of course. He told them that "his views about the market were considered by Salomon's sales managers to be 'too valuable' to be quoted in the U.S. financial press.")[9]

That same day Steve Bell, the senior Salomon Washington lobbyist, called Deputy Treasury Secretary Robert Glauber to suggest that if he was concerned about the May notes, he should call John Gutfreund and talk it over with him. On June 1, Ernest Patrikis swung into action. Senior vice-president and general counsel of the New York Fed and a stickler for details, a small, very smart man with a black mustache and a profound Boston accent, Patrikis has gone into the history books as the nitpicker who delayed the final release of the Iranian hostages because the documents relating to the release of frozen Iranian assets were not yet acceptable to him. Now he called the relevant lawyers at the SEC, the Treasury, and the Antitrust Division of the Justice Department to make sure everybody had his ducks in a row.

Sternlight of the New York Fed called Mozer and told him that the Fed did not want any "fails" after this auction and that he was counting on Salomon to make notes available in the repo market. Some reverse repos were done at the end of May with the borrower paying only 1 percent interest on his money, because the lender needed his notes to deliver against his sales on when-issued contracts. After Sternlight's call, to keep things from looking as bad as they really were, Mozer gave instructions that the "special" rate for reverse repos on the May notes should be kept within two percentage points of what Salomon was paying others in the "general" repo market.

On June 4, Basham called Mozer to discuss market conditions in the May notes. "I did tell Paul I was surprised that the May two-year note was trading on 'special' in the 'rp' market," Basham later wrote in his post-testimony replies to written questions by Congressman Jim Bunning of Jake Pickles's Committee on Government Oversight, "particularly in view of the large positions that Salomon and Quantum had to finance in that market. Additionally, Paul told me that if the Secretary were to call John Gutfreund and tell him that Treasury wanted Salomon to liquidate their May two-year note position, Gutfreund would order the position sold immediately. (Paul called me back the following morning, June 5, 1991, to tell me he had talked to Tom Strauss about this representation and Mr. Strauss had said that a call from the Secretary would not necessarily result in Salomon liquidating their May two-year note position.)"[10]

Salomon's Bell kept calling Glauber, who proved unwilling to call Gutfreund even though he was a mere Treasury undersecretary and Harvard professor and Gutfreund was the King of Wall Street. So Mahomet came to the mountain, and Bell requested an appointment for Gutfreund to meet in Washington with Glauber and Assistant Secretary Jerome Powell, a lawyer turned investment banker with little market experience who had been at Dillon Read when Treasury Secretary Nicholas Brady was chairman of that investment bank. They met on June 10, and Gutfreund made what the Treasury people considered a rambling and inconsequent presentation to the effect that what may have looked to amateurs like a squeeze was really just one of those things.

He also offered Salomon's help in any reforms of the governments market the Treasury or the Congress might have in mind, for Gutfreund now was nothing if not a statesman. And he left behind some graphs to show that the price movements in the May 1993 notes were well within the bounds of reasonable expectation in a free market. (Interestingly, these graphs apparently were not the product of Salomon's famed research department and its statistical technician Martin Leibowitz but had been pasted together by trading floor clerks. They have never been made a matter of public record, and in the light of the graph that shows the *real* situation in the May notes [on p. 195], one wonders what they look like.) Tom Strauss called Glauber a few days later to make sure that Gutfreund's presentation had taken care of the matter; Glauber was noncommittal.

The announcement of the June two-year auction did not bring forth the usual stream of May notes to be sold as the institutions rolled over into the new issue, but the auction itself was unexceptionable. Basham and the SEC had been holding their fire until after that auction, setting a trap for Salomon and Steinhardt. On the morning of the auction, Gutfreund and Strauss both spoke to Mozer and told him to keep his head down on this one.[11] On June 26, when that auction was history, the SEC sent letters to Salomon and its customers asking for information on what had happened in the May auction and its aftermarket. Salomon replied with many fewer documents and less information than the SEC wanted, and the lawyers for the two sides were back and forth for six weeks. Despite this evidence of strong government interest, Salomon and Steinhardt tightened the screws a little further on July 1, withdrawing some of the May notes from the repo market and provoking the worst panic yet among the short sellers.

The Justice Department had been aware of the SEC investigation since June 1 and thought it saw a conspiracy in restraint of trade, opening up the possibility of both criminal and civil prosecution under the Sherman Anti-Trust Act. On June 13 several Justice Department lawyers met with people at the senior vice-president level of the New York Fed. Later in the month Christopher Kelly of the Antitrust Division discussed with Norman

Carleton of the Treasury's Office of Federal Finance Policy Analysis and with two Treasury attorneys what kinds of information Justice would need to bring its case—and the FBI went off to Goldman Sachs, triggering Martin Lipton's dinner with Gutfreund in Europe.

On July 8 lawyers from Wachtell Lipton Rosen & Katz came to Salomon to do an internal investigation of the governments trading department. They soon found that $500 million of the notes Tiger, as Salomon's customer, had won at the May auction had been sold immediately to Salomon at the auction price. This was on its face an unlikely sale, because the price of the notes had jumped after the auction, and Tiger would have had no reason to give Solly a bargain. Looking at the computer records they found that Salomon had confirmed to Tiger a purchase of only $1.5 billion of the $2 billion Tiger had been credited with on the list that Salomon had submitted to the Fed following its bid. To conceal the fact that Solly had arbitrarily inflated Tiger's bid and kept the inflated portion for its own account, Mozer had arranged to have the computer system send Tiger a confirmation for its $1.5 billion and no more, and had entered the remaining $500 million as a sale from Tiger to Salomon.

There is an old story about a man who returns home to find his bossy wife in bed with another man, and upon recovering speech says, "I am surprised . . ." only to find his wife correcting him again with the words, "No, dear. *I* am surprised; *you* are amazed; *he* is astonished." On July 12 the Lipton lawyers were surprised to find the inflated Tiger bid and Salomon's expropriation of the excess notes. They were thereupon amazed to learn that in the February five-year note auction Mozer had faked a bid from S. G. Warburg's Mercury Asset Management to win a greater share of the notes than would otherwise have been awarded to Salomon. And presently they were astonished to find that Tom Strauss and John Gutfreund had known since late April about Mozer's violation of the Treasury's rules—and had done nothing about it.

Not a good day at the office. Not a good day at all.

Reinforcements were rushed from Wachtell Lipton to the team investigating Salomon's government bonds department, and the better part of a month was spent preparing a seventy-two-page report. Done for top management, the report was essentially un-

critical of top management, but it was damning to Mozer and
Murphy, both of whom got their own lawyers and stopped cooperating with the Wachtell Lipton team before the anguished what-
can-we-*do* meeting at the law firm's office on August 7.

SOLLY SQUIRMS

The end for Gutfreund and Strauss and Meriwether came with a
bang after the government regulators learned that they had failed
to report Mozer's deceptive behavior when they first learned
about it. New York Fed president E. Gerald Corrigan called his
friend Tom Strauss on Monday morning, August 12, after reading
The Wall Street Journal story about Salomon's Friday press release. At Corrigan's direction, Peter Sternlight wrote a letter that
was hand-delivered to Gutfreund on Tuesday, August 13, demanding what Corrigan later described as "a written explanation of the
circumstances surrounding the disclosures made on August 9, and
a full report on managerial and other changes that would be taken
to prevent the recurrence of those irregularities in the future."
Gutfreund and Strauss called Corrigan, who told them he meant it.
Then they called again, to tell Corrigan that a special meeting of
the Salomon board was going to be held the next day by conference call and that after that meeting there would be a press release which would tell all, including Mozer's faked "Warburg" bid
in the February notes auction, and would clean up the situation.

Treasury learned the morning of the fourteenth that more news
was to be made available, and leaked the word to the SEC, where
a steaming chairman Richard Breeden called Gutfreund at 12:45,
which interfered with his preparation time for the one o'clock
conference-call board meeting. The outside members of the board
were unhappy to the point of rebellion and demanded a real
meeting in New York the following Monday. (As it turned out, the
meeting was moved up to Sunday.) At two o'clock, in a conference room in the Treasury Department's building across the street
from the White House, Wachtell Lipton lawyers presented the
results of their investigation to people from the SEC, the Federal
Reserve Bank Board, the Treasury, and the New York Stock Exchange (though they did not at this point make the report itself

available to the government). As this meeting ended, Salomon issued its classic of black humor, explaining that Gutfreund & Co. had decided to inform the government of Mozer's misbehavior way back in April, but "due to a lack of sufficient attention to the matter, this determination was not implemented promptly."

At Salomon itself, except in a government bonds department where two managing directors had been placed on leave and in a treasurer's office that felt lenders shrinking away, it was more or less business as usual. The firm's profits in the first half had been little short of miraculous, providing a giant cushion against trouble bigger than this appeared to be; people were concentrating on their anticipated bonuses, not on newspaper stories. Salomon was known not to be loved. There had been nothing ominous in the paper on Tuesday or Wednesday, and no reason to believe that anything about the investigation was life-threatening to anybody but those immediately involved. And that category did not appear to reach very high in the firm. It was Meriwether who had been put in charge of cleansing his own department.

But beneath the surface the plates were moving, and the earthquake was coming. On Thursday the gods consulted with one another—Corrigan, Brady, Fed chairman Alan Greenspan. Salomon's borrowings to carry its portfolio involved literally tens of billions of dollars of short-term bank credit and bank guarantees behind commercial paper. A hostile Fed would give the banks the perfect excuse to pull their lines. On Friday, one week after the initial press release, the lightning flashed. The record showed no fewer than five calls from Corrigan to Gutfreund and Strauss, and a final call from Sternlight to Gutfreund to arrange a meeting with Corrigan, a meeting that never happened: Corrigan was done with Gutfreund.

Warren Buffett had $700 million of his holding company's money at risk in Salomon, Inc. He descended from his Omaha headquarters by corporate plane to meet with Corrigan on Friday afternoon and take charge at Salomon. Gutfreund, Strauss, and Meriwether would resign (Meriwether only after trying an independent appeal to Corrigan, arguing incorrectly that he had fulfilled his obligations when he told Strauss about Mozer's misbehavior); Mozer and Murphy would be fired immediately; Feuerstein would resign a week later (with a statement that he understood why his resignation had been requested); and two weeks after that event, Wachtell Lipton at Buffett's suggestion would sever its client relationship with Salomon. Buffett chaired Sunday's Salomon board meeting, made telephone calls to Treasury Secretary Nicholas Brady, held press conferences, and extended over Salomon the cloak of his folksy solidity and his unquestioned personal honesty. Among his promises to the infuriated regulators that first weekend was that Salomon would open all its files to their investigators, waive attorney-client privilege, and turn over the Wachtell Lipton report and all the notes the Wachtell Lipton lawyers had made preparing it. For three weeks Gutfreund, Strauss, and Meriwether while off the payroll continued to have offices at Salomon (in the old headquarters at One New York Plaza), limousines and drivers, secretaries, and access to whatever records they thought they might want. This got into the newspapers, and Buffett severed all relations between his Salomon and its former leaders.

The Friday afternoon of his resignation, Gutfreund summoned Solly's managing directors to a meeting in the handsome thirty-ninth-floor auditorium and told his stunned audience that he and Strauss were departing. Like most of Gutfreund's meetings with the people who worked for him, this one was brief: The boss spoke and the others listened, and that was it. "No apologies to anybody," he said, "for anything. Apologies don't mean shit. What happened, happened."

Chapter 9

THE JUDGMENTS OF SALOMON

SALOMON'S VERSION of what happened continued to be that there was a mad dog loose in its trading department, and he became suicidal. His supervisors meant to warn the government to watch him before he bit another victim, but everybody was so busy, this task fell through the cracks. By dint of hard work, Salomon sold this story, at least for a time, to most of the press and even some of the government. Sarah Bartlett of *The New York Times* swallowed it hook, line, and sinker for a Sunday article entitled "Salomon's Errant Cowboy."[1] "One brilliant woman from the *Times* figured it out all by herself," Salomon's public relations man Bob Baker said admiringly. "We never," he added with a straight face, "said that to her." But Salomon's story was simply not credible. Even if Salomon can keep the record in its present shadowy state by settling all the lawsuits from the losers in the squeeze and the stockholders claiming damages from Solly's board of directors, financial historians are not going to accept what is on examination, despite some pooh-bah artistic verisimilitude, a baldly unconvincing narrative.

To begin, the handling of customer orders in the government bonds department bore too many resemblances to Salomon's handling of program trading orders from six customers in 1987. Here trades for customers were reported back to them as executed at prices less favorable than the real prices—and Salomon itself took the more favorable executions for its own account. The New York Stock Exchange fined Salomon $1.3 million for this atrocity, the largest fine in the history of the exchange. Among the changes the exchange demanded in Salomon's compliance procedures was a rule prohibiting traders from changing the numbers in the computer without specific permission from the firm's compliance department. Like the Mozer malefaction, the equities department scandal was made possible by a computer system that could be jiggered by traders for their own benefit, a situation created by Allan Fine's refusal to spend the money to automate the compliance function. The fine was imposed in January 1991, a month before Mozer faked the two bids in the February notes auction. Gutfreund, Strauss, and Feuerstein met with Meriwether to discuss the Mozer problem four days after the deadline the NYSE had set for the implementation of policies designed to prevent a repetition of this behavior. Obviously, they didn't care. They would have cared once, but they didn't care now.

Wachtell Lipton's lawyers found out quickly the procedures Mozer had followed to hide from customers the fact that he was abusing their names. Meriwether, Strauss, and Gutfreund were all bond traders, and they all had full access to Salomon's computers. Accepting their statement that Mozer lied to them, it passes understanding that none of them so much as idly pushed some buttons to find out whether or not Mozer had pulled this stunt before—or, indeed, after. The obvious truth is that they didn't think what Mozer had done was all that serious. It was standard operating procedure to overstate bids in the auctions for paper issued by Fannie Mae and Freddie Mac in hopes of getting larger allocations in the prorations. There seemed a limit to how seriously the government could take a 35 percent rule that applied only to the auctions and permitted dealers to own as much of an issue as they could buy so long as they didn't buy it in the auction. Mozer was making money for the firm, and he passed on to the proprietary trading group more and better information than his predecessors had passed on. Management didn't tell the authorities about Mozer's misbehavior because it didn't *want* to tell the authorities, not because people were forgetful.

In the matter of the May notes, the addition of $10.6 billion to the firm's assets and liabilities position was real money even for Salomon and was the sort of thing computer screens flag for management. When the newspapers, the Treasury, even the Fed got on Solly's back about the May auction, surely someone in management should have wondered why so large a sum had been added to the company's balance sheet. Before going down to see Secretary Glauber, simple prudence should have led Gutfreund to take a peek in the computer—or at least ask Meriwether to take a peek—to see if there were any "do not confirm" orders to create suspicion that Mozer was do-do-doing again what he had done-done-done before. Surely Mozer's arguments with the Treasury over the 35 percent rule and his unauthorized bid for Warburg must have been in Gutfreund's mind when he engaged Wachtell Lipton to investigate the May auction and its aftermarket, but the law firm had no warning at all of what it was about to find. There was a cover-up not only from the government but from Salomon's own lawyers.

Finally, there was a series of arguments by Salomon's new clean-as-a-whistle management, arguments that were so disingenuous, it was hard not to call them dishonest. Discussing the squeeze in the May notes, for example, Salomon's statement to the Senate Banking Committee denied that the firm controlled the notes Quantum Fund had bought at the auction and financed by means of repurchase agreements with Salomon: "Quantum at all times was fully responsible for the economic risk of its position, determined on its own whether and when to buy or sell, to Salomon or others, and was free to terminate its financing relationship with Salomon at any time on one day's notice. . . . In determining the financing rate to be charged to Quantum, Salomon added a small service fee to the average financing rate of the aggregate positions held by both Salomon and Quantum."[2]

But the money made in a squeeze of this sort is made by putting out the notes for reverse repos at "special rates," thereby reducing the interest payments the owners of the notes would otherwise have to make to carry on their business. And the money lost by those who are squeezed is lost in their sacrifice of the interest they could otherwise earn on their funds. What was meant by the statement that Salomon financed Quantum at "the average financing rate of the aggregate positions held by both" was that Solly split with Quantum the profits on the "special rates" at which they could lend out their notes. Legally, day by day, Salomon owned the notes it had purchased from Quantum under the repurchase agreement, and as a practical matter it clearly controlled what would be done with them. Recommending in summer 1991 that all big players be required to report their positions, the committee of leaders of the industry who advise the Treasury on borrowing tactics made no distinction between positions purchased and positions borrowed.

In the same statement post-Gutfreund Salomon argued that "because the total of all 'long' positions in any security equals the total of all 'short' positions, plus the amount of securities sold at the auction, Salomon and its customer had a significantly smaller percentage of the total 'long' position than they had of the securities sold at the auction. For example, if 'long' positions totalled $8 billion in excess of approximately $12 billion sold at auction (and corresponding 'short' positions therefore also totalled $8 billion), then Salomon and Quantum, each with about $5 billion, each would have had approximately 25 percent of the total of all 'long' positions."[3] Let us extend this preposterous argument: If the when-issued market had generated $100 billion in short sales, if the hedge funds had really raided and raped it, Salomon and Quantum would have had only approximately 5 percent each of the total of "long" positions—but of course they would have had *all* the notes that could be used to satisfy the $100 billion in sales contracts the baby arbitrageurs had signed. Bond traders would be jumping off the top of the World Trade Center in despair, the few notes available to the poor shorts would be selling for much, much more than their face value, arbitrageurs would be paying people for the privilege of lending them money on the security of these notes—but Solly and Quantum could claim that they were scarcely a factor, because the notes they owned, while all the notes there were, made up, after all, only 5 percent of the total "long" position.

Nor did the Salomon arrogance end after less domineering personalities took charge of the firm. When Congressman Edgar Jenkins of Georgia suggested at a hearing that the Fed might still find it a proper penalty to suspend Salomon's status as a primary dealer, Deryck Maughan, the firm's new president, showed teeth: "We are one of America's largest investment banks. We run a balance sheet of $100 billion. We have an off-balance sheet of several more hundred billion dollars, and as a former government official I would be concerned ... with what we would term systemic risk. If you fell this tree, what other trees fall? This is a tall tree. . . . Nothing could guarantee that the market would not be disturbed and that the price of government debt would rise. . . . if one were to act brashly in this manner."

And Congressman Jenkins replied, "It may very well be a sad state of affairs. . . . If we are so subjected to one securities firm or two securities firms . . . that if you as a securities dealer are caught manipulating the marketplace, that we cannot eliminate you as a primary dealer . . . If the American people are at the mercy of one or more companies that we could not take any action, that disturbs me."[4]

THE BUFFETT FACTOR

If Warren Buffett had not been available to lead Salomon Brothers in August 1991, the firm would have gone under that fall. Foreign banks had already begun to cancel their credit lines to Salomon. ("We Germans," said one, "will never forgive Salomon. They did the unforgivable thing. They drew the attention of the government to this market.") The fury of the Treasury Department over the May squeeze and the deceptions Salomon practiced led to the cancellation of Salomon's right to bid at the Treasury auctions. This automatically meant a loss of the status of primary dealer, because one of the qualifications for that status was that the primary dealer bid at the auctions. Absent the information flow from its participation in the wholesale market for government securities, Salomon would have been disabled in its fixed-income trading departments. Customers would have fled to do business with others, and banking customers would not have allowed Salomon to bid for their business.

Buffett was distantly related by marriage to Treasury Secretary Nicholas Brady, and he was, after all, a billionaire Republican. (Gutfreund, oddly enough, was a Democrat; he had chaired the Wall Street end of George McGovern's fund-raising in 1972.) Buffett got through to Brady twice on a Sunday in August and also spoke with Alan Greenspan and Gerald Corrigan. On Buffett's assurances that Gutfreund, Strauss, and Meriwether were out and that the entire Salomon governments operation would be shaken up (which did not happen), the Federal Reserve gave Brady a green light to permit Solly to continue to bid at the auctions, but only for its own account, not for customers. (This restriction remained in effect for almost a year, until August 3, 1992.) A man who was involved with both matters said flatly that "Fred Joseph [the chairman of Drexel Burnham] made decisions that guaranteed the death of that firm; Warren Buffett made decisions that created the possibility that Salomon could survive." Leaving office, U.S. Attorney Otto Obermaier made it official: "We decided that no prosecution of the corporate entity was appropriate because Salomon had promptly disclosed its wrongdoing, reprimanded and punished those responsible, put in place a new management, and was exemplary in its cooperation with the government."[5]

The nation was in a recession in August 1991, which made the government even more reluctant than it might otherwise have been to see another major securities firm bite the dust. The Federal Reserve System had decided that the most effective way to fight the recession would be to make the banking system look and feel profitable, which meant widening the gap between the banks' cost of funds and their revenues from lending, and driving up the value of the securities in their portfolios. (The entire improvement in the profitability of the banking system in 1991 as compared with 1990 was in the sale of securities from the banks' investment portfolios, which is not the way banks are supposed to make a living.) These policies also meant greatly enhanced profits for firms like Salomon, where two-thirds of total revenues were absorbed by interest payments on the loans the firm took to carry its inventory. And, of course, the value of that inventory would go up as interest rates went down. Most of Salomon in 1991 was like Ranieri's mortgage department in 1982–85; despite the turmoil surrounding the disaster in the government bonds department, there was no way *not* to make money. Even the lagging equities department could be added to the list of no-brain winners at the end of the year when the stock market burst ahead on a tidal wave of individual investment in stocks.

Buffett made an immediate image decision that he did not wish to identify the new Salomon with the history of the firm. This may have been a reflection of the aspersions Gutfreund had cast on his former partners through the years when Buffett had trusted him. (Earlier in 1991, Gutfreund had told Gilbert Kaplan of *Institutional Investor,* explaining the blood purges at Salomon in the late 1980s, that "the people who had been made rich in 1981 when we sold our business were beginning to lose interest or think they were really worth all the money they received.")[6] Billy, age seventy-eight, whose name was still on the company, wrote Buffett a letter the day he assumed command, offering his services in whatever form Buffett might find useful—to stand beside him at press conferences or come around to buck up the staff or talk with some of the old-timers in the Fed. He never received a reply. A party was scheduled for September for the former partners and vice-presidents, to introduce them to the new headquarters at 7 World Trade Center, which Solly had occupied only in May. Buffett cancelled it. Henry Kaufman was finally invited to lunch—not with Buffett—toward the end of the year. When an old-timer still at the firm suggested at an early meeting of managing directors that one of the things the new Salomon might do was reconstruct its municipal bonds department as a symbol of the firm's return to its traditions, Buffett asked sourly who would provide the capital for such a restoration.

Although not without self-confidence, Buffett fully understood that he knew little about running a Wall Street house. He was at Salomon to protect a $700 million investment—and perhaps to take charge of protecting himself, because lawyers representing stockholders in Salomon had brought and could win a "derivative" suit against the company's board of directors for negligence in supervising the conduct of the firm. One of the most serious issues raised by the Salomon scandal, as Peter Peterson of the Blackstone Group pointed out, was the question of whether we have adequate standards for corporate governance in the United States. (Writing to Buffett to request an interview, I indicated that corporate governance was the subject I most wished to discuss with him. In his reply rejecting my request, he said he couldn't see me because he was planning to write his own book on that subject, and as a writer I would understand that he didn't wish to give away his best stuff.)

Although he did seek to restore some of the partnership ethos

Billy had created, announcing that in the future Solly would pay much of its employee bonus pool in the form of shares that could not be cashed in for five years, Buffett may not have understood the role of the Salomon compensation system in creating the scandals of 1991. Among his early acts was the appointment of an executive committee that included Lawrence Hilibrand, who had received $23.6 million under Strauss and Gutfreund's secret deal to keep him at the firm. In Buffett's first report to Salomon share-holders, in October, he reaffirmed his belief in "truly extraordi-nary pay for extraordinary managerial performance." The problem at Salomon, he said, was "a compensation plan that was irrational in certain crucial respects."

Buffett stressed "the lopsided way in which Salomon has earned its profits—a matter, indeed, on which Salomon's directors were not supplied sufficient information.... Salomon's lackluster over-all profits of recent years resulted from a combination of excellent earnings in a few areas of the business—operating in an honest and ethical manner, it should be added—with inadequate or non-existent earnings at the remainder.... In effect, the fine perfor-mance of some people subsidized truly outsized rewards for others. It would be understandable if a private partnership opted for such an egalitarian, share-the-wealth system. But Salomon is a publicly owned company depending on vast amounts of share-holders' capital. In such an operation it is appropriate that the excess earnings of the exceptional performers—that is, what they generate beyond what they are justly paid—go to the stockhold-ers."[7]

But investment banking is a business where the whole, not the parts, makes the money. Even the banker doing business with the corporate chairman who was his buddy in their final club at Princeton will eventually lose that business if his support staff isn't highly qualified. Within the securities firm, one hand is forever washing the other: The customers of the trading desks buy the securities the investment bankers underwrite; the inventors of instruments for corporate finance support both investment bank-ing and trading. As Meriwether told Ronald Freeman and David Stockman during the task force days, his proprietary trading de-partment was dependent on its knowledge of customer order flows. Indeed, Mozer's resentments may well have drawn from a belief that Meriwether and Hilibrand looked good because of the information he passed on from his customer accounts.

Buffett recognized this grudgingly: "Our compensation plans must also both reward cooperative, for-the-good-of-the-firm behavior and recognize that some business units earn relatively little in profits but deliver valuable, if hard to quantify, collateral benefits to the firm." What he did not recognize was that Salomon was also a business where, very visibly—governments trading to mortgages to junk bonds to arbitrage games—the profit sources are going to vary from year to year, regardless of who the managers are and how good they are. As the Revco deal demonstrated, investment bankers who are paid for making this year's deals—whether or not they make sense over time—may take down spectacular rewards without really contributing to the profitability of the firm. And large chunks of the profitability of an investment house lie in areas where, unless the hawks are always watching, the traders can fake their profits for their own benefit. David Tendler was undoubtedly right that whatever the compensation system for the traders, their supervisors must be on salary.

Buffett worked in the securities industry only briefly, as a lad in his father's brokerage office in Omaha, and there is reason to fear that he may have a tin ear for the music of compliance. To head the Salomon board's compliance committee, he appointed Lord Young of Graffham, who had been trained to the far less demanding ethics of the British market and had been chairman of the executive committee of Salomon Brothers International. Among the recent activities of Salomon International was the issuance of stock for Robert Maxwell's Mirror Group on the basis of an offering circular that, to quote the U.S. General Accounting Office, "did not provide adjusted financial figures in accordance with U.S. standards." Excused from American rules by the SEC's unfortunate Rule 144-A exemption for "private placements," Salomon sold 45 million shares of Maxwell's paper in May 1991 to U.S. mutual funds, insurance companies, and pension funds. Surely someone who had recently been involved with aiding the plans of Robert Maxwell was not an impeccable candidate to be top watchdog for the new Salomon. Lord Young was also embarrassed in the European Community by allegations that he concealed a government subsidy to the British aircraft industry when he was a minister in

Margaret Thatcher's government.[8] In 1993, Lord Young of Graff-ham was in the news as the intermediary and negotiator for an Iranian art dealer whose offer to "give" his collection to a British museum on a temporary basis was widely regarded in England as a fiddle to promote his subsequent profits.[9]

In June 1992 the firm hired a new compliance chief for its fixed-income traders, a young man named Charles Williams with no securities law background. He told *The Wall Street Journal* that in working with traders he wanted to "gain enough of their confidence so they can come to me and we can work out whatever we have to." If he performed satisfactorily in compliance, the *Journal* reported, he might get promoted to sales or trading.[10]

THE COST OF THE CUTS

The first victims of Buffett's insistence that departments had to pay their individual way were about 150 high-ranking professionals in the firm's equities, investment banking, merchant banking, and real estate sections. In a telephone conference call to all Salomon offices worldwide in November, Buffett identified those as the departments of the firm that had not pulled their weight in 1990–91. Before agreeing to maintain the bonuses for the people in the rest of the firm, Buffett demanded that the payroll be slashed there. Kurt Eichenwald in *The New York Times* reported statements by Buffett "that the firm could no longer afford to stay in businesses that were not making money."[11] After their year-end bonuses were cut, several dozen more Salomon managing directors and vice-presidents bailed out in early 1992.

Buffett also forced out Stanley Shopkorn, Salomon's forty-eight-year-old head of equity trading, who had held that job since Rosenthal's departure in 1982. A Bronx boy, Shopkorn was one of the few surviving Jews in the firm's senior executive cadre. Before casting him off, Buffett humiliated him by ordering him to clean out at a $98 million loss two positions he had acquired for Salomon in block trades that had lingered too long. This also made trouble with some customers who had acquired pieces of the block at the price Salomon insisted it was worth; they now learned that if they had distrusted their Salomon salesman, they could have bought it cheaper. Shopkorn's basic problem with Buffett, however, may have been that he was a big investor in Steinhardt Partners, despite the fact that Steinhardt was one of his biggest customers. After a decent interval, in fact, he would join Steinhardt as a senior trader. It was a source of some annoyance in the department that the positions Buffett made Shopkorn clean out rose in price with the rest of the market not long after he was forced to sell them.

The person Buffett chose to be his president, budget cutter, and chief operating officer (and later chief executive officer, after the government's case against the firm was settled) was a man whose identification with the firm was minimal. Deryck Maughan was a self-assured forty-three-year-old Welshman who had joined Salomon from the London office of Goldman Sachs in 1983, two years after the Phibro deal ended the partnership. Maughan had worked mostly abroad, in London and in Tokyo. Gutfreund had brought him to New York only a few months before, to share the leadership of the investment banking department with Jay Higgins. A well-liked picture-book banker with iron-gray hair who had overcome his early identification with William Agee and the preposterous Bendix deal, Higgins had been a protégé of Martin Lipton within the firm. He had not shown great talent for managing the department or creating business opportunities. Not long after Maughan became president, Higgins left.

Soft-spoken and intelligent, Maughan, like a lot of the Solly old-timers, had risen from humble beginnings—he was a miner's son—but he had never been a trader. He had made his reputation at Salomon as administrator of the Tokyo office, which was a mess when he arrived, part of an international operation poorly run from London. Maughan also had considerable shy charm. Asked soon after his appointment what he thought had caused the crisis in the government bonds department, he took his theme from Tom Wolfe's novel: "I suppose," he said, "the Masters of the Universe syndrome."

Salomon's Tokyo office—the fifth largest securities brokerage operation in Japan—had made considerable money under Maughan, but much of it came from complicated bets against the Japanese stock market. Salomon arranged "put warrants" on the Nikkei index (issued in theory by the Kingdom of Denmark, which

NIGHTMARE ON WALL STREET

was paid for allowing the use of its name), allowing their purchasers to sell the Nikkei at a pre-set price. The sellers of these warrants, which Salomon arranged to have traded on the American Stock Exchange in New York, would then cover themselves by selling the futures contract on the Nikkei, traded at the Osaka Stock Exchange. And as the prices on the Nikkei contract fell, partly in response to overseas purchases of the puts, Salomon played the index arbitrage game between the futures contract and the real stocks on the Tokyo Stock Exchange, driving down the Japanese stock market. People at the TSE who were neither fools nor amateurs believed that the severity of the decline in Japanese stock prices was in part the result of this fiddling with their markets. They were very angry (eventually, they blocked the issuance of more warrants on the Nikkei in the United States), and they have long memories. The Salomon franchise in Tokyo had less value than New York believed.

The first chore for Buffett and Maughan—and especially for CFO Donald Howard and corporate treasurer John Macfarlane—was to shrink Salomon's borrowings, which meant selling a lot of assets in a market that knew Solly had to be selling. Overnight, said Macfarlane, "our objectives changed from revenue maximization to preservation of liquidity."[12] Before the events of August 1991, Salomon had been heading for a record year, and following that track had enormously expanded its inventory, from $118 billion at the end of 1990 to more than $155 billion in midsummer 1991. In the six weeks after the disaster, selling off assets, reducing its matched book of repurchase agreements, and paying back commercial paper borrowings and bank loans, Salomon reduced that inventory to less than $100 billion, much of which was funded with longer-term debt.

Two main devices were used to force the traders to sell. First, the desks were told that the annual cost of funds shown on their profit-and-loss statements was going to be raised by four percentage points. This sounds like more than it was, because it increased the cost of holding a position for one week by only about eight one-hundredths of 1 percent (four percentage points divided by fifty-two), but it was enough to put many previously profitable trades into the ashcan. Meanwhile, Maughan conducted twice-weekly meetings of the head traders in New York, with conference-call linkages to London and Tokyo, at which everybody came clean about his or her own position—and traders critiqued one another for the common good. Like Hans Kertess and Bob Spiegel in the 1960s, they sold one another's positions. All this was carried on while there was blood in the water and the sharks were constantly circling: Bonds in which Salomon was known to have a heavy position were by no means easy to sell. Traders exult in what they call "beautiful" trades. For many on the Salomon desks, the most beautiful trades of their lives were the ones in which they ran down their positions at minimal or no cost to the firm.

Still, the shrinkage was enormously costly to Salomon, because it came at a time when the Fed was backstopping all financial intermediaries, cutting their cost of funds and not even jawboning them to cut their charges to their customers. The $155 billion inventory was earning much more than Solly had to pay to fund it—and had greater market value every day Solly held on to it. There were *probably* enough loyal lenders in Salomon's stable to have kept the firm liquid with the higher inventory, at an additional cost much less than four percentage points a year. In a meeting with analysts from institutional investors in March 1992, Buffett put a number on the 1991 profits the firm had lost by shrinking—$700 million. Henry Kaufman said Buffett and Maughan had no choice but shrinkage: "They had four billion dollars of capital, one hundred and fifty-five billion dollars of assets and six hundred billion dollars of off-balance-sheet exposure. The commercial paper issues were becoming very costly. You're in this turmoil. What are you going to have to pay as a fine? Will there be criminal charges? People are pulling their lines [of credit]. You want to be in a position to say, 'We can take care of ourselves.'"

While Salomon was cutting back its balance-sheet assets, however, it was in fact adding to its off-balance-sheet swaps and options and custom-designed forward contracts. The Salomon collection of hard-to-value exotica rose from the $600 billion that worried Kaufman to more than $800 billion in the spring of 1992. This was, stockholders and regulators were told, a "notional" exposure because the book is balanced, but the footnote in Salomon's annual statement that referred to these matters claimed a total positive valuation of almost $1.5 billion, which was about twice the pre-tax earnings of Salomon in its best prior years. And if you can win this kind of money in that casino, you can lose it, too.

Maughan's experiences in Tokyo had given him a rather strange view of what matters in the securities business. A couple of months after he took over the presidency of Salomon, "Adam Smith" asked him in an interview for his television show whether he feared that the scandal would impede Salomon's recruiting. No, he said; he thought that people who were "high-tech and very intelligent" would still wish to come to Salomon. "Smith" did a double-take—only people who were high-tech? Yes, Maughan said; "the math professors" were the people who did best at spotting the "anomalies" that cropped up when trading "complex securities."

But there are, of course, lots of math professors available to help securities firms exploit anomalies, and where such transactions are open and aboveboard, the margins rapidly deteriorate. After a while the "complex securities" are created not because they deliver an advantage to their issuers but because they are susceptible to the manipulation that creates the "anomalies"—like the put warrants on the Nikkei. In this "dangerous game," Eugene Rotberg, former treasurer of the World Bank, told a Senate committee, "profitability comes from either identifying or, unhappily, creating tiny aberrations in an arcane way which may disappear quickly before either your competitors or someone else's client realizes what has happened."[13] If Buffett believed that this was an "honest and ethical" business, he was wrong.

There is no doubt that the mathematics of these swaps and options and forward contracts is complicated, full of second-order partial differential equations and integrals, but the realities are much simpler than the abstractions. A swap that obliges you to pay a fixed interest rate while the other side pays a variable interest rate on the same amount of money will go up in value if interest rates rise, and go down in value if interest rates fall; and the fellow who takes the variable-rate side makes money if rates go down and loses money if they go up. People choosing between fixed- and adjustable-rate mortgages understand this perfectly well, and while one has to be a rocket scientist (with a computer) to measure all the permutations, the principles are not complicated. Interest-rate swaps, in other words, are similar to the very volatile IO/PO strips that Ranieri's mortgage department played with in its glory days.

Someone who writes a swap taking the unfashionable side will be paid to do so, as the British municipal councils (town governments) were in the 1980s by the American banks that thought they were exploiting the ignorance of these Labour Party politicians. The municipal councils took the money because they needed it and it looked like a gift. When the swaps proved burdensome, they reneged on their deals with the banks, and the Tory House of Lords, in an action rebuking the sharpies of the City, agreed that municipalities had never been empowered to enter into such contracts and that therefore they were not obliged to pay. The municipal councils then tried to keep the cash they had been paid to sign the deals, and now British justice got offended; the American banks that had booked some hundreds of millions of "notional" dollars in profits on their dealing with the councils had to take write-offs, but they did get back their few million in cash payments.

In 1992, the volume of swap contracts, options, and tailored forward contracts, not visible on balance sheets and reported only in footnotes, only in America (and not always there), rose to something like $4 *trillion*. Salomon and Citicorp alone accounted for one side or the other in about 40 percent of it, but banks that did not understand this stuff very well, from Credit Lyonnais in Paris to Banc One in Ohio, were using this market to generate apparent profits. A wise old hand in England said in the 1980s that the banks thought profits from swaps would save them from their Third World loans in the '90s; what they did not understand was that the swaps *were* the Third World loans of the '90s. When push comes to shove, the Aboriginal Bank of Alice Springs, Australia, will not have the floating-rate deutsche mark it has contracted to pay to Pankkibanken in Helsinki, in return for the fixed-rate Swiss francs Salomon will have to deliver to the Finns. The risks in this market are quite unknown. The only significant defaults reported to date have been by an American S&L (Beverly Hills) and the British town halls, but Salomon itself acknowledged a "non-material" loss on swaps with the Canadian-American-British development company Olympia and York. A contract with the bankrupt Macy's chain has led Swiss Bank Corporation to file an $83 million lawsuit against other lenders involved in the swap.

Worst of all, the auditors cannot find the values because each deal is individual and there is no market for the paper. The most active participants can use this market to control their apparent profit and loss. And within the firms, rocket scientists compensated according to their reported profit can determine their own numbers. To rest the future of Salomon Brothers on the income from such activities, which Maughan has said he expects to do, is riverboat gambling of the kind Buffett said his Salomon would eschew. There are also issues here beyond the question of what happens to Salomon. Henry Kaufman said, speaking of these derivative instruments in a lecture in Washington in May 1992, "I can think of no other area that has the potential of creating greater havoc on a global basis if something goes wrong."[14]

In short, someone really must keep an eye on these fellows. But who should it be, and how, and to what purpose?

Chapter 10

WHAT THE GOVERNMENT DID

In 1987, George Gould of the Treasury Department, a long drink of water with a lined face and courtly manners who had been a senior executive in the Wall Street house of Donaldson Lufkin Jenrette, came to John Gutfreund with a request. The Reagan administration felt it absolutely essential that a new banking law be written for the United States before the commercial banks foundered from lack of function. The Canadians, the English, all the Europeans, and, he then thought, the Japanese were in the process of rewriting their laws to let banks into the securities businesses from which they were barred in the United States. The Securities Industries Association was fighting the idea of such a banking law with fangs and claws and donations to congressmen and senators. Salomon was not afraid of the banks. If Gutfreund would break ranks with the SIA, it would greatly help the administration's chances.

After consultation with his kitchen cabinet, Gutfreund came back with a proposal. If Salomon were to support banking reform, the bill would have to include access for securities houses to certain services of the Federal Reserve, especially the privilege of borrowing from the Fed's discount window and the use of the Fed's wire payments system. Gould said, Of course.

And then there was something else. Solly had a big slug of profits in Switzerland, on which it had neither paid taxes nor accrued tax liabilities. In the recently passed 1986 tax act, the Bass family had gotten a one-day exemption for old Percy's estate to allow most of that dynasty's money to pass to the brothers untaxed. In return for its help with the banking bill, Solly would want a one-day tax holiday on the repatriation of profits from Switzerland by a large investment bank. And to that Gould could not say, Of course.

The next year Solly paid $180 million in taxes to repatriate its Swiss profits. Solly continued to support the SIA position, the banking bill died on the vine, and what friends Salomon might have had at the Treasury decided they weren't getting anything for their friendship.

In the end, the weakness of Gutfreund's Salomon—indeed, of Wall Street as a whole in the 1980s, but Solly was Wall Street writ large—was that it had a purely instrumental view of government. Government helped or hindered traders in their pursuit of money. Relations with government agencies were for the purpose of improving the return on equity, and they were essentially adversarial. The role of the government in establishing the legal order within which markets function was forgotten history for the new men and women of the '80s. When they thought of government, they thought of preventing or avoiding or evading or repealing rules that cost them money.

It had happened before. In 1968, Bernard Cornfeld of Investors Overseas Services, a mutual fund operation that was barred from operations in the United States by the Securities and Exchange Commission, was one of the great figures of the world of money, pouring more than a billion dollars a year from foreign investors into the American and British stock markets. His chief assistant and perhaps evil genius was Edward Cowett, a man who would have fit in well in the Salomon of the 1980s, a good family man and a brilliant securities lawyer whose weakness was that he thought the people who wrote the laws wrote them as a challenge to his cleverness in getting around them. Cowett had developed a legal argument that he told Cornfeld would *force* the SEC to re-admit IOS to Bernie's native shores. Nobody at the SEC understood these laws as well as he did; he would leave those schmucks eating his dust. Cornfeld looked at Cowett with great concern. "Remember," he said, "they may be schmucks, but they're the government."

Salomon stumbled into really serious trouble because most of the leaders of the firm and virtually all the younger managing directors thought of the government as schmucks. In the government bonds market, unfortunately, there was not much in their experience to argue otherwise.

AN IRRESPONSIBLE FEDERAL RESERVE

"The government securities market," said Jon Rotenstreich, "operated in a different environment from the rest of the securities business. In stocks and bonds the compliance officers told you what you could do. But when you jumped over the fence to governments, *the government itself* was saying, 'This is an unregulated market.' " In every other part of the securities business, firms had internal rules approved by the New York Stock Exchange or the National Association of Securities Dealers, enforced by a compliance department and often vetted by outside counsel. In government bonds trading, it was make your money how you can. For all the sophisticated defenses that could be offered for Salomon's practice that permitted the government bond trader to put a "do not confirm" into the computer without telling anyone about it, the fact of the matter was that any such order put into a computer at an investment house oriented to any instrument other than government bonds would automatically raise red flags on the screens of the compliance officers. As Assistant Secretary of the Treasury Jerome H. Powell put it in testimony to a House committee, "The government securities market is the only regulated securities market in which not all brokers and dealers are subject to sales practice rules."[1]

Salomon did cheat, and disgracefully, but a lot of the blame for what happened rested with the government agencies that failed to supervise this market at precisely the time when it most needed supervision. Prior to 1986 the supervision of the dealers in the Treasuries market was in the hands of the Federal Reserve Bank of New York, which ran the auction for new securities and did the

actual trading with the dealers in the Fed's "open market operations." And the Federal Reserve Bank of New York regulated by
lifted eyebrow, which was *always* obeyed. The Fed had the power
to recognize or not to recognize a firm as one of the "primary
dealers" with whom its open market desk did business. Part of
being a primary dealer was the submission of daily formal position
reports to the Fed and the discomfort of getting absolutely un-
dressed before the people who ran the Fed's open market desk—
every week for the larger dealers and at least once a month for the
smaller dealers. Peter Sternlight, still in charge of the desk in
1991, was considered a veritable ferret of a regulator who ran
down and eviscerated every rat that ran across his screen.

But by 1991 the Federal Reserve Bank of New York had become
essentially part of the audience for the auction and the subsequent
trading of the bonds and notes. What supervisory process survived had become pro forma, vestigial from previous administrations of the bank. The Fed permitted Salomon to enter a single
blanket bid for itself and all its customers on a "list [of customers]
to follow" basis, and even after Paul Mozer's well-publicized
blow-up at Michael Basham, it never checked whether the "customers" were really making those bids. A week after the May 22,
1991, auction, when the Treasury Department had already asked
the SEC and the FBI to look at what was going on in New York, the
Fed still had not received Salomon's list of customers for whom it
had bid—and of course it would have had no objection to Salomon's having purchased the notes from those customers in the
interim. A month or so after the Salomon story surfaced, a senior
officer of the New York Fed's division of market surveillance literally screamed at staff members of the House Banking Committee that "YOU DON'T UNDERSTAND. PEOPLE DON'T LIE TO
THE FED," provoking the astonished reply, "Why not? They lie to
us all the time."

The Fed had not known about the enormous positions Salomon's friends had taken in the when-issued market because it
sought information about such positions *only* from participants in
the auction, and the hedge funds that had purchased most heavily
in the when-issued market didn't bid in the auctions. Even the
information gathered from participants was allowed to molder on
the shelves, although the danger of market manipulation was ob-

viously greatest in this time of concentrated holdings, before the issuance of the notes began the process of actual distribution to ultimate customers. David Mullins, vice-chairman of the Federal Reserve Board, admitted in his testimony before Congressman Edward Markey in early September that "tightening up on enforcement would be efficacious in detecting and deterring future offenses. For example, the Federal Reserve regularly receives information on dealer positions in when-issued securities. These reports were not actively monitored. Though not designed for enforcement purposes, closer attention to them may be helpful in raising questions about situations with possible enforcement implications."[2] You bet.

The squeeze in the market for the Treasury's two-year 1993 notes was made possible by the vagaries of the repurchase and reverse-repurchase world, which permitted speculators as well as dealers to finance *all* their positions with borrowed money. This is presumably the Fed's proper business—but in these matters, too, the Fed was ludicrously underinformed. It solicited from the players in the market only their *aggregate* lendings and borrowings, not specific data. The system was that Joanie at Salomon called Mary at the Fed and said, "Mary, our repurchase book today totals forty-two billion, seven hundred thirteen million, ninety-two thousand, three hundred twelve dollars and seventy-one cents." Mary jotted down the number on a yellow pad, said, "Thanks, Joanie, have a nice day," and stuck the piece of paper in a file, from which it was never removed. The Fed knew from rumors in the market which bonds and notes were "on special," permitting their holders to borrow at much reduced interest rates by pledging just these bonds and notes as collateral, but it didn't investigate, even when complaints were made.

One of the things that astonished Chicago's Robert Hickey was that the Fed had once asked him, as a known Salomon customer in the auctions, to keep in touch about his larger purchases and sales but refused to give him the comfort of so much as a discussion when he called in June 1991 to complain that Solly was squeezing him. The man at the Fed who spoke with Hickey said defensively some months later, "He didn't have any solid information to back up his claims."

How could Mozer or his superiors take such rules seriously?

What happened at the Fed was the passage of the Government Securities Act of 1986. This piece of legislation was drawn up (in large part at the New York Fed itself) to prevent recurrence of several scams in the government bond business—by obscure firms with names like ESM Government Securities and Bevil, Bresler & Schulman—that had victimized municipalities, banks, and S&Ls in various parts of the country. None of these firms was a primary dealer, but the new law covered all dealers large and small, and asserted in effect the jurisdiction of the Securities and Exchange Commission over all securities houses doing business in the government bond market. Banks that did business in the market *as banks* rather than through securities affiliates were regulated by the Comptroller of the Currency, who works for the Treasury, but in 1991 only one primary dealer retained that status: Bank of America, which was not a very active player. The SEC, as always, operated through "Self-Regulatory Organizations," the New York Stock Exchange for its member firms and the National Association of Securities Dealers for everybody who did business over the counter. But there wasn't much these worthies could do in the Treasuries markets. They didn't understand the business, and if they did, they couldn't check out transactions because the government bond departments in all the securities houses didn't keep audit trails of their transactions.

"There isn't anything for us to look at," said Edward Kwalwasser, the young chief compliance officer of the NYSE. "If we go into Salomon, we can only see *their* trades. We can't see anybody else's trades.... Salomon averages eight thousand trades a day. They refinance twenty-five billion dollars of repurchase agreements every day. So for our examiners to pick up one transaction would be extraordinarily lucky."[3] When the SEC really began to look at the Treasury auctions imbroglio, it found that what audit trails there were had often been clumsily altered with white-out to deceive examiners, and not just at Salomon. Moreover, there wasn't much point in the SEC's trying to be tough, because the industry in a late display of muscle, with the usual congressional auctioneers taking their cut, had won an amendment to the bill prohibiting either the NASD or the Treasury from writing rules of trade practice for government bonds dealers.

Neither in Washington nor in New York did the Fed seem aware that the dangers of failure to supervise this market had grown exponentially in 1991. Like the Federal Home Loan Bank Board in its pursuit of making the S&Ls look solvent in 1981–82, the Fed adopted tunnel-vision policies to save the nation's banks. And just as excessive kindness to S&Ls in the early 1980s had drawn to the trough people who should not have been in the thrift business, Fed monetary policies in the early 1990s created a carnival in the government bond business.

Thanks to Fed actions in the money markets, in May 1991 the gap between the cost of funds for a big short-term borrower and the yield on the two-year notes rose to almost a full percentage point. In effect that meant the buyer of a two-year note was paid something approaching one-tenth of 1 percent a month to hold the paper. It didn't sound like much, but traders borrow at least 98 percent of the money they use in this business, which means that the gross return on capital committed to holding such paper in May 1991 was at least 5 percent a month, or 60 percent a year *before* the traders enhanced the value by doing their repo and trading things and rolling down the yield curve to higher prices as the maturity date of the notes grew nearer. Traders who thought the economy was not going to strengthen much or would fall back were also looking at a likelihood that if they held the notes, the price would rise. To be paid 5 percent a month on your capital to make a bet where the odds were with you was a dream of glory for any trader.

And it was not only the banks and the dealers who could play the game. The big "hedge funds," the Steinhardts and Soroses and Tigers and Tudors and Caxtons, could also borrow 98 percent or more of the price of their trading inventory. These people did not report to the Fed (indeed, they avoided any aspect of the government, including the IRS, as earnestly as they could). They were not interested in how much it might cost the U.S. government to fund its enormous debt as the years went on; they were interested in returns to their investors this month. Every year *Financial World* publishes a list of the hundred most highly paid people on Wall Street. For 1991, mostly thanks to the Fed, the five who topped the list, each making more than $55 million, were the players in the two-year notes market: George Soros of Quantum, Julian Robertson of Tiger, Paul Tudor Jones of Tudor Investment, Bruce Kovner of Caxton Corp., and Michael Steinhardt.[4]

Even on its own terms, Federal Reserve policy in 1991 was a failure. By making it possible for the banks to look profitable if they just bought government and government-guaranteed paper, and made no loans at all, the Fed perpetuated the "credit crunch" that afflicted smaller American business all year long. And in the meantime, the Fed inadvertently turned the most important securities market in the world into a casino where flashy types could beat the bank. Public relations director Bob Baker of Salomon sounded silly when he said that the real problem in the market was that the big nasty hedge funds were beating up on nice little Solly, and all Mozer did in May was try to get a bit of his own back—and, of course, the securities laws don't permit cheating even by people who are just trying to get a bit of their own back. But in this case his comments were not entirely unrelated to the truth.

There were a number of unpleasantnesses in Salomon's talk and action in the months after the disaster. The word "criminal" tripped easily off people's lips, obviously because if the conduct of the senior officers was found to be criminal, Salomon would not be liable for their legal expenses. (In fairness, it also seems likely that Buffett was angry.) There was a certain amount of rough stuff. At least one plaintiff's lawyer, part of a large firm, was told by a partner that a large client had suggested it would be unwise for the firm to be counsel in a suit against Solly. Another plaintiff's lawyer got an injunction from Judge Robert P. Patterson to prevent Salomon from threatening the expert witnesses the firm wished to use.

In any event, the terms of the consent decree the Justice Department and the SEC negotiated with Salomon in the spring of 1992 guaranteed that even the new, reformed, meek-and-mild Solly will not have many friends in the Wall Street community. In addition to paying out at least $290 million—$190 million to the government, the other $100 million as the minimum expectation for winners of private lawsuits—Salomon agreed to keep its books open to the Justice Department until June 1995 on both current trading and whatever past trading the investigators wished to explore, to help them build cases against others in the industry. Indeed, the deal with the SEC did not protect Salomon against anything in its past not already specified in the consent decree; if the investigators pick up any other fiddle-faddle, and they may, they can reopen the settlement.

MOUNTAINOUS PROBLEMS AND REGULATORY MICE

In the shock after the revelation of Salomon's actions, there was general agreement that something should be done. "With a carefully thought out and implemented approach," Corrigan of the New York Fed told Congressman Markey and his committee, "we believe it will be *feasible* to maintain the integrity and efficiency of this vital market."[5] The mechanism of the auctions should be automated so that billions of dollars no longer pass on the basis of slips of paper scribbled in phone booths and handed over a counter. The Treasury should have a policy that when necessary it would issue additional bonds on the same terms as those auctioned if there seemed to be a squeeze in the new issue. People other than the primary dealers should be allowed to bid on behalf of customers at the auction.

In September 1992 the Treasury launched a one-year experiment in a "Dutch auction" in which all winners received bonds or notes carrying the interest rate of the winning bid that obligated the government to pay the highest rate. This procedure was designed to eliminate the "winner's curse," the fact that those who bid the best rate in effect paid the Treasury more for the paper than those whose bids at higher rates took up the remainder of the issue. In theory, then—a theory persistently promoted by the economist Milton Friedman, who carried a lot of weight in the Bush Treasury Department—bidders in a Dutch auction would be more willing to put in bids that saved the Treasury money and would be less tempted to chat one another up in telephone calls just before the auction. This was, however, very theoretical. Had the Dutch auction system been in effect in May 1991, Salomon would have got its $10.6 billion in notes at a 6.83 percent rate, taking $4.4 million out of the taxpayers' pockets and infusing it in Salomon's.

Two more significant reforms were put into the form of a bill by the staff of Congressman Markey's committee. One would make the when-issued market in government securities much more like a futures exchange, with reports on all large trades and all large positions to prevent hanky-panky in a situation where the product being bought or sold is in limited supply but an unlimited number of contracts for its delivery can be created. The other would make the trading of government securities more like the trading of corporate stocks and bonds, requiring brokers and dealers to maintain audit trails so that their activities could be traced, if necessary, *post mortem*.

Basically, the Securities and Exchange Commission supported Markey's initiative—partly, of course, because it expanded the SEC's turf at the expense of the banking regulators but also for entirely respectable substantive reasons. "Without audit trails and market surveillance systems," SEC chairman Richard Breeden told a hearing on Markey's bill, "it must be assumed that, as a practical matter, attempts to manipulate markets in government securities will rarely be detected."[6] The "large trader reporting system" the SEC recommended would keep within the offices of the commission the information from the reports, which would be submitted not by the name of the trader but by a "large trader reporting number" that would be identifiable only within the commission.

Unfortunately, after the first burst of fear and loathing of Salomon, neither the Fed nor the Treasury was willing to take significant steps to clean up the government securities markets. The argument was that the auctions and the when-issued markets associated with them allowed the private sector to absorb more than $2 trillion a year of Treasury issues (most of it, of course, refundings of the three-month, six-month, and one-year notes, but $250 billion of it new demands upon lenders to the U.S. government). Tampering with a system that allowed big participants to game the markets might cause some of them to withdraw, adding to the federal deficit by making it more expensive for the government to sell its debt. Even the minimal reform of requiring primary dealers to identify in advance the customers for whom they are bidding at the auction had its detractors, who argued that bids from outside the dealer community had shrunk since mid-1991 because big investors were loath to let the Fed know what they were doing. Instead of bidding at the auction, they now bought anonymously from the dealers in the when-issued market or the aftermarket because they didn't want to file disclosures with the government.

Both the Treasury and the Fed in 1991–92 were essentially in the hands of academic economists who thought markets cure their own diseases. They therefore turned a deaf ear not only on

Congressman Markey and his staff but also on the official spokes-
men for the industry, the members of an oddity called the Public
Securities Association Treasury Borrowing Advisory Committee,
who had for several years been calling for reforms similar to what
Markey proposed. The eighteen members of the committee, who
served as individuals, were senior executives of the big banks and
government bond dealers. Among them was Salomon's executive
vice-president Gedale Horowitz. They met for two days four times
a year, dining richly at Washington's Madison Hotel, to advise the
Treasury Department a few weeks before the announcement of
the terms and conditions of the big ($30+ billion) quarterly
auctions of three-year, ten-year, and thirty-year Treasury notes
and bonds. The Treasury announced in its quarterly justification
for summoning these bankers, duly published in the *Federal Register,* "that the advice provided consists of commercial and financial information given and received in confidence."[7]

Among the pieces of advice given by this committee in May
1991 was that the Treasury assert much more control over when-
issued trading: "The group sees the potential for a buildup of
significant unregulated or minimally supervised credit risk. The
committee is concerned that current system checks are not organized in a way to permit the Treasury, the Fed, or others to
effectively monitor or manage this exposure.... Most OTC [over-
the-counter] markets lack standardized legal remedies for problems which might arise where the security is not available." The
discussion of this matter was phrased with reference to when-
issued trading on instruments that the Treasury had not yet announced it was planning to issue, but the recommendations were
clearly applicable to all when-issued trading.

The July meeting, two weeks before the Salomon detonation,
sent a report to the Treasury that noted the damaging "squeeze"
in the May two-year notes and urged that one of the steps to be
taken to avoid similar squeezes in the future should be a rule
requiring the reporting of large positions: "The Federal Reserve,
in its role as the supervisor of the primary dealers, should develop
a private disclosure system which allows the Fed's good offices to
be adequately informed of secondary market concentrations in
cash and financing markets for primary dealers and their clients.... Using that information in conjunction with a proactive

moral suasion posture with senior dealer management, the Treasury and/or the Fed should be able to encourage the early correction of any identifiable market problem." But that didn't mean the dealers wanted the SEC in this game—or an audit trail—and when the Fed set its face against increasing surveillance of the when-issued market, they let their suggestions for change disappear into the limbo of government documents not meant to be circulated.

Perhaps the most remarkable response to the Salomon disaster was the decision by the Federal Reserve Bank of New York to *disband* its dealer surveillance unit in early 1992. "In part because of 'moral hazard' considerations and in part because of legal and regulatory realities," Corrigan told the annual meeting of the Public Securities Association in early 1992, "it was important that the Federal Reserve Bank of New York make absolutely clear to the marketplace that the New York Fed does *not* regulate the primary dealer firms."[8] The Fed, after all, through its open market desk, was an active participant in the government bonds market, and some of its officers thought it unseemly and uncomfortable for a participant also to be the regulator. The Fed apparently believed that if it didn't pretend to supervise the players in the market, nobody would blame it for future trouble. Someone someday is in for a big surprise.

There were, in fact, a number of squeezes in the government bond market in the summer and fall of 1992, most of them associated with the massive issuance of new bonds by corporate America. The underwriters who had agreed to buy those bonds from their issuers and sell them to the public hedged their risk that interest rates might rise (pushing down the price of the new corporate bonds before they could dispose of them) by selling futures contracts on government paper, especially the five-year and ten-year notes. The when-issued market seemed cheaper than the organized futures market, and all these institutions always prefer to do business where no records are kept. Although the leaders of the hedge funds unquestionably knew what their peers were doing, there has been no accusation of active collusion in these cases. One squeeze was so bad, however, that the Treasury in November 1992 sold $10 billion of ten-year notes that would come due in August 2002 rather than the normal November to get the short sellers from the August auction off the hook.

Most astonishing was the continuing insistence of the Treasury and the Fed *both* that government bonds auctions and trading must be more computerized *and* that audit trails in the government bonds market must not be imposed because they would be too expensive for the participants in the market. Computers keep audit trails for free as a by-product of processing the transactions, and nobody knows it better than the Fed, which moves $800 billion a day over its Fedwire and keeps track of where every penny of it comes from and goes to—and when. But bankers believe in secrecy, not transparency. "The problem with the world is that there's too much transparency already," growled Paul Volcker, former Federal Reserve chairman, only half in jest. In September 1992, heavily lobbied by the Treasury and the banking regulators on a day when the currency markets were in turmoil and congressmen desperately wanted to believe that the Treasury and the Fed knew what they were doing, the House of Representatives killed the Markey bill.

Among the government's complaints against Salomon and its so-far unnamed "co-conspirators" was violation of the Sherman Anti-Trust Act by restraint of trade and market manipulation. Among the remedies sought initially by the Justice Department was an injunction to bar Salomon from "agreeing with, requesting, or directing another person to withhold securities either from the financing or secondary markets." But the Treasury, the Federal Reserve Board, the New York Fed, and the SEC sent a joint letter urging the Justice Department to back away, and Justice rather reluctantly did so, taking as part of the SEC's $290 million consent decree settlement a $27.5 million "forfeiture" by Salomon for coordinating "efforts to limit the supply of May (1991) two-year notes available in the secondary and financing market." There would be sufficient deterrent value, the Justice lawyers suggested, "because the complaint describes with particularity the unlawful activity subject to the enforcement action." But in the absence of the injunction the courts couldn't enforce this deterrent—and the financial regulators didn't want to enforce it.

Both the Fed and the Treasury have been more concerned about the profitability of the primary dealers than about the honesty of the market, because they feel that with the Japanese and the Arabs no longer buying U.S. Treasury paper the government will not be able to market its monstrous debt unless the primary dealers thrive. A veteran trader who was the head of the finance desk for one of the largest participants in the market estimated the total profitability of the primary dealers at a billion dollars a year, about $600 million on the repurchase chassis, and about $300 million of that from manipulative squeezings of the notes market. Jeff Duncan, Markey's counsel, observed of the Treasury and the Fed that "they don't care if they're getting ripped off on the spread."

At the very end of 1992, Congressman Markey sent a very tough set of interrogatories to Alan Greenspan, Gerald Corrigan, and Richard Breeden, demanding to be informed about exactly what the New York Fed had done to "expand its current market data collection program," including the gathering of information on when-issued trading, forward (futures) and options contracts, related activity in the financing markets, and large-dealer positions, and how much of that information was being shared with other agencies. The letter to Greenspan asked specifically for a report on occasions when the Fed had made itself a (doubtlessly unintentional) co-conspirator with market squeezers by holding in its own portfolio "on-the-run" notes that were elsewhere subject to "special" rates when repurchased. The answer from the Fed, in the typically disingenuous way of that institution, defined "special" as rates that were at least 50 percent below market rates on straight repurchase agreements. This meant that any Fed involvement in the May 1991 squeeze would not have to be reported, because Meriwether had ordered Mozer not to take more than a two-percentage-point reduction in the rates he demanded to lend his and Soros's notes.

The letter to Corrigan asked him to "provide the Subcommittee with copies of the FRBNY's daily 'Selected Treasury Securities on Special' Reports for the years 1990, 1991, and 1992." Finally, the letter asked, "Does the FRBNY think that efforts to date in creating its market surveillance program, changes in the auction rules, and the new reopening policy are sufficient to ensure that deliberate squeezes like those that occurred in the Spring of 1991 cannot recur? If not, what additional measures are needed? If so, how do you account for the persistence of short squeezes in the market?"[9] Here, too, the answer was somewhat dusty, announcing that at its final meeting of 1992, the board of the New York Fed had approved the purchase of computer equipment that would permit the Bank to speed up its processing of information about government securities trading. No effort was made to explain how this "market surveillance" could work in the absence of the dealer surveillance Corrigan had abandoned, especially in a market where so much of the business is done by blind brokers who don't even tell the sellers who the buyers are, where there are no audit trails, and the hedge funds are under no obligations to report. Twenty days after receiving Markey's letter, Corrigan resigned as president of the New York Fed, effective August 1993. Perhaps his successor will take these matters more seriously.

EPILOGUE

WHO STANDS FOR JUSTICE?

This book was written essentially without the cooperation of Salomon Brothers. The firm was struggling with investigations by the Treasury Department, the Securities and Exchange Commission, the Federal Reserve, the House Banking Committee, the Telecommunications and Finance Committee of the House Committee on Energy and Commerce, the House Government Operations Committee, the North American Association of Securities Administrators (as proxy for fifty U.S. and twelve Canadian state and provincial securities administrators), the U.S. Attorney for the Southern District of New York, and the Antitrust Division of the Department of Justice. Customers were raising hell, too. Its new leaders was squaring their shoulders manfully in preparation for paying out about half a billion dollars in fines and settlements of private lawsuits to seal the record of what the previous management did and failed to do in 1989–91. They were less than delighted by the thought that someone writing a book wanted to wander around and ask questions.

People were helpful as individuals, some with and some without the knowledge of the firm. Executive vice-president Dale Horowitz, whom I knew from his time as chairman of the Securities Industries Association, fed me a couple of breakfasts in the firm's lordly dining quarters, told me when he thought I was getting something wrong, talked (only) about the time before the troubles of 1991, and very kindly gave people no longer with the firm a personal assurance that I was trying to do a serious job and would not victimize them. Bob Baker talked on the phone a few times, because his role as Salomon's press spokesman made it hard for him not to take calls (he very rarely returned calls), and he was unconsciously a delicious source, because he enjoyed talking. When I wondered, for example, whether anyone at Salomon had money in Julian Robertson's very successful Tiger fund, which had been involved with Solly in the May auction, Baker said, "I wish I had money in Tiger." The partnership records on Tiger were intact at the county clerk's office, and I was able to verify that nobody at Salomon *did* have money in Tiger.

The refusal of Salomon Brothers to help was not significant in developing the story of the firm, because only three or four people who played even minimally important roles in that story still work for Solly. But it does, of course, make predicting the future of the firm even more a matter of guesswork than most such predictions. Today's Solly is an entirely different firm from what it was in the 1970s or indeed in the 1980s, although the present leadership is for all its good manners a creature of the attitudes of the '80s. There are virtually no Jews left in important positions outside the research function. It would be unthinkable now to hire somebody and tell him that if he's as smart as he thinks he is, he'll find work to do. Everybody is slotted into a box from the end of the training program, and there are few exits from the box. The compensation system still encourages people to think of their department first and last, and regard others at the firm with suspicion rather than solicitude. The ability levels are probably much reduced: The people now leading most of the departments were in the fourth or fifth rank a few years ago, frequently working for people who were no older than they were. There is still considerable bitterness about the brutal way a layer of managing directors was cut off in the early months of the Buffett regime, but the challenges of opportunity have in the end overcome past loyalties for many of the young people who were pushed up to high positions when their former leaders quit in anger or were bounced by Maughan. Still, the *exultation* people felt about working for

Salomon, about being a band of brothers at Agincourt, has completely disappeared.

New department heads have been hired from outside for equity trading in New York and for investment banking in London, but the first of these came out of retirement and the second out of Parliament after losing his seat; neither is considered a heavyweight. The consultant hired to help expand business with the European Community turns out to have been the Italian ambassador to the United States who did the dirty work of Banca Nazionale del Lavoro, urging Attorney General Richard Thornburgh to constrict narrowly the investigation into the help given to Saddam Hussein by BNL's branch in Atlanta. And Buffett is, of course, still primarily interested in safeguarding his own $700 million investment in Solly's preferred stock. The smart money on Wall Street says that Buffett will keep control (when he ceased executive involvement with the firm in the spring of 1992, he put his lawyer in as the new nonexecutive chairman of the board) until one of the nation's insurance companies is healthy enough to buy the firm, and then he will sell it for a price that makes him whole, if not the common stock holders. Meanwhile, the combination of Fed policy and the growth of the off-balance sheet "derivative" business (with new, ignorant players to be fleeced almost every day) has made the firm look much healthier than it is.

Hanging in legal limbo in the sixteen months after the explosions of August 1991, Salomon's small group of the despised and rejected mostly lived a dramatically different life. Gutfreund continued to go to an office every day, arriving early in the morning to work on his lawsuits. His wife didn't cut back by a kopeck; their friends didn't know whether to laugh or cry. Salomon contested Gutfreund's claims for reimbursement of his legal bills and for bonus money he contended was owed him in 1991. Strauss and Meriwether tended their investments and put in claims similar to Gutfreund's. Feuerstein studied French, and when the job of general counsel of Harvard became free, he applied for it but failed to win it. Mozer moved to Florida, where potential bankrupts can shelter a lot of real estate; his wife continued at her trader's job with Morgan Stanley and in late 1992 produced their third child.

The SEC in December 1992 sued Mozer and Murphy on civil charges relating to their submission of fake bids in the Treasury auctions of 1990 and 1991. It is hard to imagine the SEC permitting Mozer or Murphy to work ever again in the securities business. On the question of the false bids, the SEC in late 1992 entered a consent decree in which Gutfreund paid a $100,000 fine and agreed to seek permission from the commission if he wished ever again to become an executive in a securities firm, which he said he didn't; Strauss paid $75,000 and agreed not to work in the securities business until June 1993; Meriwether paid $50,000 and agreed not to work in the securities business until March 1993. Section II of the Administrative Order said that these penalties covered "other proceedings brought by or on behalf of the Commission or to which the Commission is a party," but SEC enforcement director William McLucas said that such words are meaningless boilerplate and do not in fact cover the potential defendants' exposure to further SEC penalties if the commission finds they were parties to rigging the market for the May 1993 notes.

In September 1992 the Antitrust Division of the Justice Department impaneled a grand jury in New York City to look at allegations of criminal behavior by the participants in the April and May 1993 note auctions, when-issued and aftermarkets. It is not clear how this grand jury will mesh with the continuing investigations of the market for these notes by the U.S. Attorney's office for the Southern District of New York, relations between the Justice Department and the U.S. Attorney's office in New York being roughly comparable to those between Iran and Iraq (they have some common enemies, but in normal times they hate each other worse). The settlement agreement between the Antitrust Division and Salomon as a corporation, which set a $27.5 million "forfeiture" as Salomon's penalty for doing things it doesn't admit doing, has an affidavit page for the lawyers in which the Antitrust Division people had to check a box saying they were not admitted to practice in the Southern District. But that settlement agreement gives these lawyers unrestricted access to Salomon's files and computer records until June 1995, which means that the subpoenas the grand jury emits may be much more than fishing expeditions. They have been hearing testimony from some very angry people. The time horizon for deciding whether and whom to indict appears to be the fall of 1993. Meanwhile, of course, both the corporations and the individuals involved in the April and May auctions are defendants in a number of private lawsuits brought by the losers as individuals and as classes.

Paul Mozer's attorney, Stanley Arkin, worked out with the U.S. Attorneys in New York a very clever plea bargain, in which Mozer would plead guilty to felony charges of lying to the government about the Warburg bid in February 1991 and to nothing else. His punishment for that offense would be determined by a judge after analysis of the losses other people had suffered as the result of this deception. As this was the note issue on which Salomon lost money because the triumph of Desert Storm pushed interest rates up in euphoric anticipation of quick recovery from the recession, Mozer would not do any jail time at all. Part of the deal as presented by Arkin was that *after* the judge had accepted the plea, he would say that it also covered the antitrust matters being dealt with by a separate grand jury, and the U.S. Attorney's office would say that it didn't. By a stroke of ill luck for Arkin and Mozer, the settlement was heard by federal judge Robert P. Patterson, in whose court had been consolidated the private suits for damages as the result of the April and May squeezes. Patterson knew what Mozer was getting away with, and the U.S. Attorney on second thought decided to incorporate in the plea bargain itself the statement that Mozer was still subject to criminal prosecution by the Antitrust Division for any role in rigging the market for the April and May notes. Arkin angrily withdrew Mozer's plea, and the next day the U.S. Attorney indicted him for several crimes carrying mandatory prison sentences, though they were still restricted to the false bids in the February auction, which was the easiest crime to prove.

One has some—but limited—sympathy with both sides in this dispute. The deal Arkin struck was too clever. Jules Brody, counsel for some of the plaintiffs in the class action suit against anybody and everybody, objected that a deal involving only the February notes where nobody lost money might confuse a future jury hearing claims of losses in the April and May notes. But the Treasury's rules were meaningless (if a firm can legally bid for a whole issue in the auction so long as it assigns some of the bids to its clients, and can legally own a whole issue on settlement day by purchasing its clients' share from them in transactions hidden from the public, it is hard to see much criminality in the faking of client bids), and the Federal Reserve Bank of New York by its refusal to supervise the market had invited the jiggery-pokery Mozer executed.

Moreover, the U.S. Attorney's office had decided that while there was reason to believe that Salomon and its friends had violated the law in squeezing the April and May notes, the case would be too hard to prove beyond a reasonable doubt, and the Antitrust Division was spinning its wheels. That conclusion came from an inadequate investigation by lawyers who did not understand this market very well, and relied on an even more inadequate SEC investigation, but it was honestly held. In early 1993 it seemed possible that the Southern District, its Republican leader departed, might be more willing to cooperate with the Antitrust Division.

For the Wall Street community, the Salomon disaster should hasten a sea change back to a more responsible view of the relations of securities houses with their clients and customers. This is, after all, a *service* industry, to be paid in a rational economy for the value of the services it performs, by those who need the services. The most important of those services has always been judgment. As Jon Rotenstreich said, "Wall Street's stock in trade was righteousness: I am your judge, your jury, and your executioner, and I will fix it for you, I will tell you the right thing to do." That service was forgotten in the 1980s, which diminished the real contribution of the financial sector at precisely the time its rewards were rising.

I have no desire to defend the quality of top management in American enterprise, but it was and it is outrageous that investment banks should be able to diddle pension fund managers and "put a company in play" for no purpose other than earning fees for themselves. Gutfreund, to give him credit, stood against such behavior for most of his tenure as Salomon's chairman, and the downfall of the firm can probably be traced to the day when his juniors—he had left himself defenseless against his juniors—convinced him that Solly should become more like Drexel.

Very few of those involved in this industry in the 1980s—not the money managers in the institutions, not the leaders of the securities houses, not the CFOs of the corporations—contributed to their economy or to their society anything like what they were paid. The misallocation of America's resources from the malfunctioning of our financial markets in the 1980s slowed the growth of the nation's productivity and diminished its economic prospects. Although the chimera of globalization will continue to be sought for a while yet, the emerging truth is that financial deregulation was harmful to the real economies (and to the long-range prospects of the financial institutions themselves) in the 1980s and that reregulation can be accomplished only nationally. The industry is going to shrink, the rewards for cleverness are going to diminish, and with luck some of the better minds that were drawn to finance will find more socially useful if less extravagantly paid employment.

About the only winners awakening from this nightmare are the lawyers (for both sides) in the cases against Salomon. Judge Patterson moved the preliminary hearings in these cases in June 1992 down to a larger first-floor courtroom in New York's federal courthouse to accommodate all the attorneys and their assistants gathering around the honey pot—and that was before Hickey's Chicago case had been consolidated into the actions before Patterson by a multi-district panel of federal judges. About fifteen lawyers were between the courtroom railing and the judge's bench, the plaintiffs widening and deepening their complaints, attacking under cover of common-law fraud, securities laws, racketeering statutes, and antitrust legislation. Cravath Swaine & Moore for Salomon tried rather feebly to limit the field on which plaintiffs could play, but Buffett in rescuing the firm had confessed enough sins to make counsel's role very difficult. At the June 15, 1992, hearing before Judge Patterson, Frederick A. O. Schwarz appearing for Salomon admitted that Gutfreund had shown poor judgment in failing to discipline Mozer, which was not news but made the plaintiffs' task a good deal easier.

The bungling that had characterized Salomon's handling of the incidents that led to these lawsuits also marked its defense against them. After the SEC took its depositions from the scores of Salomon people who knew something about the firm's behavior in the Treasuries market, the investigators asked whether Solly wanted copies of the transcripts. Somebody said yes, so when the plaintiffs' lawyers began their discovery process, everything Solly's people had said to the SEC (under Buffett's orders to be forthcoming) would have to be available to them—eventually. Solly's lawyers, being very highly paid and very skilled, maneuvered endlessly to write ironclad confidentiality agreements that would deny not just the public but the plaintiffs themselves access to the SEC depositions that would eventually be handed over to the plaintiffs' lawyers. The SEC lawyers who conducted these depositions were still pretty far down the learning curve, and apparently subjects that should have been covered were not, but there was gold in the hills. Then Judge Patterson ruled that having waived lawyer-client confidentiality on the Wachtell Lipton report and the associated notes to gain the goodwill of the government, Buffett had also inadvertently agreed to make the report and the notes available to plaintiffs' counsel. This meant that during the pretrial depositions the lawyers could base their interrogations on enormously damaging detailed material. Some of those examined—Mozer and Steinhardt's trader Ernest Theurer for sure, and perhaps others—refused to answer questions on Fifth Amendment grounds. Theurer, who had been excused from testifying to the SEC investigators for reasons of possible self-incrimination, went twice to Judge Patterson to get excused from deposition by plaintiffs' counsel, too, but Patterson refused.

As 1992 ended, it seemed unlikely that the private cases against Salomon would come to trial, because the damage to the already diminished reputation of the firm would be too great. Having told the SEC that there were virtually no documents, Salomon and its lawyers have inundated the plaintiffs with a hundred thousand of them, mostly uncatalogued. Although some of the lawyers' energy was still used for digging up stuff that would make Salomon wish to settle, most of the inventiveness was devoted to finding ways to expand the claims that could be made. One could compensate a trader for his pain and suffering when Salomon made his trades go sour. Meanwhile, Salomon's diminishing clout in the marketplace might allow some previously shy victims to enter their claims as part of the class-action suit, although Salomon could short-circuit this process by making confidential settlements with them to keep their names off the record. One large stockholder in Discount Corporation of America sued that company, which had lost money in the April and May auctions, to compel it to join the class-action suit against Salomon. In its report for the third quarter of 1992,

Salomon was still adding to its reserves against the eventual costs of the fiddle-faddle in its governments trading departments.

Perhaps this is the way the system is supposed to work. Short-term considerations of public policy—and sometimes, perhaps, political influence—too often lead government regulators and prosecutors to swallow the excuses of those who have fouled their markets. The Fed worries about what Maughan called "tall trees." The courts, bless 'em, have to deal with the case. They are not well suited to making policy. As Justice Robert H. Jackson observed, a court has to shrink the realities and concerns of a nation to the confines of a case because it cannot expand the case to the realities and concerns of the nation—but if there is a policy, the courts can make it stick.

What the courts do, moreover, is done in public, which makes them additionally effective in the securities business, where people both borrow and trade essentially on their good name. In the 1980s too much of America lost the fear of shame that used to police behavior; in the 1980s it became fashionable to respect people for putting up with shame—provided they were paid well to do so. By making dishonest conduct in the securities markets seriously expensive, the lawyers may even persuade more participants that they and the people who work for them will be better off if they internalize the rules.

As Billy Salomon did.

As virtually all those who worked for him thought John Gutfreund did.

As the securities acts, which are still the law of the land, insist that everybody must.

NOTES

PROLOGUE

1. "The King of Wall Street: How Salomon Brothers Rose to the Top—and How It Wields Its Power," *Business Week,* December 9, 1985, p. 98.
2. Transcript, Subcommittee on Securities, Senate Banking Committee, Hearing on the Activities of Salomon Brothers, Inc., September 11, 1991, p. 52.
3. Ann Monroe, "Sleepless: How Salomon Survived," *Corporate Finance,* March 1992, pp. 38, 41.
4. Jonathan Feuerbringer, "Salomon Brothers Admits Violations at Treasury Sales," *New York Times,* August 10, 1991, pp. 1, 37.
5. Michael Siconolfi, Constance Mitchell, Tom Herman, Michael R. Sesit, and David Wessel, "Salomon's Admission of T-Note Infractions Gives Markets a Jolt," *Wall Street Journal,* August 12, 1991, p. 1.

CHAPTER 1

1. In the interests of full disclosure, I should mention that Gottlieb was one of the three main sponsors (the others were Supreme Court Justice John M. Harlan and Edward Lumbard, chief judge of the Court of Appeals for the Second Circuit) of a biography of their former boss, Emory Bucker, which I wrote in the 1960s.

CHAPTER 2

1. Martin Mayer, *The New Breed on Wall Street.* New York: Macmillan, 1969, p. 89.
2. Michael Lewis, *Liar's Poker.* New York: W. W. Norton & Co., 1989, p. 167.
3. Again for full disclosure, in January 1987 I wrote a pamphlet for Sandy Lewis to distribute with his annual report to investors in his limited partnership, explaining the work of his firm.
4. "The Toughest Kid in Block Trading," *Business Week,* October 4, 1969, p. 114.
5. Chris Welles, *The Last Days of the Club.* New York: E. P. Dutton & Co., 1975, pp. 41–42.
6. Will K. Weinstein, "The Psychology of the Block Trader," *Institutional Investor,* June 1970, p. 36.

7. Securities and Exchange Commission, *Institutional Investor Study Report* 3 (1971), p. 1941.
8. William C. Rupert and Walter N. Oakes, "Interest-Rate Swap Accounting: What Is 'Market Value'?" *Bank Accounting and Finance,* January 1987, p. 3 *et seq.*
9. E. Gerald Corrigan, "Rebuilding the Economic and Financial Fundamentals: The Case for Vision and Patience," *Federal Reserve Bank of New York Quarterly Review,* Winter 1991–92, pp. 1, 5.

CHAPTER 3

1. Sidney Homer and Martin L. Leibowitz, Ph.D., *Inside the Yield Book: New Tools for Bond Market Strategy.* Englewood Cliffs, N.J.: Prentice-Hall, and New York: New York Institute of Finance, 1972.
2. Sidney Homer, *A History of Interest Rates,* 2nd ed. New Brunswick, N.J.: Rutgers University Press, 1977, p. *v.*
3. See Martin Mayer, *The Fate of the Dollar* (New York: Times Books, 1980), for an extended discussion of these subjects.
4. Irwin Ross, "How Henry Kaufman Gets It Right," *Fortune,* May 18, 1981, p. 92.
5. William Dullforce, "Rudloff Castigates World's Bankers," *Financial Times,* February 5, 1988, p. 23.
6. Corrigan, "Rebuilding the Economic and Financial Fundamentals."

CHAPTER 4

1. Siconolfi et al., "Salomon's Admission of T-Note."
2. *Salomon Inc.: A Report by the Chairman on the Company's Standing and Outlook.* New York: Salomon Brothers, October 29, 1991, p. 3.

CHAPTER 5

1. "A Maverick Pushes into Wall Street's Club," *Business Week,* April 3, 1978.
2. Vincent Carosso, *Investment Banking in America: A History.* Cambridge, Mass.: Harvard University Press, 1970, p. 451.
3. Cary Reich, "Salomon: The Spectacular Debut of an International Upstart," *Institutional Investor,* January 1978.
4. Reich, "Salomon: The Spectacular Debut."
5. Ann Crittenden, "A London Banker for Salomon," *New York Times,* September 11, 1977, business section, p. 7.
6. Robert Sobel, *Salomon Brothers 1910–1985: Advancing to Leadership.* New York: Salomon Brothers, 1985, p. 184.
7. Paul Hoffman, *The Dealmakers.* Garden City, N.Y.: Doubleday, 1984, p. 157.
8. *Final Report of Examiner Barry Lewis Zaretsky,* In re Revco D.S., Inc., et al., Debtors. 101 Park Ave., New York City.
9. Bryan Burrough and John Helyar, *Barbarians at the Gates.* New York: Harper & Row, 1990, pp. 217–18.
10. Richard Clurman, *To the End of Time.* New York: Simon & Schuster, 1992, p. 216.

CHAPTER 6

1. See Martin Mayer, *The Greatest-Ever Bank Robbery* (New York: Scribners, 1990).
2. *The Report of the President's Commission on Housing.* Washington, D.C.: Government Printing Office, 1982, p. 146. I was a commissioner and a member of the finance committee that prepared this recommendation, but it wasn't my idea.

3. Those interested in the complete story will find it in *The Greatest-Ever Bank Robbery.*

4. Peter G. Brown, Thomas A. Zimmerman, and K. Jeanne Person, *Introduction to Mortgages and Mortgage-Backed Securities.* New York: Salomon Brothers, 1987, p. 14.

5. Federal News Service Transcript, Senate Banking Committee Hearings on the Thrift Industry, Washington, D.C., August 2, 1988, p. 19–1.

6. "Through the Secondary Market Looking Glass: Fannie Mae and Freddie Mac Are Not Cheshire Cats," remarks prepared for delivery by David O. Maxwell, March 26, 1987. Fannie Mae press release, Washington, D.C., p. 5.

7. Michael McQueen and Ann Munroe, "Debate on New U.S.–Backed Mortgage Security Stirs Charges of Greed, Government Domination," *Wall Street Journal,* April 20, 1987, p. 48.

8. I was a speaker at one of these occasions in 1985. It was at Pebble Beach that Steve Joseph of Drexel Burnham, who had learned about mortgages and S&Ls at Salomon, told me and my wife that of course you wanted to put your customers' deposits in S&Ls that were about to fail, because they had to pay the highest interest rates, and when they did fail, you got another commission by doing the trick all over again.

9. Martin Mayer, *The Builders.* New York: W. W. Norton & Co., 1978, p. 353.

CHAPTER 7

1. "True Confessions," *Institutional Investor,* February 1991, p. 53.

CHAPTER 8

1. Constance Mitchell, "Salomon's 'Squeeze' in May Left Many Players Reeling," *Wall Street Journal,* October 31, 1991, p. 1.

2. Letter from Salomon, Inc., to Congressman Edward J. Markey, in Hearing Before the Subcommittee on Telecommunications and Finance, September 4, 1991, p. 70.

3. Written testimony of Thomas A. Russo, Subcommittee on Telecommunications and Finance, p. 4.

4. Salomon Brothers press release, October 24, 1991.

5. Transcript of Markey hearings, p. 108.

6. C. Barndt Hauptfuhrer, *Regulatory Implications of the Recent Intentional Manipulation of the April and May Treasury Two-Year Notes,* a submission to the SEC and others, Three Crown Limited Partnership, 25 Enterprise Avenue, Secaucus, NJ 07094, February 3, 1992, p. 40.

7. Kevin G. Salwen and John Connor, "Lawsuit in Salomon Scandal Renews Charge of Collusion in Treasury Auction," *Wall Street Journal,* November 13, 1992, p. B14.

8. SEC Release No. 34-31554, December 3, 1992, Administrative Proceeding File No. 3-7930, p. 12.

9. Michael Siconolfi and Laurie P. Cikes, "How Salomon's Hubris and a U.S. Trap Led to a Leader's Downfall," *Wall Street Journal,* September 19, 1991, p. 1.

10. Questions for the Record of Michael E. Basham by Rep. Bunning. Mss., Subcommittee on Telecommunications and Finance.

11. In the Matter of John H. Gutfreund, Thomas W. Strauss, and John W. Meriwether, respondents, SEC Release No. 34-31554, Administrative Proceeding File 3-7930, December 3, 1992, p. 13.

CHAPTER 9

1. Sarah Bartlett, "Salomon's Errant Cowboy," *New York Times,* August 25, 1991, sec. 3, p. 1.

2. Statement of Salomon, Inc., submitted in conjunction with the testimony of Warren E. Buffett before the Securities Subcommittee, Committee on Banking, Housing and Urban Affairs, U.S. Senate, September 10, 1991, p. 29.
3. Statement of Salomon, Inc., p. 30.
4. Hearings before the House Ways and Means Committee, Subcommittee on Oversight, to Review Violations in the Marketing of Government Securities, September 26, 1991, p. 85.
5. Otto Obermaier, "Do the Right Thing," *Barron's,* December 14, 1992, p. 18.
6. Gilbert Kaplan, "True Confessions," *Institutional Investor,* February 1991, pp. 43, 44.
7. *A Report by the Chairman on the Company's Standing and Outlook,* Salomon, Inc., New York, October 29, 1991, p. 3.
8. Michael Siconolfi, "Salomon Chief of Compliance Is in EC Dispute," *Wall Street Journal,* October 14, 1991, p. C1.
9. John Rockwell, "Islamic Art Collection Is Offered to Britain; Some Say, 'Refuse,'" *The New York Times,* February 15, 1993, p. C-11
10. Michael Siconolfi, "Salomon Names Charles Williams a Compliance Chief," *Wall Street Journal,* June 16, 1992, p. B12.
11. Kurt Eichenwald, "Employee Dismissals Reported at Salomon," *New York Times,* November 19, 1991, pp. D1, D4.
12. Patrick Harverson, "Salomon Begins to Pick Up the Pieces," *Financial Times,* November 1, 1991, p. 25.
13. Transcript, Subcommittee on Securities, Senate Banking Committee, Hearing on the Activities of Salomon Brothers, September 12, 1991, p. 98.
14. Henry Kaufman, "Opportunities and Challenges in the Global Capital Markets," The Walter Surrey Memorial Lecture, National Planning Association, Washington, D.C., May 1, 1992, p. 8.

CHAPTER 10

1. Statement of the Honorable Jerome H. Powell before the Subcommittee on Telecommunications and Finance, U.S. House of Representatives, October 25, 1991, p. 5.
2. Statement of David W. Mullins, Jr., before the Subcommittee on Telecommunications and Finance, U.S. House of Representatives, September 4, 1991, pp. 3–4.
3. Transcript, Hearing on the Activities of Salomon Brothers, Inc., in Treasury Bond Activities, Subcommittee on Securities, Senate Banking Committee, September 12, 1991, p. 22.
4. "The Wall Street 100," *Financial World,* July 21, 1992, p. 40.
5. Statement of E. Gerald Corrigan before the Subcommittee on Telecommunications and Finance, September 4, 1991, p. 11. Emphasis added.
6. Testimony of Richard C. Breeden, chairman, U.S. Securities and Exchange Commission, concerning the government securities market, before the Telecommunications and Finance Subcommittee, October 25, 1991, p. 22.
7. *Federal Register,* December 24, 1990, p. 592923.
8. Remarks by E. Gerald Corrigan, president, Federal Reserve Bank of New York, before the Annual Meeting of the Public Securities Association, Phoenix, Arizona, February 28, 1992.
9. Edward J. Markey to E. Gerald Corrigan, December 17, 1992, pp. 3–4.

INDEX